**Books are to be returned on or before
the last date below.**

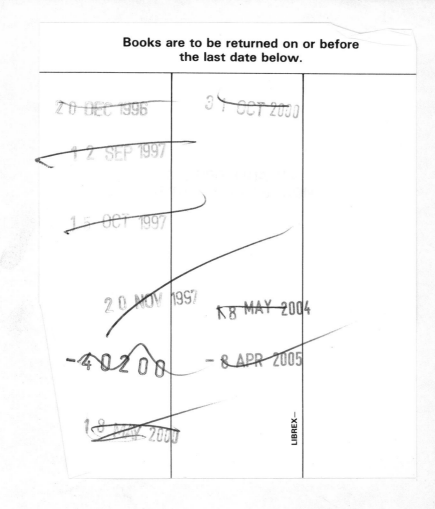

THE PERSONALITY
OF THE ORGANISATION

THE PERSONALITY
OF THE ORGANISATION

A PSYCHO-DYNAMIC
EXPLANATION OF
CULTURE AND CHANGE

Lionel Stapley

FREE ASSOCIATION BOOKS / LONDON / NEW YORK

Published in 1996 by
Free Association Books Ltd
57 Warren Street, London W1P 5PA

ISBN 1 85343 341 1 hbk

A CIP record for this book is available
from the British Library

Impression:
02 01 00 99 98 97 96
8 7 6 5 4 3 2 1

Produced for Free Association Books by
Chase Production Services, Chipping Norton, OX7 5QR
Printed in the EC by T. J. Press, Padstow

CONTENTS

PREFACE

From the outset, I want to make it clear that this is not just another book on organisation culture and change. While the subject matter may be old and familiar the approach taken here is distinctive and new. It is not simply a reworking of the many well known existing theories. On the contrary, it is an original approach based on psycho-analytic theory, and one that seeks to do what others have not done successfully: to provide an explanation to that most crucial of questions; that concerning how culture develops. Should you, like me, feel that existing theory does not provide you with all you need to know about this phenomenon, you will find this necessary reading.

As the title signifies, this book is essentially about two interrelated areas of research. The first is about the development of an explanation of the concept of organisational culture. In doing this I seek to put forward an original view of how the concept of organisational culture develops, how it is perpetuated and how it is represented. The second is the application of this concept of culture to the management of change. Here I seek to show the effect that culture has on organisational change and how an understanding of the relationship between culture and change is necessary if we are to achieve constructive change in organisations.

Organisation change has been, is, and will continue to be a continuous feature of our lives. No matter what sort of organisation we are concerned with – be it in the public, private or voluntary sector – the only thing that will remain constant will be change itself. As a consultant and a manager I have frequently discovered that to bring about change in organisations can, on the one hand, be exciting, rewarding and fascinating but can, on the other hand, be extremely difficult, unpredictable and frustrating. Having experienced some of the joys but particularly the pains that have resulted from such situations I therefore sought to gain an understanding of the processes involved.

In doing so I came to realise that in many situations what was happening had something to do with what is commonly called 'organisation culture'. In my search for a deeper understanding I discovered that there was a wide range of literature on both culture and change but it was my analysis that current theory failed to provide me with a satisfactory explanation of culture such as to enable me to be effective in attempting to bring about intended change in organisations. Consequently, it was felt that there was a need to look at organisation culture in a different light, to search for new ideas, and that an original approach might prove more beneficial. This book is the result of that research.

Such are the claims about the effects of organisation culture that it has become a matter of considerable interest and concern to consultants and managers everywhere. For example: claims about its impact on organisational change, claims about cultures that result in organisational success, and claims about cultures that are dysfunctional and liable to lead to some sort of organisational failure or even disaster. It is no surprise, then, that organisation culture has become such a hot topic of research and this has led to a situation where there are many and various theoretical approaches. Indeed, during the past twenty or so years there has been a plethora of books and articles seeking to provide consultants and managers with explanations of organisation culture.

When it comes to the matter of application, however, it has been my experience that almost none of the current explanations provided by these many theories has been really helpful. It seems that, in the main, current theory only deals with the simpler questions, the surface issues or the symptoms of culture. It makes no attempt to deal with the more complicated aspects such as the causes of culture and the underlying unconscious aspects. Admittedly, some of the more serious writers have acknowledged the part that unconscious processes play in organisational culture. Sadly, though, the frequently advised response has been for action at a rational or conscious level. For my part, I wanted to know not only *what* was happening but *why* it was happening. I felt there had to be a different and fuller explanation.

I concluded that if we were to understand this vital aspect of organisation behaviour it was necessary to look elsewhere for an explanation. I decided that I would start anew and, in doing so, seek an explanation of how the concept of organisational culture develops, how it is perpetuated and how it is represented. The crucial question appeared to be concerned with how culture develops, the rationale being that if we know how culture develops we shall in turn know how to unpack it and deal with it: we would in effect be dealing with the cause and not the symptoms. To do so I also realised that any explanation of the phenomenon must include that which previous definitions of culture failed to include, namely, an explanation of unconscious as well as conscious processes. Unless these were also understood we would have only half the story and this would be no improvement on the current situation.

At the centre of the process are the individual members of an organisation and their mental processes. Culture is a construct, and the source of that construct is the human mind. Consequently, in developing a theory and methodology we need a means of interpreting the conscious and unconscious behaviour of the individual actors of various boundaried groups within organisations. To achieve this we need to use the appropriate tools, or, as Bhaskar (1975) has pointed out, the social scientist can only say as much as the tools at his disposal, or those which he chooses to use, enable him to say.

What was needed was to find a means of establishing and understanding the feelings of members of organisations. These are less amenable to being uncovered by using conventional interviews or survey methods. I became aware that to discover what was in the 'mind' of human beings requires a different methodology from the natural sciences whose practitioners were interested in matter and would recognise that matter does not have a mind and was incapable of subjective experience. Psycho-dynamic theory has been used for the study of live objects which are seen, experienced and recognised subjectively in contrast to traditional sciences which study 'objects only'. I therefore decided to use concepts from psycho-analysis as the tools to gain an understanding of the unconscious processes and to provide the sought-after explanation of culture and change.

The application of psycho-analytic theory to organisation problems is one which is rapidly gaining ground. However, many readers may consider that such theories seem more relevant to psychiatrists and therapists than to consultants and managers in organisations. Others, possibly because of the clinical origin of the theories, may consider such concepts to be beyond their comprehension. It is true that some of the theories do, at first sight, appear complicated, but, so too was the theory that gave birth to the saying 'Freudian slip', yet we can all understand that perfectly well – it is largely a matter of familiarity. Such theories are different and are largely unknown to many consultants and managers. However, it will be encouraging for those who have limited knowledge of these concepts to know that while the author has studied and applied the psycho-dynamic theories used, he is not a clinician. It is hoped that this book will continue the process of making psycho-dynamic theories more accessible to a wider range of consultants and managers.

Organisation culture is a complicated phenomenon that cannot be reduced to a simple definition of some or all of the symptoms. To do justice to the topic requires a thorough explanation of both the conscious and unconscious processes involved. The reader should therefore not expect a simple book. However, it is intended that those with no previous knowledge of psycho-dynamic theory will be able to understand both the theoretical concept of organisation culture which is developed and the psycho-analytic concepts on which the main theory is based. It is recommended, though, that it would be best for those with little or no previous knowledge of psycho-analytic theory or practice to read the chapters in order, since the main theory builds throughout the book. Those who are more familiar with psycho-dynamic theory may choose to take a more selective route; perhaps moving in and out of the chapters as they will.

The book is organised into three parts and the structure is intended to be progressive. Part I is an introductory section which is intended to take the reader on a short journey from a consideration of the identified problem through to a new explanation. The first two chapters provide a critical look at current theory and methodology; the third provides an outline of a psycho-dynamic explanation of organisational culture. At the end of this part the reader should know what the book is all about.

Part II is concerned with concepts that are considered fundamental to the development of a psycho-dynamic explanation of culture. Each of the first seven chapters in this part deals with a separate concept. Chapter 4 looks at the nature of organisations and sets a sort of bench-mark for future reference. The next six chapters deal with the need, development and use of boundaries; symbolism; language and words as symbols; the process of learning; organisational socialisation; and creativity. These chapters provide the theoretical bases for the last chapter in this section which builds on Chapter 3 to provide a fuller explanation of the psycho-dynamic explanation of organisational culture.

Part III is an application section. The two chapters in this part apply the theory to managing change, and a case study. A fuller description of each chapter is to be found at the start of each part.

It is intended that this book will provide consultants and managers with a deeper understanding of their organisations by providing a different way of looking at organisational development and behaviour. A way of looking which provides them with an insight into things that they know about in their organisations but cannot fully understand using current theory. It is particularly intended to help them appreciate how a different understanding of organisational culture will help them to bring about change successfully. This, then, is a book for consultants who are dedicated to providing added value by helping clients to solve their problems. It is also intended for academics and students of courses on organisation behaviour and development, human resource and other management studies. In addition, it will be valued by those thoughtful managers who are constantly wanting to gain a better understanding of their organisations.

Throughout the book I refer to 'he' or 'him' when I could easily have written 'she' or 'her'. I hope this will not give offence and that the reader appreciates my desire to avoid the awkwardness of writing 'he or she' and 'him- or herself'.

Acknowledgments

I am very grateful to many people who have helped me to produce this book who I regret cannot be mentioned individually. However, special thanks are due to the following: to John McAuley at Sheffield Hallam University for his good humoured, friendly support and encouragement while completing my PhD; to those many social scientists at the Tavistock Institute who through their writing over the years have been so influential in my development; in particular to Eric Miller in his many roles but mainly as adviser, friend and colleague at OPUS (an Organisation for Promoting Understanding in Society); to Leona Henry, whose typing skill and patience through many drafts and alterations was invaluable; and to my wife, Monica, special thanks for her support, encouragement and tolerance over such a long period.

PART I

ORGANISATIONAL CULTURE: AN OLD PROBLEM AND A NEW EXPLANATION

The three chapters in this section are intended to take the reader on a journey that starts with an old and familiar problem, describes some of the limitations and failings of current theory, provides a different way of looking at that problem and then introduces the psycho-dynamic explanation of culture. In many ways this is intended to be a 'stand alone' section which describes the various processes in the simplest language possible. For those readers with a good knowledge of psycho-analytic theory it will provide a useful introduction. Those who are less familiar with such an approach will find this a basis for understanding the more complex explanations that follow.

Chapter 1 describes something of the nature of the problem that we term organisation culture and how it may affect managers and consultants in everyday life. Primarily, though, this chapter provides a detailed analysis of the main current theoretical approaches to organisation culture and introduces the need for a different approach which enables us to consider unconscious as well as conscious processes. Chapter 2 details some of the inadequacies of current methodologies and explains why it has been decided to use a psycho-dynamic approach. Chapter 3 provides the psycho-dynamic explanation of how organisational culture develops in as simple a fashion as possible. This is not intended to be a technical presentation of the theory but one which all readers will be able to understand and apply.

1

THEORETICAL APPROACHES TO ORGANISATIONAL CULTURE

The term 'culture' has been in common usage for many years and is a familiar notion. Unfortunately, this common usage has itself led to problems. For example, cultural differences are seen as being in the nature of things requiring no explanation. A result is that functions which are not easily understood are assigned to a mysterious central agency called 'culture', accompanied by a declaration that 'it' performs in a particular way. Culture is also an easy option to fall back on to solve all our unexplained problems. In addition, past uses of the word to designate a way of life of a particular society, or part of a society, such as an organisation, are exceedingly vague.

The primary purpose of this chapter is to take a detailed and critical look at how the main theories currently in use have sought to provide an answer to the question of what is meant by the term 'culture'. There are several benefits in taking such an approach, not least being the fact that it will help to explain something of the nature of the phenomenon. It will also provide an opportunity to expose the limitations of current theories and to begin to show why a different approach may be useful. However, by way of background and in order to provide the reader with an indication of what is to come, I want to start with a brief description of the nature of the problem that is being addressed in this book.

THE NATURE OF THE PROBLEM

Over the years my experience in attempting to bring about change in various organisations – whether as a consultant or manager – has caused me considerable frustration, confusion and even pain. For example, when I was the manager in charge of a police division, I walked out of my office, through the general office, down the stairs, through the operations room and into the car park passing many members of staff on the way, all of whom deliberately avoided making eye contact with me. What – I wondered – had I done to deserve treatment like this? From being a happy and cheerful place to work in, the atmosphere had changed dramatically and was quite dreadful. I just could not understand it. A similar experience was related by a friend in a large public sector organisation who said, 'It's awful here at the moment, it's just like the Russians not talking to the Americans.' The common factor in both these instances was organisation change. These examples are not unique and I have little doubt that any consultant or manager could report similar experiences.

Just how dramatic, difficult and, at times, painful the process of change can be was reported by Tunstall (1985) when he described a change at the American Telephone & Telegraph Company. The views expressed included: 'angry, sad, a little scared'; 'as if I've been through a forced divorce, and that I could not control the outcome'; 'sad and somewhat resentful'; 'a sense of loss'; 'my feelings were ambivalent, I was hurt'; 'anger, frustration, a sense of personal loss'; 'a kind of identity crisis'; and, 'a very real sense of loss'. It will be noted that, quite apart from the expression of pain that is present in these statements, there is also a strong feeling of being out of control. There are many other reported examples that support the above, and I feel certain that the reader can add to these from his or her own experiences.

From this brief description of the effects of change in organisations we should be aware that deep emotions are brought into play, but why should organisations evoke such deep emotions? People's behaviour does not automatically change in accordance with what is required or, indeed, with what they themselves may rationally believe to be right. Perception of individual roles is not simply a matter of intellectual classification, but involves the feelings and attitudes in the roles.

It is by the process of perception that we impose some structure on new input, compare it with a pool of old information, and then either add to it or eliminate it. We can only make judgements about whether we like or dislike something if it is something that we know. Our sensations must be completed by some form of appraisal before we can decide whether it is good or bad for us. What we are concerned with here is not so much 'reality' (whatever that may be), but rather how the human individual develops his or her reality concepts and uses them to live in the world.

The basis for our perceptive process is the pool of internalised information, which in turn provides the basis for our self-concepts which are the individual's views of him- or herself. They begin in childhood with the bodily self-concept and expand rapidly through object relations: first with the mother, and then with other significant family members. The object relations with the parents provide a continual psycho-social basis for learning what is pleasurable and what is distressing. The memory bank grows throughout life to produce that rich mosaic which is the individual personality.

Although no longer conscious in adult life, the imaginings and memories of infantile experience, particularly when associated with anxiety, have a profound influence on subsequent mental development and help to determine the character of personal and social relationships, cultural interests and the way of living. The growth of an infant in a human environment creates a transactional field in which most affect – or feeling – becomes oriented to human objects. Thus, even if the object is not human, it is associated with human activity.

Because of our ability to form concepts we can construct an object in the mind that is a non-human object. In much the same way that the infant creates the mother in the mind through the filters of the perceptive process which then becomes the object that the infant identifies with, the members of an organisation create an organisation held in the mind from the filtered experience of the organisation holding environment. Having created the concept of an organisation, the members of the organisation act 'as if' it exists and, because of our previous experience, even if the object is not human, it is associated with human activity. The result is that we attach to the object the same attributes as other influential objects, especially the mother.

From the foregoing, we can perhaps begin to appreciate why it is that organisational change is so complex and why it can be so painful. The dynamic configuration that constitutes the individual and his or her environment is such that all parts are closely related and in constant interaction. Thus, it is not simply a matter of making changes to the strategy or structure, it is also about the feelings of the members of the organisation. Furthermore, any consultant that wishes to intervene in such a system will also be subject to the feelings of those concerned. These and other concepts will be developed in depth throughout the book.

Having explained something of the nature of the problem, we now need to look at how others have sought to address the problem of explaining this complicated phenomenon and then to explore the need for a different approach. In doing so, it will provide an opportunity for the reader to locate the approach taken here within the existing theory.

What, then, do we mean by 'culture'? We know that the term has been used in common, everyday language for many years to designate the way of life of a society, or part of a society, such as an organisation, but what is meant by the term is far from clear. That there is a wide divergence of views immediately becomes apparent when we refer to Kroeber and Kluckholm's (1952) revelation that they had identified 164 different definitions of culture. Commenting on the fact that the concept had been borrowed from anthropology, 'where there had been no consensus of meaning' (p. 339), Smircich (1983) was of the view that we should not be surprised that there is also a variety in its application to organisation studies. More recently, Sackmann (1992) also refers to the anthropological source of the term and the problems of diversity.

Looked at from a historical perspective we discover that until about 1970 there were infrequent and often indirect references to the subject of organisational culture. For example, one of the first references to something like 'culture' was made by Sherif (1936) when he referred to a 'concept of social norms'; in 1951 Lewin referred to 'group atmosphere'; Cartwright and Zander (1953) to a 'group mind', 'collective unconscious' and 'culture' (although it was not seen as worth indexing the latter term), and Cyert and March (1963) to 'an organisation mind'. In the 1970s the notion that organisations have 'cultures' was proposed fairly frequently (for example, Turner, 1971; Handy, 1976; and Pettigrew, 1979).

In the early 1980s there was a surge of interest in organisational culture and a number of books were published on the topic. There followed a vast array of articles and publications, many lacking in theoretical rigour, seeking to popularise and simplify the phenomenon, and many making claims that a reified culture could be manipulated by managers in a manner similar to changing the structure or strategy. This, not surprisingly, led to warnings that a complex and difficult concept could be turned into a superficial fad, reducing it to an empty, if entertaining, catch-all construct explaining everything and nothing (Allaire and Firsirotu, 1984). The state of theory seems to have been influenced by the fact that this was a period of organisational history that seemed to be characterised by a belief that everything could be resolved by a 'quick fix' (Kilmann, 1989).

Little wonder that Turner (1986), catching the mood of the time, described the organisational culture literature as comprising two broad categories, 'pop culture magicians' and 'honest grapplers'. Categorising the various views is not easy as the whole field has become complicated by difficulties, such as different writers using concepts in different ways. What can be said, though, is that organisation theory of culture has been derived largely from anthropological theory. Consequently, I shall use that as my point of departure in trying to make sense of this complex data.

ANTHROPOLOGICAL THEORIES

The schools of thought in cultural anthropology can first be usefully categorised by making a distinction between those theorists who view culture as a social phenomenon and those who conceive of it as a conceptually separate phenomenon. In the former view, culture is seen as a component of the social system, manifested by behaviour and products of behaviour: the cultural and social realms are integrated into a sociocultural system that grows and changes as one. The cultural is swallowed into the social and vice versa. The ways of life, or manifest behaviour, are the product of this sociocultural system.

In examining the concept of organisations as sociocultural systems I find that it does not provide an explanation as to how such sociocultural systems can foster 'cultures' different from those of the surrounding society. If 'culture' consists of socially transmitted behaviour patterns, how do we get different patterns? Furthermore, the view that actors, who are members of these proposed sociocultural systems, are treated as passive recipients who learn 'culture' from the sociocultural systems ignores other bodies of theory that suggest that learning is an activity that is influenced by both subject and object. These include, for example, the learning theories of Piaget (1951), Bion (1967) and Bateson (1973); and the psycho-analytic theory that subject-object relations emerge out of a lifelong development, both of which will be taken up in the chapters on learning and organisational culture, respectively. These theories treat individuals as active participants in the process of learning and development; an approach more in keeping with the second view of culture.

The second view sees culture and social systems as distinct but interrelated. Culture is seen as an ideational system that is located in the minds of culture-bearers or as the products of minds in the form of shared meanings; that is, being located in the minds of, or products of the minds of, individual members of a particular society. As the various schools that view culture as systems of ideas are somewhat different I shall comment briefly on each of them. The 'cognitive school' views culture as a system of knowledge, of learned standards for perceiving, believing, evaluating and acting (see, for example, Goodenough, 1971). In the 'mutual equivalence' school, culture becomes a set of standardised cognitive processes which create the general framework for the mental prediction of behaviour among individuals interacting in a social setting (see, for example, Wallace, 1970). The 'structuralist school' views culture as made up of shared symbolic systems that are cumulative products of mind, a reflection of unconscious processes of mind that underlie cultural manifestations (see, for example, Levi-Strauss, 1973). The fourth school, the 'symbolic' or 'semiotic', takes the view that culture should not be looked for in people's heads but in the meanings and thinkings shared by social actors. Here significant symbols or products of mind constitute the raw materials for the interpretation of the ordered system of meaning in terms of which social action takes place (see, for example, Geertz, 1973).

At this stage, I would simply comment that I agree with all these views. My view is that culture may be conceived simultaneously as an idea held in the mind, as an inter-subjective phenomenon, as developed out of the interrelatedness to symbolic objects, and as an unconscious as well as a conscious process. However, it also follows that if we conclude that each of the theories is 'correct' then we may also conclude that each is only partially 'correct'. Each of the theories may be helpful in its own way but each is also self-limiting by not recognising the existence of the other. The notion of culture as an ideational system will be further commented on again shortly when I refer to organisational theories of culture, which is what I turn to now.

ORGANISATIONAL THEORIES

Organisational theories of culture have largely been derived from the anthropological theories referred to above. Many theorists have borrowed from only one of the anthropological traditions. As Lynn Meek (1988) and Allaire and Firsirotu (1984) have pointed out, the theoretical basis on which the idea of corporate or organisational culture rests is frequently that of culture as a sociocultural system, as a social phenomenon. For example, according to Allaire & Firsirotu:

A first and striking observation is that the large body of literature, including many of the classics on organisation theory, tacitly assumes that the social and structural components are (must be) fully integrated, synchronized and consonant with the ideational, symbolic dimensions of the organisation. (p. 199)

Several writers have taken the view that 'organisation culture' is a unifying force within the organisation that exists in a real and tangible sense and that management can identify and manage it as a controllable variable to enhance organisational effectiveness. For example, Peters and Waterman (1982) and Deal and Kennedy (1982) talk of 'excellence' and 'winning' by having internalised uniform corporate values. Others have produced studies that on the face of it are more sophisticated. For example, the concept of 'organisational climate' as an individual's cognitive map (Schneider, 1979); organisational learning (Argyris and Schon, 1978); the role of history and founders (Pettigrew, 1985); and basic assumptions (Schein, 1987b). However, on closer examination all of these theorists promulgate the idea that culture is the collective consciousness of the organisation and that it is available to management to manipulate.

To use Young's (1989) terminology, be they 'pop culture magicians' or 'honest grapplers', both start from the basis that there is a universal homogeneous 'culture': a unitary concept expressing, on the one hand, social cohesion and integration and, on the other hand, organisational effectiveness. Viewed in this way culture can be seen as something the organisation *has* (Smircich, 1983): something that is imported into an organisation from the broader society or something created by management that can be manipulated by them. This approach tends to ignore those anthropological schools of thought that see culture as systems of ideas where the actors play a central part in the development of culture.

The view taken here corresponds with organisation theories that are derived from the ideational schools referred to above. These treat culture as emerging from social interactions, as the product of negotiated and shared symbols and meanings, as something that the organisation *is* (see, for example, Young, 1989; Berger and Luckmann, 1966; Morgan, 1983), rather than something the organisation *has*. Following Khan (1976), human organisations are seen as having no structure other than the patterns of behaviour that are also their internal functions. When these patterns of behaviour stop, the organisation ceases to exist. Being patterns of behaviour, it therefore follows that they are contrived, and being of human construction they are infinitely susceptible to modification.

However, while it seems necessary to consider culture as something that the organisation *is*, we still need to consider the question of how (or if) culture is to be demarcated from other social aspects of the organisation (Lynn Meek, 1988). There is reason to suggest that culture and social structure can be distinguished. For example,

as an organisation consultant I have experienced many occasions
when attempts to change the formal systems of goals, structures and
strategies have – to varying degrees – been unsuccessful because what
was intended did not take place or that unintended consequences
occurred. This would suggest that in such circumstances the organisation's cultural system was not congruent with the sociostructural
system – an experience that I feel sure is shared by many others
working in organisations. In circumstances where attempts at change
have resulted in industrial disputes the lack of congruence between
the cultural system and the revised sociostructural system may be
reasonably obvious. On other occasions the distinction may be far
more subtle but nonetheless of considerable relevance.

I would therefore argue that in developing a theory of culture
that helps us to understand organisational change there is a need to
maintain a conceptual distinction between culture and social structure. In doing so, however, we need to bear in mind that culture
and structure are both constructs, not tangible entities. As culture
and social structure are not concrete entities but abstract concepts
used by members of organisations and theorists to interpret behaviour
we need to bear in mind the need of the researcher to study not
only the culture or structure developed by the members of an organisation but, also more importantly, the behaviour of individual actors
(a view also shared by Critical Social Theorists such as Habermas,
1976). An organisation, or part of an organisation, may be viewed as
an association of individuals, and it is those individuals who develop
the constructs that we categorise as structure and culture. Consequently, the behaviour of individual actors is considered to be a key
concept in the study of culture.

In viewing the role of the individual in the development of the
concept of culture, there are few references to unconscious processes of
individuals. The 'structuralist' school of Levi-Strauss (1958) believes
that there are universals in human culture which will be found only at
the unconscious level. Others, notably Mitroff (1989), and Kets De
Vries and Miller (1987), have also viewed culture from the unconscious
psychological perspective. Mitroff draws on Jung's work on archetypes
in trying to discover structural patterns that link the unconscious human mind with its overt manifestation in social arrangements. Kets De
Vries and Miller are concerned with shared fantasies, especially the
shared fantasies of a dominant coalition, which has an effect on the
culture of a group. What they do best is to describe particular types of
culture (Kets De Vries, neurotic types; and Mitroff, archetypes), but
they fail to provide any explanation of the bases of culture.

PSYCHO-ANALYTIC THEORIES

Faced with the complex situation of proposing a framework for the understanding of the human mind, Freud made the decision that it required a division into a number of portions to which it is possible to attribute a number of differentiating characteristics and methods of operating (1923, p. 343). Given the dynamic nature of the phenomenon currently under review there is a need for a similar approach. If we are to study the behaviour of individuals we need to develop a theoretical framework that relates to both conscious and unconscious processes. Over the years, psycho-analytic concepts have been used by researchers exploring various aspects of organisations (for example, Bion, 1961; Menzies Lyth, 1959; Jaques, 1953; Miller, 1976; Kets De Vries and Miller, 1987; Trist, 1990). Following their example, I intend to show that there can be a theoretical approach in which psycho-analytic ideas are used to interpret cultural data; one which is derived from clinical psycho-analysis, but independent of and parallel to it. Although psycho-analytic theory is frequently the point of origin of many of the ideas in this book, it is not necessarily their point of destination. The aim is to translate psycho-analytic concepts into a theory of organisation culture relevant to managing change in organisations.

It will be acknowledged that there are many criticisms of psycho-analytic theory. Not least is the criticism that it is a purely subjective theory that is not capable of empirical confirmation and validation, or that it is self-monitoring and self-confirming so that it 'comes out right' whichever way experimental evidence happens to point (for example, Gelner, 1985; Eysenck and Wilson, 1973). Against this, psycho-analysis has become 'the dominant idiom for the discussion of the human personality and of human relations' (Gelner, 1985, p. 5). That affect or feelings influence our behaviour is hardly contestable. It has also been accepted by even those who are most critical of psycho-analysis that, although there may be disagreement as to its form, the unconscious is a necessary construct for exploring mental processes. Psycho-analytic theory about infant development, as formulated by Melanie Klein, Winnicott and Bowlby, is considered to be particularly valuable in providing the means for greater understanding of mental activity and will be related to throughout this book.

SUMMARY

Organisational culture is a relatively new concept and until about 1970 there were few references to the subject. However, in the 1980s it suddenly became 'fashionable' and a wide range of material was published, much of which sought to popularise and simplify the phenomenon. Organisational theory has been derived largely from anthropological theory where there has been no consensus of meaning and this trend has continued in regard to organisational theory. Consequently, there are huge difficulties in categorising the various views because, for example, different writers use concepts in different ways.

However, it does seem useful to view culture as either something that an organisation *has* or something that an organisation *is*. Many writers have sought to show that culture is something that the organisation *has*: something that is imported into an organisation from the broader society or something created by management that can be manipulated by them. This approach ignores the notion that sees culture as systems of ideas where the actors play a central part in the development of culture. The view taken here is that culture is something that an organisation *is*: that it emerges from social interactions, as the product of negotiated and shared symbols and meanings.

Culture and social structures are not concrete entities but abstract concepts used by members of organisations and theorists to interpret behaviour. As such, we need to bear in mind that researchers should not only study the culture or structure developed by the members of an organisation, but also, more importantly, the individual actors. An organisation, or part of an organisation, may be viewed as an association of individuals, and it is those individuals who develop the constructs that we categorise as structure and culture. Consequently, the behaviour of individual actors is considered to be a key concept in the study of culture.

If we are to study the behaviour of individuals we need to develop a theoretical framework that relates to both conscious and unconscious processes. Over the years, psycho-analytic concepts have been used by researchers exploring various aspects of organisation. Following their example, psycho-analytic concepts will be used to interpret cultural data.

Consideration of the various theoretical approaches has provided further insights into the nature of the phenomenon that we seek to understand. In the next chapter I shall be looking at the various methodologies that are available and arguing the need for a psycho-dynamic approach that will provide us with information about the unconscious processes which come into play.

2

TOWARDS A PSYCHO-DYNAMIC METHODOLOGY

There has been criticism of psycho-analysis, some of which is difficult to refute; not least, the criticism that psycho-analysis is not a scientific methodology. In this chapter I will show that various other method-ological approaches are also far from being perfect and I will argue the case for a psycho-dynamic approach. In dealing with the issue of methodology it seems that there are two important considerations, the matter of what is being considered and the various methods that are available. Both aspects are complicated and deserve more than passing comment. Furthermore, they are both inextricably linked and will therefore shed yet more light on the phenomenon of culture.

Since this is a study of organisational culture, it may be useful to consider briefly the nature of organisations. First, we need to recog-nise, as Khan (1976) has shown, that organisations have no structure apart from patterns of human behaviour and that when an organ-isation ceases to exist there are few clues to its nature in life. The implications of this view of human organisations are many, but it will be appreciated that if organisations are essentially patterns of human behaviour, it follows that they are contrived. Furthermore, being of human construction they are infinitely susceptible to mod-ification.

In other words, what is organised is human activity and this inevitably raises the well documented and historical arguments about subjectivity and objectivity. The drawing of distinctions between the natural sciences and the social sciences and the differences between the nature of physical reality and human reality has been discussed among anthropologists and sociologists for many years (for example, Benedict, 1935; Caudwell, 1937; White, 1949; Berger and Luck-mann, 1966; Doise, 1978; Tajfel and Fraser, 1978; Berger and Kell-ner, 1981). More recently, organisational researchers have also raised the issue to a level of prominence (for example, Douglas 1976; Burrell and Morgan, G 1979; Van Maanen, 1979; Morgan, 1983;

Gummesson, 1991; Reason, 1988). However, for the origins of the arguments we have to consider the philosophical views of 'reality' formulated over the years.

EMPIRICAL-ANALYTICAL METHODOLOGIES

The dominant view of scientific method has evolved out of logical-positivist philosophy as it was formulated at the beginning of this century and is one which seeks a unified method for all sciences. This method is a logical consequence of the empirical-analytical approach to 'reality', whereby it is assumed that 'reality' may be broken up into logically independent variables. By doing so, it is theorised that these meaningful and distinct categories may be subjected to observational precision, theoretical prediction and, subsequently, validation. In other words, it is considered that statements are meaningful only when their truth can be verified and this criterion has come to be known as the principle of verifiability.

As is now well known, this view was challenged by Karl Popper (1934) who took the view that as observation is theory-laden there can be no such thing as certainty in scientific knowledge, and conclusive verification of general propositions, like laws of nature, is logically impossible. In his view a scientific hypothesis or theory must be falsifiable. Popper raised considerable doubts about the prevailing philosophy but he appears to have been insensitive to the non-rational aspects of human knowledge.

It was Kuhn (1962) who drew attention to this problem with his influential theory of scientific paradigms. In short, Kuhn concluded that scientific knowledge goes through phases. A field proceeds from an immature pre-paradigmatic phase into a period of paradigmatic science once agreement is reached concerning the proper way of study. Once such a paradigm has been created, methodological issues come to an end and scientists may proceed to solve the 'puzzles' left unsolved by the paradigm. This is called normal science. After a certain period, however, the number of anomalies that arise become a threat for the paradigm and the need for another paradigm will be felt. In turn, this state of crisis will lead to a revolution as soon as a new convincing paradigm has been articulated.

In considering how this 'scientific revolution' comes about it will be useful to recall that organisations are about human activity, and this is also the case with science. Scientific knowledge is made by people for people and the scientist as observer or communicator is an indispensable element of that knowledge system. The contents and quality of scientific knowledge depend on the powers and functions of scientists as observers, as communicators, as assessors and assimilators of knowledge, and eventually, as believers and authoritative experts (Ziman, 1978). In other words, in any scientific endeavour, subjectivity, and more particularly inter-subjectivity, will play a key role. This has long been the view of philosophers of the hermeneutic tradition who have maintained that traditional empirical-analytical research is based on implicit interpretations. Therefore scientific knowledge cannot be justified or validated by logic alone. Even the most objective research is dependent on interpretive choices which are often left implicit. Consequently, they argue that an atomistic approach is simply not adequate as it is necessary to construct or reconstruct meaning relations between significant parts of the context and the context as a whole.

Kuhn's valuable work has shown that in order to change methodology a revolution is necessary. However, this will not occur easily and this is clearly demonstrated by the fact that it was over forty years ago when White pointed out that 'we must, in short, view science as a way of behaving, as a way of interpreting reality, rather than as an entity in itself, as a segment of that reality' (1949; p.6). Yet that same debate is still going on today and the arguments between those who insist on the use of quantitative methodologies and those who insist on qualitative methods to establish 'reality' in regard to human activities are no less strong.

The relative arguments are in themselves interesting but equally interesting – if not more so – is the process. For example, we might well enquire why it has taken so long for the qualitative type of research to be acceptable – if indeed it is acceptable to all. In some ways Kuhn has explained this. However, we also need to understand the natural psychological tendency for individuals to cling to previously successful paradigms even in the face of contrary evidence. What Freud refers to as the conservative instinct is an important concept and one to which I shall return later. We also need to be aware that any change must inevitably mean unlearning much of our previous 'reality'. There are therefore implications for learning which will also be referred to in detail later.

The reliability of empirical scientific knowledge in regard to physics, chemistry, astronomy or for that matter, engineering or manufacturing, is not really in doubt. It is when we extend science to the extreme difficulties of biological behaviour, human emotion and social organisation that it becomes inherently unsound. It is then that other sources of insight and other methodologies beyond those of the empirical-analytical scientific method must be sought. In other words, the value-free, value-neutral, value-avoiding model of science that was inherited from physics, chemistry and astronomy, where it was necessary and desirable to keep the data clean, is quite unsuitable for the scientific study of life (Maslow, 1971).

HERMENEUTIC METHODOLOGIES

To provide some understanding of these other sources of insight we need to turn to a brief summary of the views of the hermeneutic philosophers. According to Kant the mind makes knowledge by forming; that is, by imposing general concepts upon the raw unstructured data of experience. So Kant internalises (or, more accurately, makes transcendental) the creation of the world. In his Critical Philosophy he sets out to reverse the old assumptions when he states that knowledge comes first and reality must then conform itself to our knowledge. Theory shapes perception. Reality doesn't come first and then get itself copied by our knowledge; rather, reality becomes itself for us in our knowledge of it. Hegel points to a world where everything is shifting, horizontal, interconnected, human, a game with constantly moving goal posts, a world without any enduring and objective meanings, values or truths.

Others, such as Gadamer (1962) and Wittgenstein (1969), have argued that human practices and rationality exist largely within frames of language and forms of life that remain unnoticed and unconscious most of the time; and even if some parts and aspects become an object for reflection it is doubtful whether they may so easily be changed, even if we would wish this. For Berkeley philosophy starts from a perceptual situation, whereby a perception is presented to a perceiver. So the world already contains two kinds of entity, perceivers and things perceived, minds and presentations, knowing subjects and objects known, spirits and ideas. This intersubjective view is shared by Habermas (1976), who considers that social action depends upon the agent's 'definition of the situation', and this is not solely a matter of subjective motivations. The meanings to which social action is oriented are primarily intersubjective meanings.

Weber was undoubtedly of the old philosophical school, nevertheless he was of the view that human phenomena do not speak for themselves; they must be interpreted. This was very much in accord with the views of Nietzsche which he expressed in his most influential slogans, such as, 'There are no facts only interpretations'. It was Nietzsche's view that there isn't any firm ready made world out there independent of us. Apart from our activity there is only a 'fuzziness and chaos of sense impressions', sometimes 'formless and unformable'. So truth is the product of our own logicalising, adapting and construing, a continuous activity which must take ever new forms. On Neitzsche's account, knowing, creatively forming, interpreting and producing truth are all different names for the same activity. The world is an interpretation – our interpretation – and it is plural and continually changing. We are continually reinventing ourselves, immersed in a world of fictions and reinterpretations.

Under the empirical-analytical philosophies it was supposed that matter could be completely described in terms of itself, and since man is made of matter, these terms would describe him also. However, when we abandon the empiricist assumption that there is a fixed reality that can be described objectively, the aims of scientific research must be redefined. This is precisely the stance of the hermeneuticians who make it clear that there is no fixed 'reality' other than that interpreted by our perception. In addition, such 'reality' as there is, is a continually changing phenomenon. It is a continuum, a stream of events, that flows freely through time. Furthermore, for it to become 'reality' it must be intersubjective, it must be a shared 'reality'. There is no taxonomic framework for human behaviour, individual or social, in which the categories are both meaningful and distinct. One of the problems with classical science when applied to psychology is that all it knows how to do well is to study people as objects, when what we really need is to be able to study them also as subjects (Maslow, 1969). Unfortunately, human behaviour is always so complex and varied that we can seldom make a sharply confirmable (or discomfirmable) prediction from the model. Consequently, the old scientific approach is of little, if any, value in researching such human activities as culture.

Not surprisingly, these hermeneutic approaches to philosophy have called for and have triggered entirely different methodologies to those employed in the empirical-analytical paradigm. A hermeneutic approach begins with the distinction between sensory experience or observation and communicative experience or understanding (*verstehen*). Observation is directed to perceptible things and events (or states); understanding is directed to the meaning of utterances. Above all, we can see that language plays a key part in any hermeneutic endeavour. The interpreter who understands meaning is experiencing fundamentally as a participant in communication, on the basis of a symbolically established intersubjective relationship with other individuals (Habermas, 1976).

In contrast to formal structures and causal laws, the hermeneutic approach seeks to elucidate and make explicit our practical
understanding of human actions by providing an interpretation of
them. The hermeneutic method is well documented (see, for example, Bleicher, 1980; Giddens, 1976; Palmer, 1969; Mueller-
Voller, 1986; Terwee, 1990; Messer et al., 1988). It is characterised by the following features. First, there is no presuppositionless
knowledge. We cannot ask fruitful questions unless we know
something about a topic. Second, in attempting to understand
other persons we must do so on their own terms. Third, both the
interpreter and the interpreted have a conception of the world and
truth. A complete understanding may aim for a fusion of horizons.
Fourth, coming to understanding involves a continuous circular
movement from the part to the whole and back again from the
whole to its parts. Thus, it will be seen that in hermeneutics
understanding only comes through dialogue. It is only through
open dialogue, that is, through the exploration of one's own as
well as the other's presuppositions, that understanding can be
improved, and this is not easy (Steele, 1979).

PERCEIVED REALITY

At this point, it will perhaps be helpful to develop the discussion on
perception that was begun in Chapter 1 in order to gain a deeper
understanding of this important concept. To do so, we need to start
at the beginning; to start from the point of the individual. According
to Freud (1921):

> Only rarely and under certain exceptional conditions is individual
> psychology in a position to disregard the relations of this individual to
> others. In the individual's mental life someone else is invariably
> involved, as a model, as an object, as a helper, as an opponent, and so
> from the very first individual psychology is at the same time social
> psychology as well. (p. 95)

Equally, the point is made by Tajfel and Fraser (1978) that 'man is
a creature both of his biological evolution and of his social and
cultural development' (p. 25). It is this issue of development that
will provide the necessary data about the nature of perception. The
following is a fairly brief and highly selective view of human development with the sole aim of providing background information with

regard to perception.It will be necessary later to refer to other aspects of development such as learning, creativity, language and symbolism in much greater detail.

Among others, Fairbairn (1952) described how, from the outset, the self-system is structured by the internalisation of the relationship with mother and child. The long period that the young child is dependent on its mother and the early structuring of the personality is inevitably dominated by the physical closeness in which the mother's attitudes are communicated through innumerable signals. Erikson (1959) describes how the individual requires constant affirmation of his or her identity from the social milieu, while Miller (1976) describes how individuals need and use social systems as means of maintaining their identity and protecting themselves against intolerable internal conflict.

Thus we can see how the child originally internalises the relationship with the mother, including the language, and then as he matures and learns to communicate with his elders and his peers, he learns certain modes and manners of expressing himself and fulfilling his requirements, and he also learns to expect consistent behaviour from others. By way of addition to Freud's comments above regarding the relationship of individuals to others, we can say that in order for either culture or personality to exist, there must be two or more individuals, with their personalities, who affect one another. Culture is the idiom of society just as it is the idiom of the personality (Bohannan, (1962). As we have seen, social reality is what somebody – usually several somebodies – may make of it. It lies in the image that the actors have of it, and teach one another about it.

As will be further explained in Chapter 5, organised life is organised in the minds of all who participate in it, and this organisation takes place by means of a conceptual framework, even though the participants may not be aware of the framework (Berger and Kellner, 1981). To do so requires communication, and the most effective means of doing so is by language. For this purpose, language is split up into bits or, to put it more eloquently, into a categorical framework. From early days on, every individual experience has a language aspect. Thus the specific language learned by a child is society specific, that is, predetermined by the social group within which a child grows up (Elias, 1991). Learning the language, we learn the local customs and assumptions so the programming within which our identity is constituted is in effect our linguistic programming, our induction into the network of human communication (Cupitt, 1990).

Because the biological disposition of humans provides for a great variety both of sound patterns themselves and of whatever they symbolically represent, the language of one human group can be completely incomprehensible to another. This means that in order to have an understanding of human beings there must be a familiarity with the particular form of life. Furthermore, whilst a people's language is itself a symbolic representation of the world as the members of that society have learned to experience it, at the same time it affects their perception, so that it would not be wrong to state that what you are determines what you see. What you see is very often a judgement upon what you are. In this way language may not only be a means of communication but may equally become a barrier to such communication.

From this brief look at development we can draw some useful conclusions. First and foremost, we need to be aware that different people see different worlds. Thus it is only through categorical frameworks that I can produce anything of my own that is intelligible to others. This consequently means that true communication is fruitless between people who do not share a categorical framework. In addition, I cannot interpret another's meaning without changing, albeit minimally, my own meaning system. Because of this ever-changing 'reality' it also means that any discovery has meaning only in relation to the knowledge available to the discoverer at the time. Thus, 'reality' is within the current knowledge of any particular human group. Hence we need to bear in mind the fundamental point that the bodily senses are the only link between a human mind and the world that he or she inhabits. I have no way of perceiving reality save through my senses and the instrumental extensions of them that I create. Therefore I must work with my perceived reality.

Quantitative and qualitative methods are not mutually exclusive; nevertheless, it has progressively become accepted that a qualitative, interpretative, or hermeneutical approach to research and analysis is a useful – if not more effective – methodology for dealing with the many variables associated with human activity. This new methodological approach has advanced our knowledge and understanding considerably, though the proliferation and variation of such methods has tended to cause confusion and may detract from its value. However, whilst there has come of age the realisation that qualitative methods are of significant value we also need to consider the time-span involved in gaining this acceptance.

It seems that one of the reasons for the long delay will undoubtedly be the 'conservative instinct' referred to earlier. Equally certain is that other matters, such as the problems of a lack of a shared language and a shared perception, will have played their part. Educated in the language of the empirical-analytical tradition, it seems most likely that the perception of scientists has been affected by limiting their understanding. However, these considerations do not relate solely to the controversy about quantitative and qualitative methodologies. The implications extend beyond the current debate because there is yet another methodology that has not thus far been referred to.

PSYCHO-ANALYTIC METHODOLOGIES

For almost a century, the psycho-analytic methodology of Freud has been available to scientists of all persuasions, especially those concerned with the problems of researching and analysing human activity. In Kuhn's terms psycho-analysis was a true paradigmatic revolution. Bearing in mind the prevailing philosophy, Healy (1990) points out that the notion of evolution of the psyche was a most dramatic development as it was a new emergent level of organisation, a psychological system; that is, a system with capacities for intelligent behaviour, perception, memory and learning, imagination and emotion. Freud showed that much of ourselves is hidden from ourselves or is not immediately given to awareness: that there were a conscious and an unconscious which are shaped by previous experiences, previous solutions, and what is unique for each individual. Freud established a new territory to be explored: the dynamic unconscious; a new science to explore it: depth psychology, and a set of new methods for the new science. This new methodology provided us with the opportunity to explain that which had previously not been possible.

Yet, why is it that this new methodology has not been embraced by all? One of the reasons could be that the lack of a shared language (and, it follows, of a shared perception) has seriously interfered with the advancement and use of a psycho-analytic approach. Indeed, it would appear that Freud himself foresaw potential difficulties and attempted to head them off by his continual insistence that his method was truly scientific. Throughout his career as a psychoanalyst, Freud maintained that he practised a natural science which did not differ in any essential way from physics. He projected this as a goal in the most unequivocal fashion in his 'Project for a Scientific Psychology' (1895): 'Psychology ... shall be a natural science' (p. 295). He stated that it was an accomplished fact in 'Some Elementary Lessons in Psycho-analysis' (1940a): 'Psycho-analysis is a part of the mental science of psychology [which is] ... a natural science. What else can it be?' (p. 282)

Doubtless being aware of the difficulties that psycho-analysis presents to their own particular brand of philosophy, it would seem that an attempt has been made by some to accommodate it within the existing perceptual framework (see, for example, Ricoeur, 1970, 1974; Habermas, 1968). Arguments surrounding its appropriate scientific category also abound. For example, while Blight argues strongly that psycho-analysis should be regarded as complementary to science and scientific explanation, there are others, such as Steele (1979), who argue, equally strongly, that psycho-analysis should be regarded as a form of hermeneutics. There is merit in both arguments but it is my view that psycho-analysis can best be viewed as differentiated from other methodologies and should be regarded as a method of its own (*sui generis*).

Building on Freud's work, others, such as Melanie Klein, Fairbairn, and Winnicott, have greatly enhanced the original theories so that psycho-analysis is now highly influential in the clinical setting. In the 1940s Foulkes and Bion began to apply the principles of psycho-analysis to group analysis. Originally used for therapeutic purposes, Bion, through his involvement at the Tavistock Institute of Human Relations, began to influence a wider application, forming groups with industrial managers and with people from the educational world. Throughout the 1950s and 1960s this resulted in many highly influential writings being published. Particularly relevant are those relating to organisations as open systems and the socio-technical perspective of organisations as developed at the Tavistock Institute. (For a full account of this work see Trist and Murray, 1990.)

In spite of their undoubted success and continued influence the concepts of group dynamics have not enjoyed the same widespread usage as personal psycho-analysis. The reason may be as stated by Trist, who was of the view that Bion's work had promised to do for group dynamics what psycho-analysis had done for personality. Yet neither he nor anyone else has contributed much to its development since 1952 (Trist, 1985, p. 34). However, personal reflection seems to suggest that a more likely reason is that it is a difficult concept and one which is not in the conceptual framework of very many people. Gaining an understanding of such matters as 'projective identification' or 'basic assumption groups' requires experiential as well as theoretical knowledge. Even then, they can be extremely difficult concepts to grasp fully.

In this respect, we should be aware that paradigms are time- and space-bound. The information (and misinformation) stored within the individual, arising from past experiences and inborn needs, sets the standards by which we both evaluate new experiences and establish their meaning. When we encounter new, or otherwise unknown, experience, we can only find the meaning by comparison with our known reality. I am especially mindful of this problem myself in trying, as far as possible, to present to the reader an understandable account of psycho-dynamic processes.

It may now be useful to take a further and much deeper look at the nature of human activity in organisations. Thus far, we have been concerned largely with conscious human activities, whereas we also need to be aware that aspects of ourselves which conflict with consciously held ideals may be denied, suppressed or disowned and become more or less unconscious. An idea may be unconscious because it is actively repressed owing to its unthinkable nature – a memory, fantasy, thought, or feeling which conflicts with our view of ourselves and of what is acceptable, and which could cause too much anxiety, guilt or psychic pain if it were acknowledged. Anxiety has been a central issue in nearly all organisational projects I have worked on. An understanding of that anxiety and the defences to it are important factors in determining human activity in organisations.

Each individual responds to and defends against that anxiety in different ways. Not only is it likely that ignoring anxiety will create a barrier in the communication process; the anxiety itself can be a valuable source of data about the significance of issues that arise in the course of the interaction. When the phenomena under study are influenced by unconscious feelings and fantasies the observer learns that he needs to attend to two levels of mental activity; the manifest conscious and the latent subconscious and unconscious. We are not so much concerned, then, with what is 'out there' to be observed, but more importantly with the careful analysis of how members of the organisation relate to the outsider, the clinician (Schein, 1987a).

When we recognise that the research encounters are, as Hunt says, 'mediated by unconscious psychological as well as conscious sociological processes' (1989, p. 17), we can appreciate that they are the counterpart of what psycho-analysts would identify as the analysis of the 'transference relationship'. In precisely the same way that the matter of how the patient relates to the therapist directly may prove more valuable as a source of information than what the patient reports about various other situations, the way that the client responds to the organisational consultant is more important than what is said about various other situations. The transference is the enactment of the unconscious.

This has been a very brief reference to the unconscious but it suffices to show that the phenomena under study are frequently influenced by unconscious feelings and fantasies. However, what this does show is that if we are to deal successfully with these important aspects we need a methodology that is able to provide us with an understanding of these complex phenomena – a methodology that will bring the irrational, the illogical, the exclusively emotional, under rational understanding and control. Clearly, this is beyond the scope of the quantitative methodologies. As for the qualitative or hermeneutic methodologies, these take us further but they are not capable of providing an understanding or interpretation of the sort of phenomena described. Any methodology for getting at this truth must include some form of what psycho-analysts call 'analysis of the resistance'. I argue that the only way to understanding, therefore, lies through deliberate intervention and the deciphering of the responses to the intervention.

In view of the nature of organisations, it is important not to use the 'old' – mechanistic – language; it is more appropriate to speak of processes of human behaviour. A process may be defined as a dynamic phenomenon that exists in a state of flux and one which is characterised by spontaneity, freedom, experience, conflict and movement. Such a phenomenon is not easy to understand. However, Bion (1961) showed that a psycho-analytic approach permitted the exposure of unrecognised, irrational, and powerful relationships that were specific to group situations.

According to Sutherland, 'The precise interpretation is not as important as long as enough of the underlying dynamics of the total situation are articulated' (1985, p. 81). The way this is achieved is by focusing exclusively on the group as a whole. That is why I choose to look at the issue of organisational culture from a psycho-dynamic perspective using, for practical purposes, an action research model. In doing so, I follow Freud's conviction that the greatest value of psycho-analysis to society in the long run will come not from therapeutic endeavour but from what it can offer as a general psychology to primary prevention in its broadest sense, as promotion of a state of individual and social well-being.

SUMMARY

In deciding on an appropriate methodology we need to consider not only the various methods available but also the nature of the organisations that we are researching. Here, organisations are essentially seen as patterns of human behaviour. In other words, what is organised is human activity and this inevitably raises the well documented arguments about subjectivity and objectivity.

The reliability of empirical scientific knowledge in regard to physics, chemistry, astronomy or, for that matter, engineering or manufacturing, is not really in doubt. It is when we extend science to the extreme difficulties of biological behaviour, human emotion and social organisation that it becomes inherently unsound. It is then that other sources of insight and other methodologies beyond those of the empirical-analytical scientific method must be sought.

There is a need to be aware that different people see the world from different perspectives. Thus 'reality' is within the current knowledge of any particular human group. It is a fundamental point that the bodily senses are the only link between a human mind and the world that he or she inhabits. We have no way of perceiving reality save through our senses and the instrumental extensions of them that we create. Therefore we must work with our perceived reality.

Quantitative and qualitative methods are not mutually exclusive; nevertheless, it has become accepted that a qualitative approach to research and analysis is a useful – if not more effective – methodology for dealing with the many variables associated with human activity.

Most importantly, however, when considering the nature of organisations we also need to be aware that aspects of ourselves which conflict with consciously held ideals may be denied, suppressed or disowned and become more or less unconscious. The phenomenon under study are frequently influenced by unconscious feelings and fantasies. Therefore, if we are to deal successfully with these important aspects we need a methodology that is able to provide us with an understanding of these complex phenomena – a methodology that will bring the irrational, the illogical, the exclusively emotional, under rational understanding and control.

Clearly, this is beyond the scope of the quantitative methodologies. And, while the qualitative methodologies take us further, they are not capable of providing an understanding or interpretation of the sort of phenomena described. In contrast to chemistry, for example, where great accuracy is both necessary and desirable, here a precise interpretation is not important as long as enough of the underlying dynamic of the total situation is articulated. In order to obtain the depth of understanding required – one which permits an understanding of both conscious and unconscious processes – it is my view that it is necessary to look at culture from a psycho-dynamic perspective, and in the next chapter I will start to develop a psycho-dynamic explanation of organisational culture.

3

A PSYCHO-DYNAMIC
EXPLANATION OF
ORGANISATIONAL CULTURE I

The first two chapters have identified some of the problems and demonstrated something of the difficulties that we face in finding a means of developing a theory of organisational culture. The aim, now, is to describe the development of a psycho-dynamic explanation of organisational culture in as simple a fashion as possible. In this chapter, I shall concentrate on what I feel is the most crucial of those questions posed in the Preface, namely, how culture develops. Until a satisfactory explanation is provided for this we shall never achieve an understanding of culture, let alone apply it to the management of change. This explanation will be added to in Chapter 11 where I shall provide a deeper and more technical explanation of how culture develops and also deal with the remaining important questions concerning how culture is perpetuated and represented.

I am not seeking to provide a short, simple definition, for the basic reason that culture is far too complex an issue to be trussed up in a conceptual strait-jacket. I shall commence by putting the process of culture into a context. In setting the scene I need to refer to another construct, namely, 'personality'. It is the view expressed here that if we are to obtain a better understanding of the characteristics of organisational culture we need to take a similar approach to that of studying personality. Hence the title, 'The Personality of the Organisation'. It will be seen, however, that there are many other factors that cause me to opt for this title.

PERSONALITY DEVELOPMENT

As with culture, there are many definitions and many uses of the notion of 'personality', some common and others technical. However, like culture it is also a complicated system and even with the theoretical frameworks that have been developed it is still difficult to gain an interpretation of this phenomenon. According to Sutherland (1985) there is no accepted means of appraising the functioning of personality in a comprehensive way. Consequently, to obtain a better understanding of the characteristics of personality development it will be helpful to look at the various aspects of individual development in considerable depth.

Culture, like personality, is less a finished product than a transitive process. While it has some stable features, it is at the same time continually undergoing change. It is this course of change, which can be of a sudden or dramatic nature or a long, slow change more in the nature of osmosis, that results in the development of culture and is our special concern. The first fact that strikes us is the uniqueness of both the process and the product. Each culture is an idiom unto itself which develops in its own particular context, and this context must be understood in order to comprehend the idiom.

The constant interaction between the individual and culture is fundamental to any study of culture or, for that matter, personality. They are indivisibly linked and consequently it will be necessary to refer to both processes. Indeed, we may take as our first premise that the function of the personality as a whole is to enable the individual to produce forms of behaviour which will be advantageous to him under the conditions imposed by his environment. We will then take as our second premise that, other things being equal, this function is performed most effectively when the advantageous behaviour is produced with a minimum of delay and involves a minimum of effort.

The conviction that personality development occurs in the context of interactions between the organism and the environment, rather than through the internal processes of maturation alone is a view supported by many. For example, it is reflected in Erikson's psychosocial approach (1950) and among object-relations theorists, who have brought the relationship of self to other (or subject to object) to centre stage. Fairbairn (1952), Winnicott (1965a), Klein (1959), Guntrip (1971) and others consider that 'object-relating' is an intrinsic interest of persons, rather than an extrinsic one. From the point of view of these theorists the very essence of ego activity is object-relations, and ego activity is presumed to begin immediately at birth.

The influences which culture exerts on the developing personality are of two quite different sorts. On the one hand we have those influences that derive from the culturally patterned behaviour of other individuals towards the child. These begin to operate from the moment of birth, a matter which will be dealt with in greater detail later. On the other hand, we have those influences which derive from the individual's observation of, or instruction in, the patterns of behaviour characteristic of his society. In summary, the fact that personality norms differ from different societies can be explained on the basis of the different experiences which the members of such societies acquire from contact with those societies.

Personality and culture are processes, that is, human 'being' is an activity. Kegan (1982) observes that it is not about the doing which a human *does*; it is about the doing which a human *is*. Both culture and personality insist on a recognition that behind the form there exists a process which creates it, or which leads to its coming into being: that is, each is not a thing but a process. The notion that we constitute reality, rather than somehow happen upon it, is most quickly and vividly brought home in the area of perception. Thus it is not that a person makes meaning, rather the activity of being a person is the activity of meaning making. There is thus no feeling, no experience, no thought, no perception, independent of a meaning making context in which it becomes a feeling, an experience, a thought, a perception, because we are the meaning-making context.

In terms of context, Erikson's (1959) related concepts of an individual and a group identity can be helpful. For Erikson, the sense of ego identity is based on the common perception of an individual's self-sameness and continuity. In other words, such basic human concerns as, Who am I? Where have I been? and Where am I going? are deeply ensconced in the individual's group experiences from the family and beyond. He also points out that we cannot ignore the fact that all individuals are borne by others and born of others; that everybody was once a child; that people and peoples begin in their nurseries; and that society consists of individuals in the process of developing from children into parents. He therefore concludes that something in the ego process and something in the social process is identical.

Having set the scene, as it were, with this preliminary but necessary discussion of context we are now in a better position to begin to answer the crucial question: how culture develops. As seems inevitable, it is necessary to commence with the processes involving the development of the young child and then to develop the findings into adult life. Individual development is an issue that will be taken up in considerable depth through the book, and especially in the chapter on symbolism. However, the following selective description of the process is necessary for our current purposes.

The newborn child lives in a completely undifferentiated world, one in which nothing is on the side of the object, in which nothing is other than the infant, in which everything he senses is taken to be an extension of himself, and where everything ceases to be once it is out of sight, touch or hearing. The child gradually moves from this omnipotent, unintegrated self, to an integrated self capable of object relating. Growth always involves a process of differentiation, of emergence from what Kegan (1982) calls 'embeddedness', thus creating out of the former subject a new object to be taken by the new subjectivity.

Winnicott (1971) would say that there is never 'just an infant'. He meant that intrinsic to the picture of infancy is a caretaker who, from the point of view of the infant, is something more than an 'other person' who relates to and assists the growth of the infant. The mother provides the very context in which development takes place, and from the point of view of the new born she is a part of the self. She provides a true psycho-social context: she is both 'psycho' and 'social', depending on whose perspective we take, and the transformation by which she becomes for the infant gradually less 'psycho' and more 'social' describes the very evolution of meaning itself.

In Winnicott's view what he refers to as the 'holding environment' is vital to the development of the infant. From the beginning of life, reliable holding has to be a feature of the environment if the child is to survive. It starts with and is a continuation of the psychological provision that characterises the pre-natal state. The function of holding in psychological terms is to provide ego support particularly at the stage of absolute dependence before integration of the ego has become established. The establishment of integration and the development of ego relatedness both rely upon good enough holding.

The notion of a 'holding environment' is seen as the key concept in providing an explanation of how organisational culture develops. A fuller explanation of the interrelatedness of the infant and mother in the 'maternal holding environment' is therefore necessary to our understanding. We need to start right at the beginning with the infant's separation and individuation from its undifferentiated state at birth. This provides us with the context to which all further considerations of object relations throughout the life-span are referred. Recurring issues of differentiation and integration throughout life come to be understood as the consequences of this earliest period. Birth itself is the first separation, the first giving up of the comfort and security of the womb for an unknown world in the service of unknown potentials of growth.

Holding in the mother's womb, then the holding in the mother's arms, is the first boundary out of chaos within which the infant's personality can develop. The mother's sensitivity to his growth provides the protection of a boundary which helps the child to extend and to expand, and within which he can include more and more experience of the world. From the outset, this is a two-way relationship, the infant signifies his needs through crying and gestures. In the beginning, needs are very few but are terrifying if they are not met. The degree of frustration that the newborn child can tolerate without disintegrating, without going back to what seems a state of chaos and distress, is minimal. Ability to tolerate frustration of needs and wishes grows very gradually. When the infant has a little more experience of having his needs met he can begin to communicate them more actively and more clearly.

The early relation in the maternal holding environment is characterised by infantile dependence, that is, a dependence based on a primary identification with the object, and an inability to differentiate and adapt. Put another way, the relation of the mother and her infant is that both are parts of a dyad: a pair of individuals who function as a unit as a result of their intimate closeness. The infant does not experience the mother as being separate and distinct but rather as part of himself. The infant is part of, what we will term, a symbiotic relationship with his mother, that is, he is both 'held' by the mother and is part of the maternal holding environment.

A relationship grows through the ability of both parties to experience and adjust to each other's natures. The relationship develops through the infant getting to know the mother as she presents herself to interpret and meet his needs, which are emotional as well as physical. The baby needs to have not only food and comfort but also the security of a loving relationship in which he can grow and learn to know himself and a range of feelings. The first need is to be held and wrapped in conditions similar to the womb-like situation so that there is the security to reach out to new experiences. In the beginning the mother is the world to the baby.

Developmental psychology (for example, Stern, 1985) has demonstrated that the infant has an innate capacity to seek out and make use of the various characteristics of a human caretaker. The infant prefers the human face and voice above other visual and auditory stimuli and feels comforted by rhythmic rocking and the sound of mother's heart and the familiar smell of her body. Yet the nature of this fit between what the infant is reaching out for and what the mother can provide is not a static phenomenon; it is intrinsically dynamic, providing the basis for a subtle reciprocal interaction between mother and baby which contains within it the potential for increasingly complex exchanges.

For the infant to develop there is a need for a 'basic trust' in the maternal holding environment and for what Winnicott (1971) has termed 'a good enough holding environment'. This 'basic trust' is developed as a result of the infant's perceived experience of his holding environment. From holding in the mother's womb this extends to holding in the mother's arms. However, what we are referring to is much more than just physical holding. It is about the mother providing boundaries which help the infant to make sense of his world.

According to Klein (1952) the meeting of instinctual needs within the infant, with an external object, that is, aspects of the mother's care, not only results in a physically satisfying experience, an interest in the external world and a rudimentary social relationship to the mother, but also initiates the beginning of mental development in the infant. Precisely because of the match between the infant's needs and the object's capacities, the external world can be brought within the infant's mental grasp and thought about as well as being available for sensual contact. Bion (1962) too saw the meeting of a 'preconception' with a 'realisation' as a crucial moment at the start of mental life.

It was Bion's thesis that the way in which a mother is able to get in contact with the infant's state of mind, and through her attention and support enable him to grow psychologically, constitutes a form of relationship in which the mother's mind acts as a container for the child. The mother's capacity to respond to the infant's experience seems to be felt by him at first as a gathering together of his bodily sensations, engendering the beginnings of a sense of bodily integrity. Winnicott (1965b) referred to this as giving the infant the experience of 'continuity of being'. This sort of close relationship with the mother provides the setting in which the infant's capacity for mental and emotional experiences can develop. Anzieu (1989) argued that in the course of development the sense of being physically gathered together, of having a physical skin, becomes the prototype through which the infant can grasp a sense of a 'mental skin' bounding a 'mental space' within himself. This, in turn, enables him to begin to make sense of his mother's mind and communication which takes place between them. The quality of early experience thus has a crucial impact on the beginnings of mental life.

As the infant grows, there then develops the use of a transitional object which leads to the recognition of external objects – of a 'me' and a 'not me'. The polarisation of symbiosis-individuation finally breaks through on the side of individuation, leading to the dissolution of the dyad, and the formation of self-concepts. With differentiation there begins the formation of a self-concept. This psychological change arises once the infant is able to experience the mother and other significant objects as separate. Gradually there develop several 'not me's' in the shape of father, siblings, playmates and other relations. At this stage there also develops the use of true symbols and the use of language and words as symbols. The infant is then capable of introjecting cognitive symbols. Here the holding environment begins to split into an internal-ised psychological part and an external social and physical part.

In order to value experience with people in the outside world, the child has gradually to make some distinction between what comes from outside himself and what he has the 'illusion of belonging' to him because he desires it to be so. The second significant stage in the infant's learning about life is the time when he realises that he is not the same as the mother who is holding and comforting and making him feel happy. He has no absolute power or control over this comforting presence. This realisation is difficult for him to accept. When the infant realises that mother comes and goes and has a life of her own, he becomes increasingly interested in how she is feeling, watches her expression, looks for liking, approval, reassurance.

The infant from all these experiences of his needs being met, gradually organises them to form a more and more complete picture of a person, his mother whom he can trust, to whom he can call for solace, for understanding, for company, for fun. By the middle of the first year his horizons are expanding. Just as he begins to be aware of the mother as a separate and more complete person, he begins to be aware of his father also as separate and distinct. His world is beginning to expand enormously. Yet, if he is safe enough in his primary relationship with his mother, he is able to return to this for strength and relaxation. It provides him with the 'continuity of being' both in the external world and in his mind. Through this he is able to cope with the intense excitement and emotional turmoil that added interests and stimuli bring.

It has been hypothesised that when the baby stores a picture of his mother's face gazing at him, or stores an impression of being cuddled, it is experienced by an infant of under three or four months as a process of actually taking in (introjecting) the percep-tion as if it were an object (Isaacs, 1952). This is partly to do with the physical nature of early memory but the view here goes beyond this to say that the 'taking in', 'summoning up' and 'holding in the mind' of these images of physical experience are also concretely felt processes. Thus the infant feels he contains within himself a world of concrete things of at least as much reality as the material world.

The infant's dependence on this sort of containment by mother will eventually be replaced by the containment offered by the sense of his own mind. Development comes about through repeated opportunities for taking in the experience of being held together by someone else and being held in the mind. Through this process the infant comes to feel the 'containing mother' as a definite presence within him. Winnicott makes it clear that the infant's relationship to a transitional object is to be seen as dependent on, and arising out of, the child's relationship to the internalised mother. Later this process within the infant is taken further as he comes to feel identified with his 'containing mother'. At this point, one might say that the infant has become self-contained and self-confident. Through this contact with the mother's capacity for containment of mental states and their transformation into thought, the basis is laid for the development of these same capacities within the infant, by means of internalisation and identification.

We have been describing a model of the relationship between parent and child which is both social and psychological. It is social in that everything is seen as developing through the complex and subtle interaction between parent and child. Yet it is psychological in that it is processes internal to each participant that are seen as essential materials in these interactions. The concern is not only with the development of the child's capacity for social experience but also the child's capacity to have mental/emotional experiences.

Although there are many different ways of describing the nature of the change, there seems now to be some consensus that at around seven months there is a major developmental shift, whereby the infant becomes able to experience himself and his mother as whole persons. This development seems to have both cognitive and emotional dimensions since what is being 'put together' is not only a physical object but also an emotional object – a human being from whom separatedness must be experienced in the midst of emotional need. For Klein (1959) this is the depressive position, a time when the infant's internal world becomes more integrated, a sense of internal continuity becomes possible. It was part of Klein's view that the establishment of the depressive position brought with it the beginning of a new relationship to external reality that was based on symbol formation.

The dawn of an object world is the consequence of the infant's gradual 'emergence from embeddedness'. By differentiating itself from the world and the world from it, the infant brings into being that which is independent of its own sensing and moving. A child's capacity to take his impulses and perceptions as an object of his meaning making not only brings an end to the liability of the earlier subject-object relation, but brings into being a new subject-object relation which creates a more endurable self – a self which does its own praising, so to speak, but needs the information that it is correct as a confirmation; a self which can store memories, feelings and perceptions (rather than being them). It is not just the physical world that is being conserved but internal experience too. As well as the emergence of a self-concept, there comes a more or less consistent notion of a 'me'.

To summarise, the 'maternal holding environment' consists first of the mother and child and later the father and other important relatives. In this 'holding environment' there is a continuing interrelationship between the mother and the child. The mother influences the child and the child influences the mother. In other words the child is part of the 'holding environment' and influences it while at the same time the child is influenced by the 'holding environment'. The maternal holding environment is not a closed system but is also open to external influences such as noise, for example. The development of the personality of the child will depend upon whether the holding environment has – to use Winnicott's terminology – been 'good enough'.

To conclude this brief look at individual development, we can describe personality in the following way:

1. It is a psycho-social process;
2. It is evidenced by sameness and continuity;
3. It is influenced by conscious and unconscious processes;
4. It is unique for each individual;
5. It is a dynamic process;
6. It is such that the individual will produce forms of behaviour which will be psychologically advantageous to him under the conditions imposed by the environment.

It should be stressed that the infant does not go from a state of absolute dependence to absolute independence – independence is never absolute for any of us. The healthy individual does not become isolated, but continues to be related to the environment in such a way that the individual and the environment can be said to be interdependent. Although the original holding phase is equivalent to the stage of being merged or of absolute dependence, ego support continues to be a need in the growing child, the adolescent, and at times of the adult, whenever there is a strain that threatens confusion or disintegration.

This is further explained by Erikson (1959) who reminds us that even in adult life we do not dare to give up our inborn need for maternal gratification. We cling to each other as if we were mothers to each other. He agrees with the view that we are never completely or successfully integrated, however healthy we may feel. The evolutionary drive for increasing integration, for improving our capabilities and capacities, brings about growth and development: and this is the principle task for a living being. Integration on any level is never total or perfect: and death – final disintegration – is always present.

This clinging to each other is further explained by Winnicott (1965a) when he describes how, in maturity, environment is something to which the individual contributes and for which the individual takes responsibility. The environment provides ego support and permits an adaptation to reality, reality testing and a sense of reality, activities as important to the adult as they are to the infant. From here we can develop the important view, as stated by Kegan (1982) with regard to personality, that there is not one holding environment early in life, but a succession of holding environments. They are the psycho-social environments which hold us (with which we are fused) and which let go of us (from which we differentiate).

THE DEVELOPMENT OF CULTURE

Building on the concept of a 'maternal holding environment', the growing infant becomes a member of several holding environments; for example, the family, the school, the university, and eventually, the organisational holding environment. Indeed, I will go further than this because I believe it is more accurate to state that there is not only a succession of 'holding environments' but that several 'holding environments' may be available for any one individual at any given time. In this regard, Freud (1921) acknowledged that individuals belonged to many groups, had identifications in many directions and a variety of models upon which to build an ego ideal.

We can perhaps appreciate the significance of the situation when we realise that for all of us the earliest experiences (and perhaps memories) are of being utterly and totally related to our maternal holding environment. It was the maternal holding environment on which we as infants were dependent for affectional support, gratification of biological needs, and protection. All of our primitive defence mechanisms were developed in that setting which had such a significance for us. It was from this very base, or embeddedness, that through a process of differentiation and adaptation we all developed into what we are today.

To further stress the significance of the 'holding environment' it may be useful to refer to what happens when there is some sort of failure. Winnicott (1965a) informs us that where there is faulty holding, this produces extreme distress which the infant may experience as the sense of going to pieces, the sense of falling for ever, the feeling that external reality cannot be used for reassurance, and other anxieties that are usually described as 'psychotic'. Faulty handling results in disruption to the development of muscle tone and co-ordination. And, where the infant's creative impulses are stifled, this blocks the development of the infant's capacity to feel real in relating to the world of objects and phenomena.

Where the individual has experienced his holding environment as good enough his personality may develop to the extent that he is capable of progression. Thus, we may now have an individual who is capable of using true symbols, and of mature dependence based upon differentiation of the object from the self, and who is a member of multiple holding environments: a unique individual who might be termed an artificial creation that has developed out of his interrelatedness with the multiple holding environments to which he belonged. The unique mosaic that is the individual personality is made up of introjects from all of the holding environments of which he has been a part.

Having demonstrated the importance of the maternal holding environment in the process of personality development, I shall now show how the concept of an 'organisational holding environment' is central to the approach taken here. It is my contention that in a manner similar to the relationship of the individual with his maternal holding environment, so the organisation becomes a partly conscious and a partly unconscious holding environment for its members. As with the maternal holding environment, the organisational holding environment may usefully be seen as two parts. The conscious part of the holding environment may be termed the external holding environment, while the unconscious part may be termed the internalised holding environment.

Viewing organisations as open systems, the partly conscious and partly unconscious holding environment is influenced by activities in the external environment of the organisation. The interrelatedness to symbolic objects may include those 'outside' the organisation. The degree of influence will depend on the degree of boundary control exercised on behalf of the members of the organisation. If there is a clarity of purpose external influences are unlikely to be great, whereas if the boundary is weak external influence may be considerable. Unless there is some sort of discontinuity, there can be no boundary region and thus no sense in which activities carried out within the supposed system are insulated from other activities 'outside' (Miller and Rice, 1967).

Organisations are essentially seen as processes of human behaviour. As part of the organisation holding environment – and in common with the maternal holding environment – we each influence the organisations we are in and they influence us and our behaviour. But, of course, the reader will appreciate that, unlike the maternal holding environment, there is no 'mother' in the organisation setting. So why is it that as members of an organisation we perceive them as being in existence and as real as our mother? We identify with the organisation 'as if' it were real; it is what might be referred to as an 'organisation held in the mind'. It is a construct that we identify with and treat 'as if' it were real.

To explain further, in psycho-analytic terms, other people are given the rather unfortunate term of 'objects'. By object relations is meant the relationships of the person with other human beings in the world; but not only with human beings, and I think that is why the term 'objects' is used, since one can have relationships with animals, and also with inanimate things, such as automobiles. For example, many of us have relationships with our cars, we get very attached to them and may become upset if someone else drives them. We may feel that it does not run quite the same afterwards. When we have to sell it we have a period of mourning as though we have lost a loved object. So, also, do we get attached to organisations.

In much the same way that we interrelate with the maternal holding environment, so we interrelate with the organisational holding environment. We use it so supply the same needs as the maternal holding environment and we apply the same affect to it and create the same defences when it is seen as 'not good enough'. Ego support continues at times to be a need of the adult, particularly whenever there is a strain that threatens confusion or disintegration. There is never total independence, the healthy individual does not become isolated, but continues to be related to the environment in such a way that the individual and the environment can said to be interdependent. In much the same way that there is a need for a 'basic trust' in the maternal holding environment and for what Win-nicott (1971) has termed 'a good enough holding environment' if the infant is to develop, so there is a similar need here in the organisa-tion holding environment. Such 'basic trust' is developed as a result of the perceived experience of the organisation holding environment by the members of the organisation.

We can say, then, that the organisational holding environment con-sists of the totality of the organisation including the members of the organisation themselves. However, there are various aspects within that totality that will have a particular influence on the members' perceived notion of the organisation. In the maternal holding environment, the particular influence was the mother and later the father and other important relatives. In the organisational holding environment these particular influences are seen to be the task, strategy, structure, leader-ship and management of the organisation that are in existence at the relevant time. The perceived view of the organisation, 'the organisation held in the mind', that the members of the organisation identify with and interrelate with is the organisation holding environment.

In adulthood, each of the holding environments of which we are members consists of an internalised psychological part and an external social and physical part. It will be recalled that in the maternal holding environment the relationship between mother and infant is not only social but psychological as well. In the normal infant there is both physical and psychological growth. In the last chapter I described how an idea may be unconscious because it is actively repressed owing to its unthinkable nature – a memory, fantasy, thought or feeling which conflicts with our view of ourselves and of what is acceptable, and which could cause too much anxiety, guilt, or psychic pain if it were acknowledged.

For all of us, there exists a whole world of ideas that we are not normally conscious of: an unconscious part of our mind that exerts a very strong influence on us. Furthermore, this part of our personality sets up a resistance to most of these ideas coming into consciousness and therefore they tend to remain unconscious. All of us contain an internal phantasy world, first developed as a child. Each individual in an organisation brings with them their own history, their own phan-tasies. But there are common concerns that may emerge once they are faced with a common holding environment. In the same way that unconscious forces are operating in the maternal holding environment, so they are at play here in the organisational holding environment.

Consequently, it is not only helpful but is also necessary, there-fore, to view the organisational holding environment as consisting of two parts. In this respect, the 'iceberg' analogy previously used by other writers may be a useful way of viewing things. The sociological part of the holding environment is that part which is exposed or is conscious: That part I have previously referred to as the 'external holding environment'. The psychological part of the holding environment is internalised and largely unconscious: That part that I have previously referred as the 'internal holding environment'.

The external holding environment. This is basically the sociological holding environment. It includes the formal structures and strategies, the ruling coalition or leader and the organisational tasks – that is, the reason why the organisation exists, the roles of the various members, all forms of knowledge and skills, values and attitudes shared by the members. Trist (1990) points out that for each of the members of the organisation there are external social objects which exist within them as material which they can use, of which they are partially aware, and which they are able to make available to themselves by the normal process of recall. In addition, an organisation does not exist in isolation, it is an open system that interacts with the external world and, depending on the degree of openness, this provides some of the external social objects.

The internalised holding environment. This is basically the psychological holding environment. Here we are referring to internal objects which are regarded as part of the self and compose the basic social character of the individual. They relate to the deeper character level and derive from the phantasy activity of unconscious systems of internal object relations. According to Trist: 'They act as an internal source of influence on the patterns at a more conscious level and reach into society through them. They may also be directly, though still unconsciously, projected onto various types of external social objects which themselves are then partly fashioned by these investments' (1990, p. 542).

In the same way that the 'holding environment' provided by the mother influences the personality of the infant, so the 'holding environment' of the organisation influences the culture. The holding environment is not the culture, it is how the members of the organisation interact or their interrelatedness with the holding environment that results in the culture. It is how the members of the organisation perceive the holding environment that results in the unique and distinct culture that is the feature of every organisation. If they perceive it as 'good enough' and they have a 'basic trust' in it they will develop a task

supportive culture. The specific 'holding environment' provides the
context in which development of the culture takes place.

It is out of the interrelatedness of the members of the organisation and the organisational holding environment that organisational
culture develops. In effect, what happens is that members of the
organisation adopt forms of behaviour that they feel are appropriate
to them under the circumstances imposed on them by the organisational holding environment. In other words, the behaviour of the
members of the organisation will depend upon their psychological
perception of the organisation holding environment.

From this view of organisations it is considered that we may also
describe culture in a similar manner to the description of personality:

1. It is a psycho-social process, which was explained by reference
   to the interrelatedness of the members of the organisation with
   the organisational holding environment;
2. It is evidenced by sameness and continuity to provide for the
   self-esteem of the members and their sense of reality with
   others;
3. Being a psychological as well as a social process it is influenced by conscious and unconscious processes;
4. Both the uniqueness of the collective, perceived view of the
   members of the organisation and the organisational holding
   environment results in a unique culture in every organisation
   and part of an organisation;
5. Because groups are ongoing structures as opposed to finished
   ones, it is a dynamic and changing process;
6. The members of the organisation will produce forms of behaviour which will be psychologically advantageous to them under
   the conditions imposed by the environment.

The end result is what has been referred to in the past as 'the way that
things are done around here'. Thus, in very simple terms, we can say
that the way that organisational culture develops is out of the interrelatedness of the members of the organisation and the organisational
holding environment. In other words, it is not a 'thing', it is a process.
It is not something that the organisation *has* but something that the
organisation *is*.

Organisational culture can be seen 'as if' it were the 'personality
of the organisation'. It exhibits many of the same characteristics and
presents us with the same sort of problems. For the organisation
consultant (as for the analyst in regard to individuals) it is very

much a matter of treating every organisation or part of an organisation as being unique. However, by an awareness of the characteristics outlined above, it should be possible to establish sufficient knowledge of the situation to provide an understanding of the culture.

SUMMARY

The constant interaction between the individual and culture is fundamental to any study of culture or, for that matter, personality. They are indivisibly linked and consequently it is necessary to refer to both processes. Culture, like personality, is less a finished product than a transitive process. While it has some stable features, it is at the same time continually undergoing change. Each culture is an idiom unto itself which develops in its own particular context, and this context must be understood to comprehend the idiom. Both the product and the process (of culture and personality) are unique.

Essential to an understanding of organisational culture is the concept of a 'maternal holding environment' which consists first of the mother and child and later the father and other important relatives. In this 'holding environment' there is a continuing interrelationship between the mother and the child. The mother influences the child and the child influences the mother. In other words the child is part of the 'holding environment' and influences it while at the same time the child is influenced by the 'holding environment'. This 'maternal holding environment' is not a closed system but is also open to external influences, such as noise, for example. The development of the personality of the child will depend upon whether the holding environment has been 'good enough'.

The newborn child lives in a completely undifferentiated world, one in which nothing is on the side of the object, in which nothing is other than the infant, in which everything he senses is taken to be an extension of himself, and where everything ceases to be once it is out of sight, touch or hearing. The child gradually moves from this omnipotent, unintegrated self, to an integrated self capable of object relating. Growth always involves a process of differentiation, of emergence from 'embeddedness', thus creating out of the former subject a new object to be taken by the new subjectivity.

Starting from birth, the early relation in the maternal holding environment is characterised by infantile dependence, that is, a dependence based on a primary identification with the object, and an inability to differentiate and adapt. The infant is part of a symbiotic relationship with his mother, that is, he is both 'held' by the mother and is part of the maternal holding environment. For the infant to develop there is a need for a 'basic trust' in the maternal holding environment and for what Winnicott (1971) has termed 'a good enough holding environment'. This 'basic trust' is developed as a result of the infant's perceived experience of his holding environment. However, what we are referring to is much more than just physical holding. It is about the mother providing boundaries which help the infant to make sense of this world.

As the infant grows there then develops the use of a transitional object which leads to the recognition of external objects – of a 'me' and a 'not me'. Gradually there develop several 'not me's' in the shape of father, siblings, playmates and other relations. At this stage there also develops the use of true symbols and the use of language and words as symbols. The infant is then capable of introjecting cognitive symbols. Here the holding environment begins to split into an internalised psychological part and an external social and physical part.

The infant does not go from a state of absolute dependence to independence. The healthy individual continues to be related to the environment in such a way that the individual and environment can be said to be interdependent. As the infant grows he becomes a member not only of a succession of holding environments but, later in life, of multiple holding environments.

Where the individual has experienced his holding environment as good enough his personality may develop to the extent that he is capable of progression. Thus, we may now have an individual who is capable of using true symbols, and of mature dependence based upon differentiation of the object from the self, and who is a member of multiple holding environments: a unique individual who might be termed an artificial creation that has developed out of his interrelatedness with the multiple holding environments to which he belonged. The unique mosaic that is the individual personality is made up of introjects from all of the holding environments of which he has been a part.

In a manner similar to the relationship of the individual with his maternal holding environment, the organisation becomes a partly conscious and a partly unconscious holding environment for its members. As with the maternal holding environment, the organisational holding environment may usefully be seen as two parts. The conscious part of the holding environment may be termed the external holding environment. This is the socio-structural part which consists of the ruling coalition or leader, the formal goals, structures, strategies, policies and processes, roles of members, knowledge and skills, the shared private language, beliefs, values and attitudes. The unconscious part may be termed the internalised holding environment. This is the psychological part which consists of internal objects derived from phantasy activity about the holding environment, that is, by introjection of external objects. It is that part of the self which composes the basic social character of the individual.

It is out of the interrelatedness of the members of the organisation and the organisational holding environment that organisational culture develops. In effect, what happens is that members of the organisation adopt forms of behaviour that they feel are appropriate to them under the circumstances imposed on them by the organisational holding environment. In other words, the behaviour of the members of the organisation will depend upon their psychological perception of the organisation holding environment.

We may thus describe culture in a similar manner to the description of personality:

1. It is a psycho-social process, which was explained by reference to the interrelatedness of the members of the organisation with the organisational holding environment;
2. It is evidenced by sameness and continuity to provide for the self-esteem of the members and their sense of reality with others;
3. Being a psychological as well as a social process it is influenced by conscious and unconscious processes;
4. Both the uniqueness of the collective, perceived view of the members of the organisation and the organisational holding environment results in a unique culture in every organisation and part of an organisation;
5. Because groups are ongoing structures as opposed to finished ones, it is a dynamic and changing process;
6. The members of the organisation will produce forms of behaviour which will be psychologically advantageous to them under the conditions imposed by the environment.

Reliable holding is as important to the self-esteem of the members of an organisation as it is to the infant. If there is a basic trust in the holding environment there is likely to be a task supportive culture. That is, the culture is likely to be in synchronicity with the socio-structural system. However, if there is no basic trust and the holding environment is viewed as being either socially, physically and/or psychologically 'not good enough', there is likely to be an anti-task culture. These are matters that will be developed in some depth in Chapter 11.

PART II

DEVELOPING A PSYCHO-DYNAMIC THEORY OF CULTURE: FUNDAMENTAL CONCEPTS AND THEORY

Having read the chapters in Part I, the reader will now have an understanding of the theory developed and be able to apply it to his or her thinking about their own organisations. It is appreciated, however, that it will have raised as many – if not more – questions than answers and that some readers are likely to have queries about various aspects of the theory that they would wish to be explained further. This part is designed to provide that further explanation by providing, first, in Chapters 4–10, a discussion of those concepts that are considered fundamental to the development of the theory, and, second, in Chapter 11, a fuller and more technical explanation of the theory itself.

Chapter 4, on 'The Nature of Organisations', is written from the point of view that it is important not only to know what we are talking about in terms of organisations, but also to know the nature of the phenomenon: it sets a sort of benchmark. Relying on psycho-analytic writings on individual development and relating this to the psycho-dynamic writings of group relations practitioners, it concludes that what is organised in human organisations is human behaviour, and thus when an organisation ceases to exist, its traces – buildings, equipment and the like – will give very few clues to its life. Perhaps more importantly, from the perspective of culture, it adds to previous arguments to show how the members of organisations or parts of organisations treat them 'as if' they are real.

A particular development arising from the fact that organisations are perceived as objects is the issue of boundaries, which is dealt with in Chapter 5. The significance of boundaries is highlighted by the fact that it is at the boundary that differences are expressed. In this relatively short chapter I seek to explain the processes involved, why and how boundaries develop, and their nature. By relating a wide range of views to the subject matter it is shown that boundaries, like organisations, are artificial creations. It is the need to reduce the whole rich world of infinite variability to a manipulable and bearable size which leads to the formation of boundaries. This should not disguise the fact that boundaries should be seen as momentary points in a dynamic process; however, for those concerned it is the boundaries that matter.

The system that we mainly choose to categorise our world is that of naming. Chapter 6 deals with the issue of symbolism. One of the results of symbolism is the development of condensed symbols that have significance for an organisation. This account will provide some explanation of condensed symbols, but it seeks to go much deeper than this in order to understand not only the symbols themselves but, more importantly, how those symbols come about. Chapter 6 attempts to provide an explanation of organisational symbolism by tracing the process of its development in the individual with reference to the psycho-analytic theory of symbolism.

Klein (1930) pointed out the importance of understanding symbolism when she concluded that symbolism is the foundation of all sublimation and of every talent, while Winnicott (1971) concluded that the transitional object is the first use of a symbol and that this object gradually gives place to an ever-widening range of objects and to the whole cultural life. The psycho-analytic account of this process therefore provides us with useful information about the development of culture. Understanding the developmental process also provides us with information about what happens when an individual or a group regresses to infantile behaviour.

From an organisational perspective, the use of language and words as symbols is highly significant. Chapter 7 looks at this specific issue. Here I recognise particularly the fact that we may experience different uses and meanings of the same language. I explore the issue of how condensed symbols are developed and I also show that the usual way for an individual constantly to affirm his identity with those around him is through the use of words or language as symbols. Thus language is society specific. The language is a symbolic representation of the world as the members of that society, or part of society, such as an organisation, have learned to experience it at that time. A difficulty may be that if we are not familiar with the particular way of life, we may not understand the symbolic representation and thus language may be a barrier to communication.

Any change involves some level of learning, we therefore need to understand what is involved in the process of learning. Chapter 8 looks at the process in terms of how we learn, the levels of learning, and the possible blocks to learning. Using a mixture of personal reflection and theory, the interrelatedness of subject and object is demonstrated. By linking various theories, such as Bateson's Hierarchy of Learning and Kuhn's Paradigms, some useful insights are provided. Looking at the various situations that can create blocks to learning provides us with information regarding change.

Not only does change involve learning, it inevitably involves loss as well. Chapter 9 examines this aspect of loss by looking at organisational socialisation. Again, a mixture of personal experience and theory is used to show the effect of socialisation on individuals, and this provides an unusual perspective for viewing organisational change and the effects of culture. By examining the phenomenon of 'culture shock' we are able to view culture from a perspective which shows the effects of the loss of loved objects and the problems of adjusting to and acquiring new loved objects.

Chapter 10 deals with another of those factors that shed light on the phenomenon of culture – creativity. Here I commence with a substantial review of other writers, viewing creativity in the most commonly used categories: as a mystical process, as a drive, as similar to play, as requiring an holistic view, as resulting in something new, and as involving imagination in bringing about this something new. I then put my own original interpretation of creativity which includes an explanation of the anxiety and guilt associated with the process which is seldom, if ever, referred to by others. Creativity is highly relevant to organisational culture and change because it is largely through creativity that growth can occur. Creativity is about testing reality and, as we shall see, the drive to create is one of the factors that results in the dynamic nature of culture.

In Chapter 11 we return to an explanation of the phenomenon that we refer to as organisational culture. This chapter expands on the information contained in Chapter 3 to provide a more detailed account of the theory developed. In addition, I go beyond the question of how culture is developed to answer the remaining questions posed at the outset, regarding the perpetuation and representation of culture. The explanation for the way that culture is perpetuated is provided by using the concept of infantile and mature dependence and that of representation is explained by reference to symbolism.

4

THE NATURE OF ORGANISATIONS

We all have some experience of organisations and many of us work or participate in them in some way. On the face of things, they are varied in size and shape, in their task and purpose, and in many other less obvious ways. For example, they may be viewed as systems of communication, power and politics, strategy, technology and structure. Alternatively, they may be viewed as functional groupings, such as marketing, finance, personnel, research and development, and manufacturing.

Traditional text books and academic courses on organisational behaviour tend to regard organisations as mechanistic. For example, Child (1984) refers to 'decision mechanisms' and to 'operating mechanisms' (p. 4), while Buchanan and Huczynski (1985) refer to 'instruments to accomplish the purposes for which they were intended' (p. xi). The language and approach used leaves one with the impression that if only we could find the part of the machinery of organisation that needs fixing, we would be OK. This even seems to be the approach to human problems which are addressed by such responses as stress training, leadership training, management competencies and courses on how to achieve success.

In many ways the empirical-analytical paradigm reigns supreme when it comes to the analysis of organisations. Yet this is the least suitable paradigm for this purpose. As I will show, what is organised in human organisations is human behaviour. Consequently, even viewing organisations from the hermeneutic or interpretive paradigm will still not provide an understanding that is more appropriate to issues of change. My proposition is that this only becomes possible when we view them from a psycho-analytic perspective, one that provides explanations for human behaviour in unconscious processes rather than only in stated intentions.

ORGANISATIONS AS PROCESSES OF
HUMAN BEHAVIOUR

As Khan (1976) points out, biological and mechanical structures have a physical boundedness so that when the animal dies or the automobile stops running, the physical parts are still there, connected to each other as before, and the mechanic or pathologist can perform a post-mortem analysis. In contrast, human organisations have no structure other than the patterns of behaviour that are also their internal functions. When these patterns of behaviour stop, the organisation ceases to exist. Not even the traces of equipment and buildings that remain will provide us with many clues as to its nature in life.

From this view organisations are essentially patterns of human behaviour. It therefore follows that they are contrived, and being of human construction they are infinitely susceptible to modification. They do not conform to the laws of growth and death that characterise biological organisms; there is no particular size and shape they must attain, or lifecycle that they must follow. Organisations are not held together by functional branches or systems, the cement that holds them together is ultimately psychological. In order that the organisation is to exist, people must be motivated to engage in the stable recurring patterns of behaviour that define the organisations and give them continued existence.

Both Khan (1976) and Rioch (1985) considered that a useful concept for describing these patterns of behaviour in organisations and for understanding their motivational bases was to view them as systems of interrelated roles. Astrachan and Flynn (1976) take the view that almost every organisation or institution is a group of groups, formal or informal. Sadler (1976) refers to influences, such as values, beliefs and attitudes, which members of the organisation share in common – values and beliefs which will vary from group to group and from role to role. A further, most valuable view is that of Turquet (1974), who stated that an institution was an idea held in the mind.

It will be seen that these ways of looking at organisations are all very different from the traditional approach. From this view we should perhaps conclude that organisations are what their members make them. They exist only in the perceived reality of the members of the organisation. It is very much a matter of an idea held in the mind of the members, of people held together by a psychological cement. The groups of people, formed for all manner of reasons, are artificial creations. Some of the influences, such as values, beliefs and attitudes, may operate against effectiveness. It is a view of organisations as perceived objects. As we shall see later, this concept is very much in line with the view expressed regarding boundaries – they are artificial conceptions. Be they spatial, temporal or whatever, they are artificially constructed in the mind.

In this chapter and elsewhere I use the terms 'group' and 'organisation' as interchangeable on the basis that organisations consist of 'groups of groups'. It is with these groups that individual members of the organisation primarily identify even though they may also identify with the larger organisation. It is my experience, and the reported experience of others, that the culture of different groups in the same organisation varies from group to group, sometimes considerably. Consequently, for the purpose of viewing organisations from the perspective of culture and change, it is felt that this approach will provide the most useful data.

In spite of their artificial creation, we all treat institutions as if they exist, and for all of us they are exceedingly real. The family, the school, the college and the Metropolitan Police are all very much real objects for me. However, to be aware of the phenomenon is one thing, but to understand it is another. To be able to explain it and get a better understanding of why this should be so, we need to look at the processes that lead to this 'idea held in mind' and at how a group identity is created. In doing so it will inevitably be necessary to look at the manner in which an individual identity is formed.

One of the processes is undoubtedly identification, and Freud points out that this 'is known as the earliest expression of an emotional tie with another person' (1921, p. 134). He further explains that during the process of emotional maturation, the child gradually adopts the standards and values of the parents by identifying himself with them. This is added to by Flugel (1921), who explains that the identification with the parents is transferred to other important individuals. Later, however, this identification may no longer be with individual persons, but through a process of identification of the individual with a group or institution. Here we can see that identification can equally be with a perceived object, for example, the school, the college, the university or the Metropolitan Police.

In his explanation of groups Freud spoke of intense identification of group members with both the leader and the group as a whole. The libidinal ties arising from these intense identifications and strongly dependent mutual attachments make what he terms a psychic cement that, although operating outside awareness, often leads to the adoption of a common ideology. The result of the individual's group identification is that he reacts to the attributes of the group as if these attributes were also his.

The concept of an 'idea held in the mind' was previously referred to as an artificial creation. A different term is that used by Anzieu (1990), namely, a 'group illusion'. This he describes as a necessary illusion, one which sets up a group object that is at once internal and external to each member creating a collective consciousness. He explains that the group illusion corresponds to the founding moment in which the group forms itself as such. That is, a collection of individuals becomes a group when they are gripped by the collective imaginative belief that the group exists, as a reality that is both immanent and transcends each of them. In Anzieu's terms, 'there is no group without a common skin, a containing envelope, which makes it possible for its members to experience the existence of a group self' (1990, p. 97) – that is, a notion of 'other'; 'not-us'.

If we accept the notion of a collective consciousness we are getting very close to treating the perceived group object 'as if it were an individual. Indeed, Anzieu goes on to make the link between individual and group object-relations when he tells us that Klein's description of the individual psychic apparatus is still at present the best available model both for thinking about groups and the phenomena that unfold in them, and for building up an effective method. By this account we are needing to consider groups in terms of a self, containing somehow or other an innate ego, an acquired super-ego, and disparate internal objects that are more or less accepted or rejected by the ego and variously cathected by the drives.

A further view also tends to offer support for treating an organisation 'as if it were an individual. Reed and Palmer (1976) explain how the displacement of attachment instinct from mother to an illusory object, such as a work group, can result in organisations becoming a subordinate attachment-'figure' for some people, and a principal attachment-'figure' for others. If that is the case, we need a better understanding of the process preliminary to this displacement on to the illusory object. In order to gain this understanding, and to prepare our understanding for what is to follow, it is necessary to digress at this point to look at various aspects of individual personality development.

PERSONALITY DEVELOPMENT

In various publications Melanie Klein refers to the process of integration with regard to object-relations theory (see Klein, 1948, 1952,

1955 and 1960). She shows how, from the earliest stages of life, there is an instinctual need for an integration of the self as a whole person with boundaries. She describes how, even during the paranoid-schizoid position, that is, during the first three or four months of life when splitting processes are at their height, such splitting processes are never fully effective; from the beginning of life the ego tends towards integrating itself and towards synthesizing the different aspects of the object. There appear to be transitory states of integration even in very young infants – becoming more frequent and lasting as development goes on.

As the small child begins to be aware of himself as a separate entity, and at the same time begins to be aware of other people as separate, another important mechanism comes into operation. Until this time the infant is in a state of primary identification: that is, when the distinction between 'I' and 'you' is meaningless. Awareness of separate identity results in secondary identification: that is, the process of identifying with an object, the separate identity of which has been discovered. Unlike primary identification, secondary identification is a defence since it reduces hostility between the self and the object and enables experience of separation from it to be denied. Nonetheless, secondary identification with parental figures is held to be part of the normal development process.

According to Jacobson, 'the adult ego will make extensive use of introjective and projective mechanisms, based on such fusions between self and object images, for the special purpose of establishing feeling and fantasy identifications at any level, not only with our love objects but with our whole environment' (1964, p. 40). These are temporary fusions induced in the service of the ego and do not normally weaken the boundaries between the images of self and objects.

When the infant enters into what Klein called the depressive position and is able to establish the complete object, increasing integration brings about changes in the nature of his anxiety, for when love and hatred become more synthesized in relation to the object, initially the mother, this gives rise to great mental pain – to depressive feelings and guilt. Here, as Anna Freud explains, 'the instinctual impulses can no longer seek direct gratification – they are required to respect the demands of reality and, more than that, to conform to ethical and moral laws by which the superego seeks to control the behaviour of the ego' (1966, p. 7). At the same time the progress in integration and in object-relations enables the ego to develop more effective ways of dealing with the destructive impulses and the anxiety to which they give rise.

Storr (1963) is of the belief that the realisation of separateness leads to anxiety and fear; for, in the infant, this realisation is necessarily attended by the simultaneous realisation of dependence and helplessness. He claims that the fear of being abandoned leads to an attempt to re-identify with the parents and to an introjection of their standards and attitudes. 'I must be the same as they are or they will be angry', is the operative phrase. 'Good' is what parents approve of; and 'bad' is what they dislike; and, naturally, they like themselves and their opinions.

A different view of the same process is provided by Winnicott (1988), who explains that there then develops the theme of a 'me' and a 'not-me'. There are now 'me' contents that depend partly on instinctual experience and a meaning comes to the term 'relationship' as between the person, 'me', and objects. He describes how the infant develops from what he terms an unintegrated state at the theoretical start, at a time when there is a lack of wholeness both in space and in time, indeed, when there is no awareness. What he appears to be saying is that in the beginning there are no temporal, spatial, or other boundaries − just a continuum − but gradually, out of the inner world, there is produced some sort of pattern: order out of chaos.

In common with Klein, he also describes how progress is made when out of the unintegrated state comes integration for moments or brief periods, and only gradually is a general state of integration achieved. During this process dependence becomes lessened. Gradually, as integration becomes a maintained state of the individual, so the word disintegration rather than unintegration becomes appropriate for the description of the negative of integration. Disintegration, as we shall see, is a chaotic and painful experience.

Both Klein and Winnicott explain the importance of integration. For example, according to Klein (1955):

> One of the main factors underlying the need for integration is the individual's feeling that integration implies being alive, loving, and being loved by the internal and external good object; that is to say, there exists a close link between integration and object-relations. Conversely, the feeling of chaos, of disintegration, of lacking emotions as a result of splitting, I take to be closely related to the fear of death. (p. 144)

And, according to Winnicott (1988), 'Integration feels sane, and it feels mad to be losing integration that has been acquired' (p. 118).

Winnicott (1988) makes the point that integration means responsibility, and, accompanied as it is by awareness, and by the collection of memories, and by the bringing of the past, present and future into a relationship, it almost means the beginning of human psychology. This point is confirmed by Klein (1960) who claims that a well integrated personality is the foundation for mental health. She then goes on to enumerate some of the elements of an integrated personality: namely, emotional maturity, strength of character, a capacity to deal with conflicting emotions, a balance between internal life and adaptation to reality, and a successful welding into a whole of the different parts of the personality.

It is Winnicott (1988) who provides the best explanation of what happens in disintegration, when he points out that 'disintegration is chaotic, being an alternative to order, and it can be said to be a crude kind of defensive organisation, defensive against the anxieties that integration brings' (p. 135). In a far less dramatic way, many of us will have experienced individuals who have almost literally 'gone to pieces' when faced with a sudden traumatic experience. And, while it may not appear a very sympathetic response, the advice to 'pull yourself together' may not be entirely inappropriate.

A somewhat different view of the process is put by Anzieu (1989, 1990), which provides us with a further valuable insight. His approach has been to view the body boundary in conjunction with the boundary of the psyche. In *The Skin Ego* (1989) he explains the titular notion as follows:

> By skin ego, I mean a mental image of which the ego of the child makes use during the early phases of its development to represent itself as an ego containing physical contents, on the basis of its experience of the surface of the body. (p. 40)

It is Anzieu's view that the psyche gradually comes to terms with the body, so that in health there is eventually a state of affairs in which body boundaries are also the psyche boundaries. From his perspective, the skin is universally obviously important in the process of the localisation of the psyche exactly in and within the body. Anzieu (1990) claims that the baby's original fantasy in relating to his mother is one of having a common skin with her. In imagination each of them develops in different parts of a single skin, which allows them immediate exchange and contact.

For Anzieu, the boundaries of the body image are acquired in the course of the child's detaching itself from its mother and they are, according to him, to some degree analogous to the ego boundaries. He suggests that we take the body image not as a physical agency or function, but simply as a representation elaborated at a quite early stage by the ego itself while in the process of becoming structured. He therefore considers that what is involved here is a symbolic process of representing a boundary which functions both as a stabilising image and as a protective envelope. This procedure, he suggests, poses the body as an object which must at all costs be kept intact. Here he seems to be in agreement with both Klein and Winnicott by suggesting that the function of setting boundaries connects with the necessity for bodily integrity.

I have referred to the chaotic state of disintegration as described by Klein and Winnicott. Thus far the discussion has been largely theoretical. However, Menzies Lyth (1988) provides practical examples of the very real terrors experienced by young children and the need for maintenance of various boundaries. These provide us with an explanation as to why adults need and form all manner of temporal and spatial boundaries. As to temporal boundaries, she explains how the child's rudimentary time sense and the connection of the mother's absence with his own aggression make it only too easy for him to believe that she has gone for good. This, of course, is an unbearable and terrifying experience which may act as a dreadful confirmation of the fantasy of permanent loss and lead to obvious states of depression and despair even in quite small babies.

In referring to children in hospital she provides a fine example of the need for spatial boundaries in the development of children. She shows how the importance of boundary control gives a stronger sense of belonging to what is inside the infant, of there being something comprehensible for it to identify with, of there being 'my place', or 'our place', where 'I' belong and where 'we' belong together. If there are no boundaries or the boundaries are drawn too wide children cannot get identity from or identify with such a large institution. It does not offer enough sense of being bounded and contained within something comprehensible. Menzies Lyth explains that small children need this holding together not only by space but also by attached people in terms of consistency in modes of communication and response. If not, they may feel lost internally as well as possibly getting lost in fact. Recalling the chaotic state described earlier she tells us that they literally feel all over the place.

In other words, there must be clear boundaries of various categories in order that the child has a consistent picture such as will permit integration. It is this process of constant testing of reality that helps the child to build an effective identity. The baby comes to be and to know himself as he is known and reflected back to himself by others; both the quality of the other's response and its consistency being important. An aspect of healthy development in the individual is therefore the establishment of a firm boundary for the self and others across which realistic and effective relationships and transactions can take place and within which a sense of one's own identity can be established.

This need does not cease with development to adulthood. For example, whilst carrying out the research for this book my father was admitted to hospital in a terminal condition. After an initial admission to a general hospital he was moved to a geriatric unit. My father was very ill, and unable to communicate verbally, but my mother seemed quite certain that he was informing her that he was not happy in this location. In discussing this with my wife, who had recently retired from a career in nursing, she stated that it was a well known phenomenon that elderly patients frequently reacted badly to a change of location. In many cases, their condition would be seen to deteriorate quite dramatically following a move. It would appear that the likely explanation is that the boundary changes from familiar to unfamiliar result in disintegration, in a feeling of chaos; this coupled with increasing physical fragility results in the rapid deterioration.

A further example is provided by Bruno Bettelheim (1960) who recounts how, despite the dreadful conditions of the concentration camps at Dachau and Buchenwald, with all their horrors, he still suffered terrible anxiety because he was unable to put into being temporal boundaries in relation to the work activities that he was forced to carry out. The experience of disintegration was also vividly portrayed by the hostage Brian Keenan, who, describing his experience just after his release from Lebanon, said, 'A hostage is a man clinging with his fingernails over the edge of chaos', and, 'It's like someone comes and tears your right arm off and walks away' (*The Times*, 28 August 1990). There can be little doubt that this shows that throughout life the matter of integration is vital to all of us. A violent disruption to the individual's identity will appear as chaos and result in disintegration. No one who saw Keenan or his fellow hostages on their release can doubt this.

There is another aspect of personality development which is felt to be relevant to the issue of boundaries. In common with Freud, Marris (1974) referred to a conservative instinct which results in an attachment to objects which remains with us through life. In this sense he tells us that conservatism is an aspect of our ability to survive in any situation: for without continuity we cannot interpret what events mean to us, nor explore new kinds of experience with confidence. He goes on to explain that the process of attachment influences our perceived reality of the world. He describes how, in order to construct meanings, a growing child must be able to identify, classify and compare, to perceive relationships and conceptualise them in abstraction. Attachment influences the development, not only as our first and for a long time our most crucial experience of security and danger, order and predictability, but as the guarantor of all other learning.

Freud (1921) referred to the conservative instinct as paramount, but he also acknowledged that there may be others which push towards progress and the production of new forms. This is the view of Bowlby (1969) and others, who show that the child has an instinctual need for attachment. This is more than just conservatism: Bowlby's concern is with the nature of the child's tie to its mother. In Bowlby's view this bond manifests itself in attachment behaviour. This is behaviour, on the part of the young child, directed towards gaining proximity to certain specific people referred to as 'attachment figures'. The infant's first attachment figure is usually his mother. Bowlby identifies a number of patterns of attachment behaviour: sucking, clinging, following (bodily or with the eyes), crying, calling and smiling.

These relationships of attachment are crucial to a child's well-being, even its survival. Because we are born very helpless and throughout childhood remain primarily dependent on our parenting figures to protect, feed and care for us, the attention of our parents is our only weapon of defence. Hence a child's most crucial task, for its own survival, is to make its attachment relationships secure. Since attachment is so overwhelmingly important to us, above all in the early years, it underlies all our understanding of how to survive in and manage the world we inhabit.

It is difficult for us as adults to imagine the feelings associated with infancy. However, according to Anzieu (1989), the catastrophe haunting the nascent psyche of the human baby would then be that of letting go of this clinging grip. When that happens the child is plunged into what Bion called a 'nameless dread'. Menzies Lyth (1989) explains what happens when the attachment is broken and the effect that this has on the child when she describes the experience of separation of the young child from its mother, notably when the child is put in an institution. The effect, according to Menzies Lyth, is that immediate and often inconsolable distress is almost universal.

The foregoing has been a brief and selective view of individual personality development, but it has nevertheless described some important aspects which it will be helpful to summarise. We can say that, right from the start, the infant has an instinctual need for an integration of the self as a whole person with boundaries. From an unintegrated state, there is gradually produced some sort of pattern – order out of chaos. An order in terms of space and time, which eventually leads to a state of affairs in which the body boundaries are also the psyche boundaries. This is a precarious state and one which is protected with great care, as disintegration is experienced as madness. Out of this process the individual builds an effective identity which is itself a reassurance against fears of death or madness. To achieve this, there must be spatial and temporal boundaries that limit the degree of inconsistency experienced by the infant. There must also be a consistency in the authority boundaries and of the consistency of the mother. Hence a child's most crucial task, for its own survival, is to make its attachment relationships secure. This is aided by an attachment instinct which results in both conscious and unconscious processes of attachment, and both physical and psychological attachments.

From the foregoing, we can see just how crucial to individual identity formation and retention are both the attachment instinct and the instinct for integration which must be supported by the formation of boundaries. The boundaries are essential to preserve the wholeness of the individual, both physically and psychologically, without which we would not be able to function properly. The attachment instinct by clinging to those boundaries supports this process by defending the predictability of life and our very survival. For without this continuity we should not be able to interpret what events meant for us, nor explore new kinds of experience with confidence. However, in making these points I should not wish to infer that this is in any way anything other than a dynamic process. Integration is a continuing process that is never complete even in adult life, as is the case with introjection and projection. Conservatism and adaptability are both necessary for survival.

GROUP IDENTITY

Having shown how integration and attachment are so vitally important to individual identity, the question is, can we also relate this to group identity? I believe we can, and will show that the perceived group object is treated by the group members in more or less the same way. The basis for this belief is the interdependence of the individual with the group. Freud (1921) asserted that there was no dichotomy between individual and group psychology because the psychology of the individual is itself a function of the individual's relationship to another person or object. According to Bion (1961), the individual is a group animal, and in order to study the individual, it required that he be looked at from the position of the group and the group from the position of the individual. There were 'socio-' and 'psycho-' perspectives which were interdependent.

In a paradoxical way, the need of the individual constantly to affirm his identity with those around him results in the perceived group object. Bion stated that the interdependence of group and individual was the subject of his enquiries. The individual perpetually requires and seeks personal relationships for his development and maintenance. The anxieties inherent in the primitive phantasies, described earlier, are instinctively responded to by an attempt to find 'allies', figures with whom the feeling of a close contact can bring reassurance. Thus, as Sutherland (1985) claims, the origin and nature of the individual's 'groupishness' is no problem. From the very start he cannot survive without his needs for social relatedness being met.

The logical extension of this view is that put by Erikson (1959): that of a group identity which refers to the group as a social collective with a sense of shared human qualities, a commonality with others, an ideology, goals, and refers in a broader sense to the group's basic way of organising experience. Thus the ego identity is based on the common perception of an individual's self-sameness and continuity. Put another way, personal identity is based on two simultaneous observations: the immediate perception of one's self-sameness and continuity in time; and the simultaneous perception of the fact that others recognise one's self-sameness and continuity.

I feel quite sure that our personal reflection provides us with confirmation of the foregoing but, by way of affirmation, Marris (1974) describes research where students were studied when taking their places at university. It was found that the students looked for their own kind, on the basis of signs which were immediately perceptible: for example, accent, manner, and dress. The greater the differences, the more likelihood of difficulties between the students. Many of these perceptible signs were centred upon language. Students from different social backgrounds felt the strain of communicating across subtle distinctions of class-bounded cultures. Konig (1985) explains that when we enter 'stranger groups', we try to manoeuvre the other group members into positions which correspond to our internal objects.

A slightly different approach is taken by Anzieu (1984), who referred to a 'skin ego' in regard to the individual. In much the same way, he refers to a 'group envelope'. He explains that the only way a group can protect itself from the extreme anxieties that it faces is to fabricate an overarching group psychical apparatus on top of those of the individuals composing it. According to Anzieu:

> to exist at all the group needs an overarching agency that envelops it. Thus the group is organised around the same agencies as the individuals composing it. The conscious and unconscious functioning of the group will differ depending on the agency that serves as envelope to the group psychical apparatus; the enveloping agency also affects the behaviour of the group, its goals and attitudes towards external reality. (p. 101)

At this point I should wish to stress that while these matters of integration and group membership are important and are thus accentuated to make the necessary points, equally important is the dynamic nature of the process and the fact that we pass through a series of identifications which are constantly changing and shifting. As to the group, we need to appreciate the interrelatedness between the group and the individual. Thus the individual is required to be looked at from the position of the group and the group from the position of the individual.

Anzieu (1984) also helps us to understand the formation of the group illusion when he explains how the group situation awakens the image of limitless fragmentation or splitting of the individual's body and personality. He tells us that it summons up the oldest of phantasies, that of dismemberment and that the group draws the individual far into his past, to early childhood where he did not yet have consciousness of himself as subject, where he felt incoherent. We are aware that one of the deepest anxieties is that of losing one's physical and psychological unity. Experience such as that described by Anzieu has led us to realise that the group constitutes a primary threat to the individual. A human being can exist as a subject only if he feels physically and psychologically coherent.

This leads us to one of the most important developments in group relations training: the observation of Turquet that the possibility of a participant emerging from anonymity and isolation and becoming a subject involves establishing contact (visual, gesture or verbal) with his neighbour or his two closest neighbours. In this way is formed what Turquet calls 'the relational frontier of the "I" with my neighbour's skin' (1974, p. 99). This tends to support Bowlby's theory by showing how the attachment drive operates in humans. We all look for protection both against external dangers and against an internal psychical state of distress; in doing so we search for contact (in the double sense, both bodily and social, of the term) which enables signs to be exchanged in a reciprocal process of communication in which each partner feels himself recognised by the other.

What we are saying here is that the boundaried group serves as a defence against both external dangers and internal distress. This aspect is touched on by Marris (1974) who refers to the setting up of tribal and territorial boundaries to withstand the threat to the meaning of our lives. Turquet (1974) also introduced the concept of bodily and social attachment. It is upon the skin that a first picture of reality is registered – that is, biologically. Socially, an individual's membership of a social group is shown by incisions, scarification, skin painting, tattooing, by make up and hair style, and by clothes, which are another aspect of the same thing.

These boundaries do not resolve the problems of social coherence. But they protect people from having to confront the confusion as an aspect of their own uncertain identity, unmediated by any given sense of where they belong. If these boundaries are threatened, the tensions will once again press upon people directly, and may provoke panic-stricken violence or flight. Conversely, the more nakedly people are exposed to the anxieties of change, the more uncompromisingly they will try to erect protective barriers about their precarious sense of self. That is, they may, as Marris (1974) has suggested, seek to invent a tribe – a collective identification – where none has existed, and project their internal conflict upon society in these terms.

It seems that the foregoing provides support for Bion's assumption that there is a 'socio-' aspect of interdependence between individuals and groups. The issue that now arises is whether the group can be seen to have a 'psycho-' aspect in a manner similar to an individual. Some positive indication is provided by Anzieu (1989), who, talking about his findings from group work, describes how participants tend to fill up empty space by huddling in a corner, by putting tables in the middle, or by removing empty chairs. I believe that what is being described here shows quite clearly the need for the group to create a clear spatial or territorial boundary. It will doubtless be noted that the activity described by Anzieu is very similar to the needs expressed earlier by Menzies Lyth in relation to children in hospital. Faced with a broken boundary, there is considerable effort to reduce the anxiety caused. It would seem then that the individual needs groups to be 'integrated'; indeed he needs several groups to enable him to feel integrated.

A further description of how members of groups act in a manner similar to individuals is provided by Anzieu (1984) when he describes how participants in any group situation may regress to the situation of the infant. In Anzieu's view this explains the phenomenon, which Freud discovered, of the common substitution in a group of the group ego ideal for the individual ego ideal. This idea of group regression was very much a part of the theory of Bion in his view of groups. He regarded a group in the state of basic assumption as acting irrationally because of regression. The basic assumption states are ways of dealing with impulses so as to satisfy the defensive needs of the group.

Bion postulated that the basic assumption states were based on the processes which established themselves in earliest infancy. He saw the anxiety that provoked them as deriving from much earlier phases in which the fears were of disintegration, a loss of the self or madness. They crystallised for him replicas of the emotions with which the infant related to the mother and, later, the family. Sutherland explains that the task of establishing contact with the emotional life of the group would appear to be as formidable to the adult as the relationship with the breast appears to be to the infant, and the failure to meet the demands of this task is revealed in his regression.

Bion describes how the work of the group, its functioning and task performance, is impaired with deterioration of the ego functioning of the members. The realities of the situation and the task are lost sight of, reality testing is poor, secondary process thinking deteriorates and more primitive forms of thinking emerge. There is new organisation of behaviour which seems to be determined by fantasies and assumptions which are unrealistic and represent a failed struggle to cope with the current reality situation. Thereby the group survives as such at the expense of the individual though its essential functioning and primary task are now altered in the service of a different task.

It will be appreciated that there is an element of defence in the regression described by Bion. Likewise, Anzieu referred to the need for an envelope as a means of protection for the group. A different view is put by Menzies Lyth (1988) and Jaques (1953), who have developed a concept that they have referred to as 'social systems as a defence against anxiety'. They describe how, in its development, a social organisation is influenced by a number of interacting factors – above all, for the support in the task of dealing with anxiety. To this extent the nature of the organisation is determined by the psychological needs of the members. The characteristic feature of the social defence system is its orientation to helping the individual avoid the experience of anxiety, guilt, doubt and uncertainty.

Bion's argument is that basic assumption activities are difficult to sustain beyond the small group level; therefore the members of the larger group need a more complex configuration to deal with their anxieties. What is being described is not a regression or a sudden reaction to an anxiety provoking threat to the group. On the contrary, a social defence system develops over time as the result of collusive interaction and agreement, often unconscious, between members of the organisation as to what form it shall take. It is a gradual build-up more in the nature of a seeping into the group fabric like a process of osmosis. However, once in place, the socially structured defence mechanisms then tend to become an aspect of external reality which old members of the institution take for granted and with which new members must come to terms.

In 'normal' organisations we still find the same anxieties. However, in these cases there are various institutional defences which serve to reduce the danger of identity loss. We go to considerable lengths to ensure that anxiety is reduced to a minimum. This is achieved by various defensive structures: for example, participants identify themselves before they speak, the roll is called, name tags are distributed, lists of participants are handed out. This is the world as we commonly see it on the surface, but we should be aware that these are only defences to those not-so-easily-seen phenomena.

It would appear then that there is also a prima facie case for regarding the group 'as if' it were an individual. As we have seen, in precisely the same way as in relation to individuals, we also go to great lengths to create and maintain our boundaries in institutions. It is just as important to protect the group boundaries as it is to protect individual boundaries. The institution as a whole must control its external boundaries and regulate transactions across them so as to protect and facilitate the maintenance of the primary task. In addition, any institution is divided into subsystems, some of which perform different tasks. The way these subsystems control their boundaries and conduct transactions across them is of equal importance for the performance of the subgroup task.

It can be seen that integration and synthesis are as relevant to the group as they are to the healthy individual. In terms of managing change this would appear to be vital. Should we not be aware of the need to control anxiety, those involved will undoubtedly suffer from some form of disintegration. An example of this, witnessed by myself, concerns a change situation in the Metropolitan Police, where two different members of the group involved were heard to comment, 'It was just like going through a divorce', and, 'I don't mind bleeding, provided they (senior management) are also prepared to bleed.' In both instances, it will be noted that quite apart from the very real expressions of pain, there is also a very strong feeling of being 'out of control', of chaos.

There are many other reported cases that support the above, some even more dramatic than those already expressed. The problem is that we rarely recognise that changes in the nature of work also create losses that trigger powerful individual or collective reactions. The costs may not be immediately obvious nor reflected in tangible ways, but left unattended over a period of time, pressure builds up and can become a silent killer in organisations – much like hyper-tension in the human body (Deal, 1985).

SUMMARY

Through a process of identification, which first applied to the mother, attachment feelings and instinct are displaced on to groups. The group becomes either a subordinate or a principal attachment figure. The result is that a collection of people become a group when they come to the illusory agreement that the group exists. Thus, the group is to be regarded in the same manner that any other object is in object relations. This object is seen to have a common skin in the same way as an individual and the members of an organisation have the same needs as an individual to create spatial, temporal and other boundaries. Indeed, we can say that integration and synthesis are just as important to the group as they are to the individual.

Furthermore, the need to protect the boundaries of the group is the same, and, should there be a breach of these boundaries, the result is precisely the same for the members of the group as for an individual – disintegration, and it will be recalled just how painful this is. In addition to the reasons for identification with the group given above, the group itself creates anxiety for individuals which in turn results in a stronger identification. The attachment instinct leads to a search for both a bodily and social contact, and this in turn helps us to withstand the threat to the meaning of our lives.

The outward signs of dress – hair styles, and so on – permit a ready recognition of other like-minded persons, of others in the same social boundaries, and this reduces the confusion and the anxiety. Should the group boundaries be threatened, the result may well be a regression to an infantile state, perhaps even more so than in the case of an individual.

From the foregoing, I believe that we can state, with some confi-dence, the existence of a group identity. Whether we call it a common skin, a containing envelope, an idea held in the mind, or whatever, the actions of groups indicate such an identity. In the same manner as individuals, it is essential for the group to create and maintain boundaries such as will ensure a continuity and thus reduce or avoid anxiety. It is equally clear that should change be imposed on the group the members will experience the same chaos and suffer the same dreadful anxieties as individuals. These boundaries are the social structures which are created as a defence against the group's anxieties. Again, as with the individual, these boundaries may be spatial, temporal, psychological, or in terms of authority, role, or whatever. They may be based on phantasy or illusion and, to others, appear to be nonsensical. However, to the group, they are all important.

I believe that it is also reasonable to state that the structures resulting from the boundaries created as a defence against anxiety are what may be termed the group identity, that is, an unconscious and partly conscious construct of its members. In order, then, to understand the culture of the group we need to understand the boundaries. That is, what boundaries exist, and why. Some, such as spatial or temporal, may not be too difficult to discover. However, this should not diminish our understanding of the effect that will result from changing them. Others, such as psychological boundaries, may be more difficult to locate and understand.

It will be appreciated that this view of organisations is most relevant to organisational culture. Precisely how, will be developed further in Chapter 11, where the explanation of organisational culture outlined in Chapter 3 will be expanded. In the next chapter, the issue of boundaries will be looked at in greater detail.

5

THE NEED, DEVELOPMENT AND USE
OF BOUNDARIES

An old proverb tells us that you cannot swim in the same river twice. In like manner, experience is kaleidoscopic and the experience of every moment is unique and unrepeatable. This means that unless we are able to classify our experience on some basis of similarity we will be unable to make sense of that experience. Without some sort of categorisation we would be imprisoned in the uniqueness of the here and now. Such categorising activity is aptly described by Sapir (1961) as the reduction of experience to familiar form.

In Chapter 6, 'Symbolism', I will describe in some detail how the infant develops to a position where he or she is able to distinguish the complete object; to a position where there is increasing integration, a greater degree of awareness of differentiation and of the separateness of the ego. A situation where the infant is able to distinguish between 'me' and 'not-me' and meaning comes to the term 'relationship' as between the person 'me' and objects. At the same time, the infant develops the use of symbols – in particular, speech symbols – which enables the infant to make rapid progress. In the meantime, however, I shall largely assume this situation.

The significance of boundaries has already been referred to particularly in the last chapter. I now want to take a closer look at this phenomenon, to try to establish why and how boundaries develop and to learn more about their nature. The establishment of a personality system as a separate entity with a well functioning boundary across which input and output are possible is vital to the healthy development of any individual. This is further explained by Lofgren (1975) who points out that personality boundaries and reality testing – that is, the ability to discern the outside from the inside so that the individual has adequate perception and the ability to deal with incoming material – are vital features if there is to be progression.

MAKING SENSE OF OUR WORLD

Without some system of making sense out of total chaos the uniqueness of the here and now would be intolerable. The result is that we classify or categorise. As Tyler (1969) puts it, 'It is through naming and classification that the whole rich world of infinite variability shrinks to manipulable size and becomes bearable' (p. 67). This, of course, is a highly selective process. We do not live in a world where we discriminate among all the possible sensory stimuli in our environment, nor do we react to each stimulus as if it were new and foreign. In effect we choose to ignore many of those perceptual differences which make each object unique. The system that we mainly choose to use for this is naming. By doing so we put objects which to us are similar into the same category, even though we can perceive differences among them.

It will be appreciated that the objects of our world do not present themselves to us ready classified. The categories into which they are divided are categories into which we divide them. The anthropologist Leach (1976) makes this point, claiming that when we use symbols to distinguish one class of things or actions from another we are creating artificial boundaries in a field that is naturally continuous. In other words, we are still referring to perceived objects, or ideas held in the mind. Moving on from here it will not be too difficult to imagine that some experiences could not be classified if it were not for the use of language. Language is our principal means of classifying the representations of our experience.

In principle the created boundaries have no dimensions yet they are as real for you and me as the groups referred to earlier. Leach explains that these boundaries apply to time as well as space. By way of example he cites neighbouring gardens and national frontiers as spatial boundaries, and the segmentation of time into hours and minutes as temporal boundaries. He also explains how social time is similarly segmented as an individual moves from one social status to another in a series of discontinuous jumps. For example, from child to adult, from unmarried to married, or from sick to healthy. The occupancy of each status constitutes a period of social time of social duration, but the ritual that marks the transition – wedding, funeral, healing ritual – is an interval of social timelessness (Leach, 1976).

Gestalt Theory. The view that people seek to impose order upon what they see is also shared by the Gestalt psychologists. For example, according to Nevis (1987), complex human behaviour cannot be explained as an additive building up of simple components. For Gestalt psychologists, the true data of experience are organised wholes. The world of sensory data is arranged in an organised manner, and people react to the overall pattern of unitary organisation of objects, not to specific bits or parts. In his view this is not a passive response: on the contrary, people work hard to impose order on what they see.

Gestalt psychology also maintains that we often comprehend objects as units before we have any way of knowing what they are like. It is the view of Katz (1969) that this applies to vision in comparative darkness and to strange surroundings when we come upon objects we have never seen before. This tendency to perceiving wholes leads to what Nevis refers to as the fixed Gestalt, which in turn leads to the difficulty for individuals of forming fresh, new figures in the present moment. In his view, hanging on to past perceptions of people or events prevents comprehension of what would be the most useful behaviour in the here and now.

Nevis also came to realise that people cannot have appropriate interactions until tensions derived from the past are released in some way. It seems that in order to confirm this concept we have only to attempt to complete a crossword puzzle. Anyone who has experienced the situation where the insertion of a wrong entry has prevented new thinking, or where they have erased a wrong entry thus permitting new thinking, will be aware of the correctness of this assertion. The interesting thought is how we 'erase' old thinking when it comes to managing change.

The nature of a boundary is that it separates two zones of social space-time which are normal, timebound, clear-cut, central, secular, but the temporal and spatial markers which actually serve as boundaries are themselves abnormal, timeless, ambiguous, at the edge, sacred. Consequently, the ambiguity which exists at the boundary is a source of anxiety, and it is the boundaries that matter. We concentrate our attention on the differences, not the similarities, and this makes us feel that the markers of such boundaries are of special value, or, as Leach (1976) has observed, 'sacred' or 'taboo'.

A further valuable approach to the nature of boundaries is the Gestalt view of individual boundaries of Merry and Brown (1987), who point out that contact is the point where the boundaries of the individual meet other boundaries, such as those of social systems. The boundary is at the location of a relationship where the relationship both separates and connects. In contemporary terms the boundary is at the interface. Without interrelation of some kind, there can be no boundary. The contact point, at the boundary, is where awareness arises. With awareness the individual can mobilise energy so that the environment can be contacted to meet a need. The contact boundary is where one differentiates oneself from others.

This is further explained in a more general way by Nevis who says that 'boundary' is a term used to designate the phenomenological moment in which one entity is experienced as separate or different from another. To have a boundary of any kind is to define or set the limits of interaction (contact) between the individual or system and its environment. Thus, for Nevis, boundary is a relational concept that summarises the state of affairs between reasonably discrete objects or people but it is important to see these states as momentary points in a dynamic process, not as fixed structural conceptions. The concept of a dynamic process is similar to the concept of a 'boundary region' referred to by Miller and Rice (1967).

Systems Theory. Systems theory as described by Miller and Rice also deals with the concept of boundaries. In regard to 'systems of organisation', they describe a system of activities as that complex of activities which is required to complete the process of transforming an intake into an output. The term 'system' as they use it here, implies that each component activity of the system is interdependent in respect of at least some of the other activities of the same system, and the system as a whole is identifiable as being in certain, if limited, respects independent of related systems. Thus a system has a boundary which separates it from its environment.

In common with the views previously stated they also observe that a system boundary implies a discontinuity. This discontinuity of the boundary may constitute a differentiation of technology, territory or time, or some combination of these. They further explain that in a simple system there are no internal boundaries either between one operating activity and another or between operating activities on the one hand and maintenance and regulatory activities on the other, whereas a complex system contains such internal boundaries, which is the nature of most enterprises. Such complex systems include a number of identifiable subsystems of activities through which the various processes of the enterprise are carried out. These constituent systems, like the enterprise as a whole, are open systems which acquire intakes from the environment, transform them and export the results.

Group Relations Training Theory. The notion that groups distinguish boundaries is one of the most important characteristics that students of group relations experience and study. Group relations training has therefore provided some very useful data in regard to the concept of boundaries. For example, Redlich and Astrachan (1975) distinguish three types of boundaries: spatial, temporal and psychological. The spatial boundary is the most obvious one. Here the group begins to consider the room to be its own territory and is often willing to safeguard it against strangers. Within the group territorial arrangements are observed and seating arrangements are important to the group. Anzieu reported similar behaviour. Temporal boundaries refer to how the study group learns to appreciate time boundaries. This is experienced quite vividly when – out of a group of strangers – a cohesive and distinctive group emerges and ends quite abruptly at a given time. In addition, the 'death' of the group is usually experienced with anxiety, anger and, most of all, with some grief, expressed overtly and covertly. However, the most important boundaries are the psychological boundaries of the group, which define who belongs to the group and who does not. They explain how the group members distinguish external boundaries, separating members from non-members, and internal boundaries where the phenomenon of scapegoating is frequently observed. This acceptance and rejection of group members is related to the development of inner psychological boundaries.

CONVENTIONALISED SYMBOLS

These three types of boundaries, spatial, temporal and psychological, are social structures created by the group. It is of passing interest to note that I am using the words 'spatial', 'temporal' and 'psychological', to categorise or classify groups of sensory data, that is, to put boundaries around them. Without doing so I could not possibly comprehend them myself, let alone communicate them to the reader. I am also using conventionalised symbols, symbols that are known both to me and, hopefully, to the reader. Furthermore, had I chosen to create totally new symbols for the sensory data that I refer to as 'spatial', or whatever, I should have needed to explain that.

Our system of conventionalised symbols provides us with various categories for explaining organisations. For example, Goodenough (1964) concentrates on the division of organisations by means of rights and their duty counterparts. Every individual has a number of different social identities. What his rights and duties are varies according to the identities he may appropriately assume in a given interaction. A further categorisation is that used by Lofgren (1975) who prefers to use the classification of roles. He describes roles as being claimed labels, from behind which people present themselves to others and partially in terms of which they conceive, gauge and judge their past, current and projected action. Roles are also imputed labels, towards which, and partially in terms of which, people likewise conceive, gauge and judge others' past, present and projected action.

Yet a further view is also put by Goodenough (1964) – that of identities; some of which are ascribed and some 'achieved'. In describing how one comes to possess a particular social identity as a matter of social fact, he explains how everyone has many more identities than he can assume at one time in a given interaction. This means that the individual must select from among his various identities those in which to present himself. Several considerations govern the selection of identities. An obvious consideration is an individual's (or group's) qualifications for selecting the identity. Does he in fact possess it? An individual may masquerade as a policeman, for example, donning the symbols that inform others of such an identity, and yet not be one.

OUR NEED FOR BOUNDARIES

It seems clear that we all need to create boundaries, either individually or as groups, and that we are in some difficulty when we cannot do so. The feelings of disintegration referred to earlier that were experienced by Bruno Bettelheim (1960) are partially explained by the fact that life in the concentration camp resulted in the removal of temporal boundaries which brought him severe hardship. He informs us that nobody had a watch. Consequently, in regard to most of the work, it was not possible to gauge how soon the horror of forced labour would end. In this case the 'anonymity' of time was a factor which was destructive to personality. On the other hand, it was possible to know, in regard to one particular type of work, that 'each trip of the carrier column took half an hour which meant that one knew exactly when the noon break would come with its half hour rest, and when the work day would finally be over in the evening' (p. 140). In this case the ability to 'organise time' was a strengthening influence as it permitted some initiative or some planning.

While I should not wish to draw comparisons with the experience referred to above, the question of boundaries also causes me to reflect on life as a young boy, when I often had to walk along a country road for about a mile in total darkness. In such circumstances I was frequently very frightened, because I could not distinguish anything. I could not put boundaries around anything. This is, of course, precisely what Katz (1969) was saying above. Taking this forward I cannot help thinking that to metaphorically keep people in the dark about change could be equally frightening for them.

SUMMARY

It is important to understand the need to impose order on our world and it is also important that we understand the process involved. The function of boundaries is to create separate entities, and a well functioning boundary permits logical thinking. However, disintegration will result in malfunctioning boundaries and regression. A boundary is a relational concept that summarises the state of affairs between reasonably discrete objects or people. The fact that groups have boundaries is an essential factor; these boundaries may be of various types, and between subgroups. Gestalt psychology shows that we comprehend objects as units before we have any way of knowing what they are like. It is as though everything has to be an object. People work actively to impose order upon what they see.

The boundaries created are to be seen as momentary points in a dynamic process; they are artificial interruptions to what is naturally continuous. Yet to us it is the boundaries that matter. Concentrating on the differences makes us feel that the markers of the boundaries are 'taboo'. These boundaries are created by feelings, assumptions and fantasies, which in many cases are unconscious. In order for change to occur, the boundary must be confronted in order that a new experience of the avoided or unknown can take place. In order to do this we use language which has been used to categorise our world, by now tying the component elements together again, by putting things and persons into relationship with one another.

By naming we classify and put objects which are similar into the same category. We classify because life in a world where nothing was the same would be intolerable. It is through naming and classification that the whole frightening world of infinite variability becomes manageable and bearable. Naming can refer to rights, to roles or to social identities: all permit us to make sense out of the world and to reduce anxiety. Whatever the categories are that we create, be they spatial, temporal, psychological or social structures, they all result in 'the way that we do things around here'.

Naming and classification are achieved by the use of language and words as symbols. This is a matter which I shall revisit in Chapter 7. Chapter 6 looks first at the concept of symbolism, with a view to understanding how culture is expressed.

6

SYMBOLISM

The relevance of the concept of symbolism immediately becomes evident when we refer to the following views of Klein and Winnicott. Klein (1930) came to the conclusion that symbolism is the foundation of all sublimation and of every talent. Winnicott (1971) concluded that the transitional object is the first use of a symbol and that this object gradually gives place to an ever-widening range of objects, and to the whole cultural life. On these views, we can begin to see that the development of symbolism shadows the development of culture. Consequently, the study of symbolism is of the utmost relevance if we are to understand culture.

PROCESSES OF INFANT DEVELOPMENT

To develop an understanding of symbolism I shall trace it as a process in the individual through the various psycho-analytic writings. However, in order to provide some sort of context I first need to describe two different periods of infant development. Freud referred to two types of mental functioning, primary and secondary processes: the former being characteristic of unconscious mental activity and the latter being characteristic of conscious thinking. The primary process is governed by the pleasure principle, which leads to avoidance of pain and unpleasure by hallucinating the satisfaction necessary. This process ignores categories of space and time, and images tend to become fused and can readily replace one another. This is a period before ego formation and integration. The secondary process, on the other hand, is governed by the reality principle, which leads to the avoidance of pain and unpleasure by adaptive behaviour: that is, the capacity to discriminate between subjective images and external percepts. Freud considered that the secondary process developed at the same time as the ego and that this was closely connected to verbal thinking.

Roughly analogous with the primary and secondary processes are the Kleinian concepts of the paranoid-schizoid position and the depressive position. In the former the individual deals with his innate destructive impulses by primitive defensive responses: by splitting both his ego and his object representations into good and bad parts and by projecting his destructive impulses on to the bad object by whom he feels persecuted. In the depressive position the individual becomes aware of his ambivalence when he realises that both his love and hate are directed towards the same object. In this position, the individual is able to distinguish the complete object and is able to progress towards integration.

These two periods of development, whichever choice of terminology we use, are relevant not only to an understanding of symbolism but also to the wider issue of culture. The significance will perhaps be appreciated if we recall that earlier we referred the issue of regression – of both individuals and groups – to the situation of the infant. It will also be recalled that this regression brought about fears of disintegration, a loss of the self or madness. In other words, the regression referred to is from the depressive position or secondary process, to the primary process or the paranoid-schizoid position.

As explained in Chapter 3, in the first instant the infant progresses from a situation of unborn dependence to one of born dependence. Ferenci (1952) postulates that in the former situation the infant must be under the impression that he is omnipotent: that he has all that he wants and there is nothing left to wish for. This continues after birth, but now this is achieved in a hallucinatory way. The infant feels himself to be in possession of a magical capacity that can realise all his wishes by simply imagining the satisfaction of them. Ferenci calls this 'The period of magical hallucinatory omnipotence' (p. 222). He then describes how the child makes use of crying and gestures with the same result: that is, satisfaction promptly arrives. He calls this 'The period of omnipotence by the help of magical gestures' (p. 225).

During this period the thinking is not in accordance with reality but has all the archaic and magical features that have been described. This is explained by Fenichel (1946), who considers that primitive symbolism is a part of the way in which conceptions are formed in pre-logical thinking. At this stage, comprehension of the world radiates from instinctual demands and fears. The first objects are possible means of gratification or possible threats; stimuli that provoke the same reactions are looked upon as identical; and the first ideas are not sums built up out of distinct elements but wholes comprehended in a still undifferentiated way, united by the emotional responses they have provoked.

It seems that the child passes through an animistic period in the apprehension of reality, in which every object appears to him to be endowed with life, and in which he seeks to find again in every object his own organs and their activities. It will be recalled that this period is governed by the pleasure principle, and, during this period the pleasure is derived from bodily functioning. As Ferenci reminds us, the child's mind is at first exclusively concerned with his own body. This is in line with the view of Anzieu previously expressed. During this period the child is also experiencing many 'unpleasant' experiences as Ferenci would describe them. This is further referred to by Klein (1930) when she describes how the wholly undeveloped ego is faced with a task which at this stage is quite beyond it – the task of mastering the severest anxiety.

This anxiety leads to the use of primitive defence mechanisms. This is perhaps best explained in regard to the infant's first object relations. According to Segal (1981):

> It is the time of the hallucinatory wish-fulfilment, described by Freud, when the mind creates objects which are then felt to be available. According to Melanie Klein, it is also the time of the bad hallucinosis when, if the ideal conditions are not fulfilled, the bad object is equally hallucinated and felt as real. (p. 53)

This leads to the defence of splitting, where the object is seen as split into an ideally good and a wholly bad one. The aim of the ego is total union with the ideal object and total annihilation of the bad one, as well as the bad parts of the self. Omnipotent thinking is predominant and reality sense intermittent and precarious. The concept of absence hardly exists. Whenever the state of union with the ideal object is not fulfilled, what is experienced is not absence; the ego feels assailed by the counterpart of the good object – the bad object, or objects.

It is the anxiety arising in this early stage of mental development which also operates the mechanism of identification. The child passes through an animistic period in which every object appears to him to be endowed with life, and in which the child seeks to find again in every object his own organs and their activities. Klein (1923) was of the view that it may very well be this that makes possible the comparison between different organs and areas of the body, and that this comparison would subsequently be followed by the process of identification with other objects. From this she developed the view that we are probably justified in assuming that these objects and activities, not in themselves sources of pleasure, become so through identification, a sexual pleasure being displaced on to them.

A further leading defence mechanism in this phase is projective identification. Segal describes how, in projective identification, the subject in fantasy projects large parts of himself into the object, and the object becomes identified with the parts of the self that it is felt to contain. Similarly, internal objects are projected outside and identified with parts of the external world which come to represent them. Here the infant deals with discomfort and anxiety by projecting it into mother, who feels the discomfort on the infant's behalf. This is an important concept that will be referred to again later.

SYMBOLIC EQUATIONS

From here we can begin to understand how these first projections and identifications are the beginning of the process of symbol formation. We can see how the 'severest anxiety', as Klein refers to it, leads to the infant equating the organs in question with other things. Because of this equation, these other objects in turn become objects of anxiety, and so the child is constantly impelled to make other and new equations. This process forms the basis not only of the child's interest in new objects, but also of symbolism. Ferenci is of the view that earlier processes explain the origin of symbolism: that is, the impulse to represent infantile wishes as being fulfilled, by means of the child's own body. He points out that 'In all probability this is even the more primary kind of symbol creation' (1952, p. 275). Whichever view we take, not only does symbolism come to be the foundation of all fantasy and sublimation but, more than that, it is the basis of the subject's relation to the outside world and to reality in general.

It is important to remind ourselves, however, that these early symbols are not felt by the ego to be symbols or substitutes but to be the original object itself. It will be recalled that in the paranoid-schizoid position – or primary process – the differentiation between the self and the object is obscured. The object is identified with the parts of the self that it is felt to contain. Since a part of the ego is confused with the object, the symbol – which is a creation and a function of the ego – becomes, in turn, confused with the object which is symbolised. According to Segal:

> In the symbolic equation, the symbol-substitute is felt to be the original object. The substitute's own properties are not recognised or admitted. The symbolic equation is used to deny the absence of the ideal object or to control a persecuting one. It belongs to the earliest stages of development. (1981, p. 57)

In like manner Winnicott (1971) reminds us that at the earliest stage the symbol is at the same time both the hallucination and an objectively perceived part of external reality. He was therefore of the view that this way of stating the meaning of the transitional object made it necessary for us to use the word 'illusion' – the fact being, as referred to by Anzieu (1984), that an external object has no being for you or me except insofar as you or I hallucinate it. Winnicott felt that this gave us a meaning for the word 'omnipotence' which we really need, because when we talk about the omnipotence of early infancy we do not only mean omnipotence of thought but also an omnipotence which extends to certain objects and perhaps extends to cover the mother and some of the others in the immediate environment.

THE TRANSITIONAL OBJECT

The transitional object is a symbol of the union of the baby and the mother (or part of the mother). Winnicott tells us that this symbol can be located at the place in space and time where and when the mother is in transition from being (in the baby's mind) merged in with the infant and alternatively being experienced as an object to be perceived rather than conceived of. In other words, the transitional object forms the link between the two phases described at the beginning of this chapter.

Thus the 'transitional object' is very much as the term implies. In the first instant we can see that the infant's use of an object can be in one way or another joined up with body functioning, and indeed one cannot imagine that an object can have meaning for an infant unless it is so joined. What is more, here Winnicott (1971) is in almost direct agreement with the later views of Anzieu (1984), who considered that this is another way of stating that the ego is based on a body ego. As the child develops, so do the object relationships: the infant has a fist in the mouth, then a thumb, then there is an admixture of the thumb or fingers, and some object which is chosen by the infant for handling. Gradually there is a use of objects which are not part of the infant nor are they part of the mother.

Klein (1923) explains that when the step is taken from identification to symbol formation, this process affords an opportunity for libido to be displaced on to other objects, hence we arrive at the mechanism of sublimation. The progressive use of transitional objects as described above results in energy being displaced from the self on to other objects. This process initiates the infant's capacity for using symbols, and where growth is straightforward the transitional object is the first symbol. The piece of blanket (or whatever it is) is symbolical of some part-object, such as the breast. Nevertheless, the point of it is not its symbolic value so much as its actuality. Its not being the breast (or the mother), although real, is as important as the fact that it stands for the breast (or mother).

Winnicott (1971) makes the important point that the gradual use of objects extends to teddies, dolls and hard toys. Indeed, this is eventually extended so that in favourable conditions this object gradually gives place to an ever-widening range of objects, and to the whole cultural life. That is, into activities of play; of artistic creativity and appreciation; of religious feeling; of dreaming; of fetishism, lying and stealing; the origin and loss of affectionate feeling; drug addiction, and the talisman of obsessional rituals.

Thus we can draw a direct link from symbolism right through to the whole of cultural life. When we witness an infant's employment of a transitional object, the first 'not me' possession, we are witnessing both the child's first use of a symbol and the first experience of play. Cultural experiences are in direct continuity with play, the play of those who have not yet heard of games. Klein also explains how the child constantly advances from his original primitive symbols, games and activities, so that we find symbols at work in increasingly complicated inventions and activities, leaving the former ones behind. This brings her to the conclusion that symbolism is the foundation of all sublimation and of every talent. Accordingly, we see that identification is a stage preliminary not only to symbol formation but at the same time to the evolution of speech and sublimation.

The child's use of symbolism progresses through early object relations to games and other more advanced activities, to the point where it is regarded as the basis of those skills by which we relate to the world around us. This continues until we reach the stage where there is a recognition that words, which started to develop in object relations, are in fact symbols by means of which the world is comprehended.

DEVELOPMENT OF SPEECH

Just as there is a steady transition from 'bodily' objects to objects which are not part of the child or mother, so there is a gradual transition from gestures to speech as a means of representation. Ferenci (1952) explains that speech is originally imitation, certain series of sounds are brought into close associative connection with definitive objects and processes, and are gradually identified with these. Hence, as the infant starts to use organised sounds, there may appear a 'word' for the transitional object. Speech symbolism thus gets substituted for gesture symbolism. Having reached this stage, the child then thinks himself to be in possession of magic capacities and is in what Ferenci calls 'The period of magic thoughts and magic words' (p. 230).

The acquisition of the faculty of speech, of the understanding that certain noises are used as symbols for things, and of the gradual capacity for rational use of this faculty and understanding, is a decisive step in the formation of the ego. However, we are reminded by Fenichel (1946) that we still need to bear in mind that at this stage symbolic thinking is vague, as it is directed by the primary process. It is not only a method of distortion; it is also a part of the primal pre-logical thinking. However, from the development of words as symbols accrues the great progress. The imagination and representation of the series of sounds that we call words allow a far more specialised and economic conception and expression of the wishes. At the same time conscious thinking makes speech symbolism possible by becoming associated to thought processes that are in themselves unconscious, and lending them perceptual qualities.

With the development of words the infant is able to make much faster progress towards the development of the ego and to integration. The main characteristic of object relations when the depressive position has been reached, as explained by Segal (1981), is that the object is felt as a whole object. In connection with this there is a greater degree of awareness of differentiation and of the separateness of the ego and the object. This brings with it other problems: since the object is recognised as a whole, ambivalence is more fully experienced. The ego in this phase is struggling with its ambivalence. New anxieties are experienced; its relation to the object is characterised by guilt, fear of loss, or actual experience of loss or mourning, and a striving to re-create the object. At the same time, processes of introjection become more pronounced than those of projection, in keeping with the striving to retain the object inside as well as to repair, restore and re-create it.

TRUE SYMBOLS

Segal (1981) points out that the word 'symbol' comes from the Greek term for throwing together, bringing together, integrating. She claims that the process of symbol formation is a continuous process of bringing together and integrating the internal with the external, the subject with the object, and the earlier experiences with the later ones. According to Segal the ego in the depressive position has the important task of dealing not only with the depressive anxieties referred to above, but also with unresolved earlier conflicts. In the depressive position the individual has the capacity to symbolise, and in that way to lessen anxiety and resolve conflict.

By 'symbolise' I mean the use of the symbol proper, which is now available for sublimation and furthering the development of the ego. Here the symbol is felt to represent the object; its own characteristics are recognised, respected and used. According to Bion (1967) the capacity to form symbols is dependent on:

> The ability to grasp whole objects; the abandonment of the paranoid-schizoid position with its attendant splitting; and the bringing together of splits and the ushering in of the depressive position. Since verbal thought depends on the ability to integrate, it is not surprising to find that its emergence is intimately associated with the depressive position which, as Melanie Klein has pointed out, is a phase of active synthesis and integration. (p. 26)

True symbolism develops when depressive feelings predominate over the paranoid-schizoid ones; when separation from the object, ambivalence, guilt and loss can be experienced and tolerated. Here the symbol is used not to deny but to overcome loss. Anxieties which could not be dealt with earlier because of the extreme concreteness of the experience with the object and the object substitutes in symbolic equations, can gradually be dealt with by the more integrated ego by symbolisation. In that way they can be integrated.

When a substitute in the external world is used as a symbol it may be used more freely than the original object, since it is not fully identified with it. In the depressive position the symbol is distinguished from the original object and recognised as an object in itself. Its own properties are recognised, respected and used because no confusion with the original object blurs the characteristics of the new object used as a symbol. The symbols, created internally, can then be re-projected into the external world, endowing it with symbolic meaning. And as the symbol is acknowledged as a creation of the subject, unlike the symbolic equation, it can be freely used by the subject. In Segal's view, the formation of symbols in the depressive position therefore become available for sublimation.

The development of symbols as speech brings rapid progress. Symbol formation governs the capacity to communicate, since, of course, all communication is made by means of symbols. However, there is another important aspect to symbols: that is, the fact that they are needed not only to communicate with the external world, but also in internal communication. In regard to this internal communication Segal (1981) points out that the capacity to communicate with oneself by using symbols is the basis of verbal thinking. However, as she informs us, not all internal communication is verbal thinking; symbols already formed and functioning as symbols may revert to symbolic equations.

When this stage of development has been achieved, it is, of course, not irreversible. If the anxieties are too strong, a usually temporary regression to the paranoid-schizoid position can occur at any stage of the individual's development and projective identification may be resorted to as a defence against anxiety. Then symbols which have been developed and have been functioning as symbols in sublimation revert to concrete symbolic equations. This is mainly due to the fact that in massive projective identification, the ego again becomes confused with the object; the symbol becomes confused with the thing symbolised and therefore turns into an equation.

SPEECH SYMBOLS

It seems that apart from the vital knowledge that anxiety can result in regression to child-like behaviour, the other important aspect is the use of symbols as speech. Rycroft (1968b) points out that words are a special class of symbol, which, when operating as words, form part of the secondary process. They arise in exactly the same way as other symbols; that is, by displacement of cathexis from the imago of the object on to the imago of the word.

For Rycroft, words owe their special significance to three characteristics which enable them to be differentiated from other symbols. One of those characteristics is particularly significant, the fact that they are conventionalised symbols. The way in which they are acquired, that is the simplest instance, by the child repeatedly hearing their sound made in connection with what they signify which then leads to the development of a community of symbols: that is, to a tendency for each individual to use symbols which are common to him and to other members, both past and present, of his group.

Here we have another important point: 'the tendency for each individual to use symbols which are common to him and to the other members, both past and present, of his group'. This has a distinctly Wittgenstinian flavour – 'The limits of my language are the limits of my world' – save that to be more accurate this should perhaps be reversed to read, 'The limits of my world are the limits of my language.' This appears to be precisely what Kuhn (1962) was saying when he referred to paradigm changes. It also tends to signify 'limits' or more appropriately 'boundaries'.

Before speech there is no conception: there is, as Langer (1951) points out, only perception, and a readiness to act according to the enticements of the perceived world. It is by means of symbols that we form concepts. This is a remarkable advance because once we have a concept of a piece of reality, we can play with it, think about it and, most importantly, relate it to other pieces. As Storr (1972) points out, this interrelating of concepts is the principal way in which new scientific discoveries are made. The symbol, therefore, increases our grasp and mastery of reality.

As stated in Chapter 1, for an experience to come into awareness, it must be comprehensible in accordance with the categories in which conscious thought is organised. According to Fromm (1962), we can become aware of any occurrence, inside or outside of ourselves, only when it can be linked into the system of categories in which we perceive. A similar claim is made by Jaques (1970), who maintains that the process of verbalising percepts requires that they be organised in accord with man-made rules to form concepts. In effect what we do is to agree among ourselves that this percept and that, and any others like them, shall be included within a given concept which we identify and to which we allocate a word. The perceptions may be things, actions, or relationships.

One of the most significant benefits of the use of words as symbols is the fact that words can symbolise instinctive acts and objects and carry cathexis ultimately derived from them. Rycroft points out that it is this which makes psycho-analytical treatment possible. More importantly in the context of this book, it is this that makes it possible for the organisational consultant to analyse how the client responds to him, to analyse from the transference the enaction of the unconscious.

SUMMARY

In our development we all go through two different periods of infant development – the primary process, or paranoid-schizoid position, and the secondary process, or depressive position. At first sight, as adults, it might not appear relevant as to why we need to refer to such distant events. The fact is that these events have a direct bearing on our life as adults and affect the way we behave.

Freud referred to primary and secondary processes as two types of mental functioning. The former is characteristic of unconscious mental activity and the latter is characteristic of conscious thinking. The primary process is governed by the pleasure principle, which leads to avoidance of pain and unpleasure by hallucinating the satisfaction necessary. The secondary process is governed by the reality principle, which leads to the avoidance of pain and unpleasure by adaptive behaviour: that is, the capacity to discriminate between subjective images and external percepts.

Roughly analogous with the primary and secondary processes are the Kleinian concepts of the paranoid-schizoid position and the depressive position. In the former the individual deals with his innate destructive impulses by important defensive responses: that is, by splitting both his ego and his object representations into good and bad parts and by projecting his destructive impulses on to the bad object by whom he feels persecuted. In the depressive position the individual becomes aware of his ambivalence when he realises that both his love and hate are directed towards the same object. In this position, the individual is able to distinguish the complete object and is able to progress towards integration.

In the primary process the infant goes through periods of 'hallucinatory omnipotence' and omnipotence by the 'help of magical gestures'. During this process the child is subject to extreme anxieties which lead to the use of important primitive defence mechanisms whenever the holding environment is not felt to be good enough. These are: identification, splitting (where the object is split into ideally good and wholly bad), and projective identification. It is through these processes that symbolism begins to develop. However, we are not referring here to the development of true symbols but of concrete symbols or 'symbolic equations'. These early symbols are not felt to be symbols or substitutes but are felt to be the original object itself.

Such omnipotence therefore extends to cover the mother and some of the others in the immediate environment. Gradually the infant comes to perceive the mother and other objects as separate. The transitional objects, which progress from thumb to blanket to teddy bear, form the links between subjective and objective experience. This continues until we reach a stage where there is a word for the transitional object. Just as there is a steady transition from bodily objects to objects which are not part of the child or mother, so there is a gradual transition from gestures to speech as a means of representation.

With the acquisition of words, there is a rapid progress in infant development. The main characteristic of the depressive position is that the object is felt as a whole object. It is something separate and distinct from the subject. This brings new anxieties as the child's relations to the object are experienced as guilt, fear of loss, or actual mourning and a striving to re-create the object. At the same time the process of introjection is used to retain the object inside; to repair, re-create and restore it.

When depressive feelings predominate over the paranoid-schizoid ones, anxieties can be dealt with by the more integrated ego by the use of true symbols. In this position the symbol is distinguished from the original object and recognised as an object in itself. The development of symbols brings rapid progress, not least the capacity to communicate. That is, to communicate not only externally but also internally. Having successfully reached the depressive position the child will have progressed towards integration. Now there is a need for reality testing and ego support, for continuity, consistency and confirmation.

Where these matters become important to the adult and to organisational change is the fact that when this stage of development has been achieved, it is, of course, not irreversible. If the anxieties are too strong, a regression to the paranoid-schizoid position can occur at any stage of the individual's development and projective identification may be resorted to as a defence against anxiety. Then symbols which have been developed and have been functioning as symbols in sublimation revert to concrete symbolic equations. This is mainly due to the fact that in massive projective identification, the ego again becomes confused with the object; the symbol becomes confused with the thing symbolised and therefore turns into an equation.

Another important aspect is the use of speech as symbols; here the symbols are conventionalised symbols. The way in which they are acquired leads to the development of a community of symbols, that is, to a tendency for each individual to use symbols which are common to him and to other members of the group, both past and present. The means of categorising the order that we impose on our world is by the use of words as symbols.

This is an important area as it is the means of confronting or testing the boundaries in order that a new experience of the unknown or avoided can take place. In doing so, we also create boundaries by the language used and by the designation of identity relationships, status relationships and the ways in which they are mutually described. In looking at words it is important to remember that they are symbols, that they represent individual or group views, and are not themselves objects. They are not the only symbols that we use; nevertheless, they are the most frequently used and therefore the most important. It seems right, then, that we should look at this matter next.

7

LANGUAGE AND WORDS
AS SYMBOLS

It may be useful to recall, as was explained by Ferenci (1952), that words are originally imitation and, as Rycroft (1968b) further explained, that they are conventionalised symbols. They are acquired by the child repeatedly hearing their sound made in connection with what they signify which then leads to the development of 'a community of symbols': that is, a tendency for each individual to use symbols which are common to him and to other members of his group.

This is very much in accordance with the views of Bion in regard to the interdependence of the individual and the group. The usual way for an individual constantly to affirm his identity with those around him is through the use of words and language as symbols. A 'community of symbols' has a highly distinctive nature in regard to particular groups. This point was made by Leach (1976), who explained that the grammatical rules which govern speech utterances are such that anyone with a fluent command of a language can generate spontaneously entirely new sentences with the confident expectation that he will be understood by his audience.

This is to be distinguished from non-verbal communications which will only be understood if they are highly familiar. Furthermore, private symbols, such as language symbols not familiar to the individual concerned, will fail to convey any information until they have been learned. It will be recalled here that language is society specific, that is, predetermined by the social group within which the individual is situated. In order to have an understanding of human beings there must be a familiarity with the particular form of life. The language is a symbolic representation of the world as the members of that society have learned to experience it at that time.

CLASSIFYING AND CONCEPTUALISING REALITY

The world we respond to, the world towards which our behaviour is directed, is the world as we symbolise it, or represent it to ourselves. Changes in the actual world must be followed by changes in our representation of it if they are to affect our expectations and, hence, our subsequent behaviour. As Britton pointed out, 'I look at the world in the light of what I have learned to expect from my past experience of the world' (1970, p. 15). In Chapter 5 it was noted that we put objects which to us are similar into the same category, even though we can perceive differences among them. Britton explains that without such patterns the world appears to be such an undifferentiated homogeneity that man is unable to make any sense out of it. Even a poor fit is more helpful to him than nothing at all.

The great benefit, or – as we have referred to it – progress, lies in the fact that symbolic expression can yield the possibility of prospect and retrospect. What is fixed in consciousness is there to go back to: a prediction, an expectation, is formulated by reference back. It is a continuing sense of the world that is continually brought up to date. We habitually use talk to go back over events and interpret them, to make sense of them in a way that we were unable to while they were taking place. However, we may opt out of the handling of reality for a time and improvise to our own satisfaction upon our represented world. That is, we may operate directly upon the representation itself.

By the use of language and words as symbols we impose a scheme for classifying and conceptualising our reality. This scheme of things has been referred to by several authors who have commented on the 'taken for granted' nature of language. For example, Whyte and Braun (1968) claim that the most important things about a people are the things they take for granted. One's own language and culture fall into the category of things taken for granted. Schein (1987b) has used the term 'taken for granted assumptions' in describing culture, while Langer (1951) tells us that they fit so neatly into the frame of our ultimate world picture that we can think with them and do not have to think about them.

This is graphically illustrated by Koestler (1964), who considers that there is less difference between the routines of thinking and bicycle riding than our self-esteem would make us believe. Both are governed by implicit codes of which we are only dimly aware, and which we are unable to specify. A further example might be a soldier who carries out his drill whilst fighting a battle. Or indeed, a consultant who deals with his own anxieties whilst dealing with those of the client. Without these indispensable codes we would fall off the bicycle, or whatever, and thought would lose its coherence.

However, the fact that we, who are familiar with our symbols, do not have to think about them when we think with them should not hide the fact that all these symbols have to be supported by a vast intellectual structure. This structure is composed of the stock of knowledge that results in our perceived reality. Because the symbolic representation is as the members of a particular society have learned to experience it, we can appreciate that words are used differently in different societies. In this way language may not be a means of communication but rather a barrier to such communication.

DIFFERENT USES OF WORDS

Whyte and Braun (1968) describe the different use of words in the US and Peru. In the former, words are looked upon as instrumental, as a means of getting things done. In this society, actions speak louder than words. In Peru, however, words are not instrumental nor can they be taken lightly. Words carry more weight and are fraught with peril. This is a good example of words and language as symbols. From my casual knowledge of both societies I feel that I could also say with some certainty that the various non-verbal symbols, such as gestures, are also totally different. I might also add here Winston Churchill's famous quotation regarding Britain and America, 'two nations divided by a common language'.

We normally think of a speech community as one whose members speak closely related varieties of the same language. This may be the norm, but the distinctiveness of the language may not be confined to one language. According to Gumperz (1969), there is ample reason to suppose that whenever two or more languages are regularly employed within the same social system, they differ significantly from the same languages that are spoken in separate social systems. Thus the particular society applies its own distinctiveness to the language, a distinctiveness that reflects the society that they have learned to experience – their perceived reality.

When we refer to different groups speaking different languages it is not readily obvious that the words and language are different. There would be no problem accepting this if we were speaking in two very different languages, such as German and French. The difficulty arises in accepting that different versions of any particular language are in fact very different. The fact is, we would be better advised to treat them as being just as different as German and French. As Wittgenstein (1953) stated, 'If a lion could talk, we could not understand him' (p. 223), on the basis that, in the end, understanding human beings depends on a familiarity with a particular society.

If speech and words are but symbols it is not surprising that one homogeneous group uses a different language or languages from another homogeneous group. Reflection of my early experience in the police service provides a good example of this. When I joined I was confronted with a private language of reliefs, beats, area cars, serials, CRO, CO and many others. All this was totally mystifying and left me confused and, no doubt, not a little anxious. I was not part of this organisation. I could not share with them, and could not communicate with them. I was at the boundary and it was uncomfortable. I then joined the CID and was confronted with another private language, of blaggers (robbers), peters (safes), and plenty more. Again, I was not part of it; I could not communicate with them. I was at the boundary and again it was not very comfortable.

From this we can conclude that if two groups show marked differences at certain points, then we can also expect to have difficulty in finding exact translations at these points. At first sight this would seem to have grave consequences for organisations where there is disagreement between different groups of workers. However, since our reality is not static but constantly changing, we can expect to find changes in the meanings of words and phrases and changes in the style of discourse. It therefore follows that it is possible for both parties to change their perception of reality and, in doing so, to adopt a shared language.

Though there is a clear need to categorise and to create boundaries in order to make sense of our reality, these are a matter for constant negotiation. The explanation by Winnicott of the 'me' and the 'not-me' infers an experience of 'discovering' a boundary, the infant creating the mother and vice versa. This implies that there is a period of 'negotiation' before the boundaries are drawn. This leads us to look at both sides of the boundary, because, as is implied by the word, negotiation is a two-way event. For example, negotiation from inside can be achieved by the impact of an individual in a group on the boundary of the whole group. We also need to look at the nature of influence in the negotiation: for example, reinforcement of the boundary from outside can be negative or positive.

This leads us to the consideration that every interpersonal relationship is a political relationship. It is useful, therefore, to look at the nature of the negotiations. In this regard Szmidla and Khaleelee (1975) helpfully explain that negotiations or transactions can occur across four different boundaries. That is, between: Me (my inline) and you as I see you (your outline); You (your inline) and me as seen by you (my outline); Me (my inline) and me as seen by you (my outline); and, You (your inline) and you as seen by me (your outline).

Quite apart from the influence of negotiation or transaction, there is also the issue of the influence of the environment on our perceived reality and its symbolic representation in words and language. Bettelheim (1960) writes of the influence of the environment in a most powerful manner when he states, 'I could no longer doubt that environment can and does account for important aspects of man's behaviour and personality' (p. 14). Within a very short time his experience in the concentration camps taught him that he had gone much too far in believing that only changes in man could create changes in society. He had to accept that the environment could, as it were, turn personality upside down, and not just in the small child, but in the mature adult as well.

CONDENSED SYMBOLS

In Chapter 5 it was explained that our perception of reality is a very selective process. We choose to ignore any perceptual differences and put objects which to us are similar into the same category, even though we perceive differences in them. We learn by assimilating experiences and grouping them into ordered schemata, into stable patterns of unity in variety. They enable us to cope with events and situations by applying the rules of the game appropriate to them. The matrices which pattern our perceptions, thoughts and activities are condensations of learning into habit.

Condensation of habit, assimilation and grouping into stable patterns recognisable to the individual and other members of his group, leads to the development of theories, myths and ideologies. Lawrence and Miller (1976) describe the reassuring nature of such condensed symbols which they point out are insensitive to change. When they are built into the structures of relationships, they provide the participating individuals with mechanisms of defence against anxiety.

According to Kaes (1971) myths and ideologies are compromise formations to be found only in group or social situations. This process is explained by Anzieu (1984) who observes that the primary psychic processes, which, in the group, become objects of wishes shared by its members, are displacement, condensation, symbolisation, and reversal into the opposite, in the same way as in dreams. Furthermore, again as in dreams, secondary elaboration rearranges the results of the primary processes; in groups this takes the form of the production of myth-like narratives or intellectual constructions of an ideological type in which forbidden wishes are displaced.

A further explanation is provided by Erikson (1968) who sees it as a product of identification and integration when he describes how the synthesising function of the ego constantly works on subsuming in fewer and fewer images and personified 'gestalten', the fragments and loose ends of all infantile identifications. In doing so it not only uses existing historical prototypes but also employs mechanisms of condensation and pictorial representation which characterise the products of collective imagery. Here we have the myths and ideologies referred to above. Indeed, I am reminded of the tidying up operation referred to by Anzieu (1989) whereby the group stopped up gaps and shut windows in a physical attempt to draw boundaries. Whereas here, by mechanisms of condensation, the loose ends are tidied up so that we are left with images of good and bad. It is between good and bad that the boundaries are drawn.

According to Erikson (1968), the ego, in the course of its synthesising efforts, attempts to subsume the most powerful ideal and evil prototypes (the final contestants, as it were) and with them the whole existing imagery of superior and inferior, good and bad, masculine and feminine, free and slave, potent and impotent, beautiful and ugly, black and white, tall and small, in one simple alternative in order to make one battle and one strategy out of a bewildering number of skirmishes. He therefore concludes that the unconscious associations of ethnic prototypes of good and evil with moral and sexual ones are a necessary part of any group formation. In this way, men who share the concerns of an ethnic group, who are contemporaries in an historical era, or who compete and co-operate in economic pursuits are also guided by common images of good and evil. Infinitely varied, these images reflect the elusive nature of societal differences and of historical change.

INHIBITIONS TO CHANGE

The concept of condensed symbols is valuable in terms of providing us with clues with regard to the representation of culture. However, there are problems associated with condensation. One of these problems is that condensation, habit, or whatever we choose to call it, can be inhibiting to change. Thus the question for Laing (1967) is whether we remain the masters of the rules by which we want to make things more manageable or whether the rules master the ruler. Maslow (1970) points out the paradoxical nature of condensed symbols when he describes how habits are simultaneously necessary and dangerous, useful and harmful. They are problem solutions, and yet in the long run they are the antonyms of fresh, uncategorised thinking, that is to say, of solutions to new problems. To the extent that language forces experiences into categories, it is a screen between reality and the human being.

Koestler agrees that habits have varying degrees of flexibility which, if often repeated under unchanging conditions, in a monotonous environment, tend to become rigid and automatised. Yet a further view is that of Jaques (1970) who makes the point that knowledge is man-made and therefore we can be sure of it as we have made the rules and set the limits. It is these rules and limits which allow us to re-duplicate it with such precision. However, the constant danger is that the word to some extent becomes the thing, and we dull and inhibit to the same extent our capacity to perceive.

Thus we can see how an inhibiting situation arises if we reify the myth, habit or ideology, or if we become so comfortable with them that we do not wish to conceive of change. This leads to another problem which is related to the activity just described. We resent having our cherished illusions shattered, that is, illusions in regard to myths and ideologies which are defences against chaos and disintegration. Should these (ideological) boundaries be disturbed it may result in the group regressing in the manner previously described. It is only when the group is acting in the secondary process, in the reality principle, that words are used normally, that is, with their symbolic significance. Where the group regresses into primary process behaviour, words, by contrast, are used by the group as a mode of action – that is, as concrete symbols – and are thereby deprived of the flexibility of thought that progression requires.

This was the experience of Bion (1961), who, in regard to 'basic assumption activity', explained how he had been forced to the conclusion that verbal exchange was a function of the work group. Furthermore, the more that the group corresponded with the basic assumption group, the less it made any rational use of verbal communication. Words served as a vehicle for the communication of sound. For Bion the work group understands that particular use of symbols which is involved in communication; the basic assumption group does not. He also observes that the language of the basic assumption group is primitive and, in the group state that he is describing, appears to be relevant to Klein's breakdown of a capacity for symbol formation.

In terms of managing change it should become evident that a knowledge of symbolism is relevant to any consultant. Regression to the primitive behaviour referred to by Bion means a reversion to the paranoid-schizoid position and to infantile defences of splitting and projective identification – a world opposed to the world of progression that we should be seeking. It literally prevents the group from conducting meaningful communication, as the members revert to near primary processes of the sort used in infancy. Furthermore, it also removes the ability of the group and the individuals concerned to accept their own authority.

SUMMARY

The usual way for an individual to confirm his identity with those around him is through the use of language and words as symbols. Non-verbal communications will only be understood if they are highly familiar. Private symbols, such as language symbols not familiar to the individual concerned, will fail to convey information until they have been learned. Language, which is society specific, may be understood by those who are familiar with that particular way of life.

A language imposes its own scheme of classifications and concepts for describing the world. Language is part of our taken for granted assumptions. Each boundaried group either has a different language or has a different version of a language. The concept of private languages in homogeneous groups is important in displaying the diversity of groups. Language, being the most widely used symbolic system, is thus vital to our understanding of culture. The synthesising function of the ego constantly works on subsuming in fewer and fewer images. In doing so it employs mechanisms of condensation and pictorial representation which characterise the products of collective imagery.

Condensed symbols are valuable in terms of providing us with clues with regard to the representation of culture. However, condensation or habit can be inhibiting to change. To the extent that language forces experience into categories, it is a screen between reality and the individual. Where these habits or myths become so ingrained that we do not wish to change, we resent having our cherished illusions shattered and resist change. Should this be the case, there is a likelihood that the group will regress to primary process-type behaviour. This may well be identified by Bion's 'basic assumption activity', in which case there will be no progression and the language will be in the nature of concrete symbols. Members will be prevented from conducting meaningful communication.

We can draw a direct line from the development of symbols right through to the whole of cultural life. The capacity to communicate with oneself by using symbols is the basis of verbal thinking. With the development of speech, conceptualisation becomes possible, the symbol thus increases our grasp and mastery of reality. However, as the language is a representation of the world as we have learned to experience it at that time, what happens when we want to change something? What happens when the world as we know it changes? In the next chapter I shall be looking at such matters with regard to learning.

8

THE PROCESS OF LEARNING

To obtain an understanding of culture we need to understand how it develops and how it is perpetuated. Here I want to build on the previous chapters by taking a specific look at learning. I shall do this by looking at three particular aspects: namely, the process of learning, the levels of learning, and possible blocks to learning. I shall commence with a personal reflection on some of the more difficult moments that I experienced when I was first studying psycho-analytic material. In doing so I shall describe in my own words what that learning process meant to me. Having done so, I shall then use this reflection as a basis for a theoretical understanding.

A PERSONAL REFLECTION

First the personal reflection of the process, which I believe was something like that described below:

1. On the first read, I sometimes did not understand what I was reading. It was almost as though I was reading a foreign language.
2. On the subsequent read I understood the words and tried to link them. In this respect I could understand them in the context in which they were written.
3. At the next reading I struggled to make sense of the meaning of what was written. I could read the language but did not understand the meaning of it.
4. I then wanted to use it but could not until I had fully mastered the reading: this was usually after verbalising my understanding. By discussion and assimilation the text gradually made sense.

5. It was only at the stage of understanding the material fully that I was able to conceptualise and to use elements to create new meaning.

Let me start with the position of not understanding what I was reading. Bateson (1979) explains that what is subliminal will not be grist for our mill. Knowledge at any given moment will be a function of the thresholds of our available means of perception. It follows therefore that what we can perceive is always limited by threshold. It also follows that a response is always a response of a living organism, always something constructed in part according to determinants that are intrinsic to its own structure. A stimulation is something intrinsically related to the structure, or, as Piaget (1951) points out, something that can be 'assimilated' by the structure.

Taking Piaget's view of a response being determined by the organism's own structure, it is clear that my structure, my world of reality, my boundaries, the threshold of my knowledge at that given moment, was such as to limit my perception of the material that I was studying. From this we can also conclude, as does Furth (1981) in interpreting Piaget, that a reaction of an organism is therefore not merely a response to an outside stimulation, but is always and at all levels also the response of the underlying structure within the organism. In order to explain a response, one must investigate the underlying structure that makes that response possible and adaptively appropriate.

In this respect, Piaget holds that behaviour at all levels demonstrates aspects of structuring, and he identifies structuring with knowing. This is also the view of Bettelheim (1967), who observes that 'human experience is built up out of our sense of space, time, and causality, Kant's a priori categories of mind' (p. 51). He explains that it is our ability to extract from contiguity in time and space a sense of causality that takes us into the human adventure. What makes us what we are is not simply that we recognise causal relations, but what follows from it: the conviction that a sequence of events can be changed through our influence.

Yet a further view is that of Bion, who described the process through which a new idea is born as the mating of a preconception with appropriate sense data (a realisation) to produce conception. Palmer (1972) explains that the word preconception here has no negative overtones; merely that it is impossible to enter any experience without preconceptions, and that if it were possible it would, by the same token, be impossible to make sense of the experience. Again referring back to my first point, it seems clear that my preconceptions were such that at that time I could not mate them with the sense data that I was reading. Thus I could not produce a conception at that time.

Here I want to add to the views expressed earlier that the infant gradually develops a concept of the self as an entity that has continuity and direction. The reality principle and secondary processes become more dominant. Or as Bettelheim (1967) would have it, to begin to function as human beings, one must have learned how to arrange one's life in terms of space, time and causality. He explains that 'These categories of mind are not just metaphysical; there is a definite histori-cal-genetic sequence in which they appear' (p. 52). Orientation in space and time precedes a sense of causality but there is some doubt as to which of the two comes first. Most certainly the infant's feeding is a crucial time experience because it brings some order into life by creat-ing temporal boundaries at a very early age. However, if we take a Gestalt view we come to the conclusion that spatial boundaries take precedence by an ordering in space on the basis of visual, auditory and kinesthetic experiences.

To return to Piaget, these boundaries, or, as he calls them, 'regu-lations', serve to keep the organism in a 'state of dynamic equilibra-tion'. That is not the static equilibrium of an unchanging, rigid balance which needs an outside pull to make it move. Rather, the living equilibrium of a biological organisation, as described by Piaget, is ever in a state of flux, if not growing, at least constantly interacting with new elements of the environment, always exercising previously acquired structures. This is borne out by the fact that the boundaries that I had formed, which were initially stopping me from understanding and conceptualising the data, were not of a rigid nature. If this were not so I should not have been able eventually to reach a stage where I could conceive the information presented.

From here we can conclude that learning is not solely a matter for me, but equally it is not a matter for the subject matter to be learned. This notion corresponds with the thesis that knowledge is neither solely in the subject, nor in a supposedly independent object, but is constructed by the subject as an indissociable subject-object relation. According to Furth (1981), knowledge is, in Piaget's theory, never a stage, whether subjective, representative or objective. It is an activity. It can be viewed as a structuring of the environment accord-ing to underlying subjective structures or as a structuring of the subject in living interaction with the environment.

From the foregoing we can conclude that learning does not appear now to be a process during which the subject's activity is limited to receiving or reacting automatically to what is received;

rather, learning seems to be a complex construction in which what is received from the object and what is contributed by the subject are indivisibly linked. This is very similar to the interdependence of the group and individual described by Bion. In regard to my learning experience, it seems clear that the process described shows how, in the subsequent stages, my contribution and the construction of the object of my study were indivisibly linked to form a new concept.

That is not to say that this produced a new static concept: on the contrary, this was a new concept which would now permit further concepts to be developed. This is in common with Piaget's view that everything that we commonly connect with objective, stable reality, such as perception, identity, spatial co-ordination, objective time, and causality, are constructions and activities, that is, living operations. In his view the more differentiated and the more diverse the objective contribution of operational intelligence is, the more differentiated and the more objective the resulting knowledge becomes.

At this stage it will be helpful to explain two of Piaget's most important terms, that is, 'accommodation' and 'assimilation'. 'Accommodation' operates in an outward direction, and it defines the object of knowledge, while 'assimilation' operates in an inward direction, and it defines the subject of knowledge. Here we can see that before I could assimilate the knowledge that I sought to learn, I had to accommodate it. Put another way, knowledge is therefore a relational concept; it relates the subject to the object.

The relative use of these terms is helpfully explained by Marris (1974), who describes how normal events can be assimilated, roughly at least, by the present structure, which then accommodates to features of the event for which its previous experience had not prepared it. However, when we are faced with critical events these cannot be assimilated at all until the structure accommodates. It will be appreciated that this is much more difficult, because the less assimilable events are, the harder it is to see what kind of accommodation will be successful. I would suggest that this was the situation that I was in. The difficulty is that in trying to accommodate, the ability of the structure to grasp events which were formerly assimilable may be undermined. While I would hasten to add that this was not my experience, the whole structure may then be threatened by radical confusion.

Perception has to do with the appearance of the external world in its momentary, yet ever-changing characteristics. It thus constitutes a particularly clear form of accommodative behaviour, accommodation being the outward-directed activity of intelligence adaptation that applies general schemes to the particular here and now situation.

Assimilative activity transforms a given input into objects that correspond to the person's structure of knowing. Accommodative activity
transforms the organism according to the particular characteristics of
the input.

Although opposed in direction, assimilation and accommodation
by no means function against each other. On the contrary, it is
characteristic of biological, and particularly of human, knowledge that
they go together in depth and extent. In simple language the better
you understand a particular topic, the better you attend to its particular characteristics. Furthermore, accommodation by itself does not
mean the permanent change of a scheme in response to external
pressure, rather, the near opposite: the episodic adjustment of the
same scheme to the constantly changing contents to which it is
applied. Obviously both assimilation and accommodation can and do
become obligatory occasions of developmental changes of schemes.

Thus we can see that the process of learning is an activity that is
governed by the indivisible relationship of the subject and object. Our
learning is affected not only by the threshold of our perception, but
also by the nature of the object. Should our preconceptions be too few
or too rigid, or should the nature of the object be new to our existing
reality, then the learning experience is likely to be difficult.

LEVELS OF LEARNING

The foregoing, particularly the references to Piaget's theory, provides
us with a sound basis for understanding the process of learning. I
want now to extend that understanding by looking at what is being
learned. In doing so I shall rely greatly on 'Bateson's Levels of
Learning'. As Palmer has explained, one of Bateson's interests is in
our apperceptive habits, how we acquire them, and how we modify
them. Palmer explains that by the term apperceive we mean 'to unite
and assimilate a perception to ideas already possessed, and so comprehend and interpret' (1979, p. 169). From this definition it will be
seen that this terminology is very much in line with the indissociable
subject-object relation described earlier. I shall also relate Bateson's
views to my personal experience as appropriate.

Palmer points out that the value of Bateson's theory of learning is
that he brings together in a single scheme the processes of learning
which give rise to the complexities of our apperceptive habits, and
the more simple learning processes which have been described by
experimental psychologists. If now we accept the notion that all

learning (other than zero learning) is in some degree stochastic – that is, contains components of 'trial and error' – it follows that an ordering of the processes of learning can be built upon an hierarchic classification of the types of data which are to be apperceived in the various learning processes.

The first of Bateson's logical categories of learning is 'Zero Learning'. At this level the person simply absorbs more facts, more simple information. There is no progress and no change. Zero Learning is shown in habituation. There is no new habituation, only the pre-existing known categories of meaning. Information in Zero Learning expands only arithmetically. This is most certainly not the type of data that I was seeking to learn. At this level of learning it is almost a matter of assimilation only.

The second category he calls 'Learning One'. At this level this is learning when one has progressively more clues to fit facts into, and hence one's learning expands geometrically. This is learning of habituation, that is, one is aware of one's habituation, or as Palmer explains, the individual finds a new response or pattern of responses to a given situation: 'The process is one of correcting errors of choice within a set of alternatives' (1979, p. 174). One acquires new connections between 'stimulus' and 'response' but always in familiar patterns of connection. There are no new patterns of connection. Palmer tells us that rote learning is of this sort. May (1977) informs us that most of what we call learning in psychology is also of this variety. The important thing here is that one is aware of the context markers, but the context itself does not change.

The third level, 'Learning Two', is learning 'propositions about contexts'. At this level the context itself changes. The premises on the basis of which one learns now shift. Contexts which are new to the learner may induce such learning. One 'learns to learn' in a new way. An example given by Palmer is transference in psycho-analysis, when the context (the background, the screen against which one is learning) and all of the facts one has learned take on a new meaning. This is the changing of the 'context' through which one sees the facts in a new light. People can avoid this learning – that is, they can cling to the old 'context' – by hallucination or repression.

This was my experience with regard to the data that I was seeking to learn. It was a new experience to me and one which totally changed my context. As explained by Bateson in the original text, 'Learning Two is a change in the process of Learning One, for example, a corrective change in the set of alternatives from which choice is made' (1973, p. 264). Using Kuhn's terminology, this type of learning is a true 'paradigmatic revolution'. The objects do not fit into the subject's known categories or classifications and therefore this type of learning requires the subject to revise his known boundaries before he is able to assimilate the material. My struggle to make sense of this data meant that I had to develop a new context, to advance to a new level of learning. However, it is of significance that when learned, I could reasonably expect the context to remain 'the same' when I encountered the material again. This also raises the important issue of loss of known and loved objects. This will be referred to in greater depth in the next chapter but suffice to say at this stage, that this is why people may avoid learning at this level and cling to the old context.

The fourth level, 'Learning Three', occurs in such situations as religious conversion or in Zen experience. According to May, when there is a contradiction of 'contexts', Learning Three may occur and be the discovery that all that pain and joy of fitting one's self to the perceived world was premised upon personal perceptions of the world – a system of 'glosses'. Or perhaps some other discovery about 'glosses' (1977, p. 87). At this level the context as a matter of fact may be somewhat fluid. Learning Three may involve a oneness with nature, or an identification with what one is learning. There is an absorption in life in a new and different way. This seems to require a kind of eruption of the unconscious, that is, some kind of conversion.

Bateson also included a fifth level which is of little use for our purposes but nevertheless deserves mention. It is best described by May when he explains that 'there is a fifth level, Learning Four, which Gregory Bateson says human beings perhaps never attain. I then asked him why he put it in. He assured me it was to keep the learning categories open ended, and to indicate that his learning theory takes in not just human beings but the whole of nature' (1977, p. 87).

The open-ended nature of the categories is an important aspect of Bateson's theory. From the application of my own experience, it seems clear that different processes of learning are necessary in regard to the type of learning involved. However, once the learning has taken place the process of learning may revert to a lower level. This is precisely what Kuhn indicated when he explained how following a paradigmatic revolution there is a period of 'normal science' when puzzles may be solved using the new paradigm. Having reached the last stage referred to in my reflection, I am able to understand and use the concepts of my new paradigm. In doing so I am now able to operate at the level of Learning One.

In regard to the object of knowledge which the subject will 'accommodate', to use Piaget's terminology, this will also vary and may usefully be distinguished. The distinctions (referred to by Miller, 1976), made by William James between 'knowing about' and 'knowledge of acquaintance' are particularly relevant. The former type of knowledge we could refer to as cognitive knowledge; this can be communicated through words and symbols which may be understood in the same way. In all probability, learning this type of knowledge will not cause great anxiety, though should it be inconsistent with the subject's current perception, it could be anxiety provoking. As to the latter, this presents a totally different problem. Knowledge of human behaviour cannot be communicated as if it were an extraneous, objective entity: it cannot be learned by reference to a textbook.

Knowledge of acquaintance is an important concept: it is a prerequisite to knowing more about the roles and relationships that we are involved in. According to Miller (1976), learning by experience – acquiring knowledge of acquaintance – starts with oneself. As a prerequisite of knowing more about the roles and relationships in which I am involved, and about managing myself in them, I have to learn more about me. This is not easy, as it affects the personality boundaries and can therefore be threatening. The responsibility and authority for forming his own views rest with the individual. He is learning when he catches a glimpse of the way in which a unique patterning of his own internal world is affecting his perception of phenomena.

A further view of the nature of the object of knowledge is that of Jaques (1970), who points out that real life problems are open-ended in the sense of not having correct answers – that is, answers that may be shown by subsequent experience to have been better or worse. Here lies the difficulty, because open-ended problems are inevitably accompanied by worry and uncertainty, and never end with a reassuring sense of completeness. As Rice (1963) has observed, this being a process of 'internalisation', of incorporating felt experience into the inner world of fantasy and reason, the individual will resist learning if the process makes him anxious or frightened or if the rewards are insufficient.

BLOCKS TO LEARNING

This leads me to the third aspect of learning that I wish to cover in this chapter: the blocks to learning. Jaques makes the observation that because knowledge is man-made there is a constant danger that the word to some extent becomes the thing, and that this dulls and inhibits to the same extent our capacity to perceive. He describes how the acquisition of knowledge brings with it a sense of closure, as described by the Gestalt psychologists, and claims that it is this sense or sureness, of completeness, of reproducibility, that gives the psychological experience of the concept being the thing itself – a fact of experience as against a psychological fact. This sureness can block creative perception and inhibit flexibility in thought.

This was also the point made by Blay-Neto who observed that knowledge can be utilised as a property and that once acquired, it confers on its owner the same sensation that one feels when obtaining the advantages of retirement. 'That means, no more work to be done, no more thinking, and no more progress' (1985, p. 254). Much depends therefore on the preconceptions with which we work. They constitute the spectacles through which we view the world. If our preconceptions are too few or too rigid, then learning will be blocked.

It seems, then, that in situations concerning human behaviour there will always be a temptation to take what might be termed the easy way out. Freud suggested many years ago that it is not necessarily to be assumed that the reality principle will inevitably dominate in human affairs. At best there will always be some conflict between the demands of reality-testing and the demands of those more primitive qualities within us that seek for magical solutions in accord with what Freud termed the pleasure principle. A particular expression of these magical impulses is the process of reification. To know the word is to possess control over outer concrete reality. To control the word is to control the thing.

This may be so, but we should not forget the purpose of forming boundaries as defences against anxiety. It is also important to recall that those boundaries were created to enable us to distinguish inside from outside and that any disturbance of the boundaries may be seen as chaos and result in disintegration. This point is made by Maslow (1943), who claims that any thwarting or possibility of thwarting of these basic human goals, or danger to the defences which protect them or to the conditions upon which they rest, is considered to be a psychological threat. With a few exceptions, all psychopathology may be partially traced to such threats. In Maslow's view, a basically thwarted man may be defined as a 'sick' man. This is a very powerful statement and one which is very relevant to our discussion of culture and change. He explains that in children it may be particularly obvious and be represented by vomiting for example.

However, when adults feel their safety to be threatened, we may not be able to see this on the surface.

Anxiety has always been a response to perceived danger. The threat to the boundaries, that of disintegration, is danger. Seen in this light it may be easier to understand why there may be blocks to learning. A child confronted with a difficult situation may recourse to a temper tantrum. On the other hand, by acquiring certain skills, a person can retain boundaries even in difficult situations. As we have seen, the concept of boundaries touches on learning theory in general. The real problem arises when we feel our boundaries threatened but have little or no control over the activities posing the threat. Bettelheim also makes this point when he states, 'It is when we feel we cannot influence the most important things that happen to us, when they seem to follow the dictates of some inexorable power, that we give up trying to learn how to act on, or change them' (1967, p. 51).

On the other hand, knowledge can be used as a stimulus to approach the 'not knowing', allowing us to put up with ignorance as a basic condition for achieving mental development. The word 'learning' undoubtedly denotes change of some kind. To not learn means to stay in a state of sameness. If sameness is preserved, time must stop in its tracks. Thus time is the destroyer of sameness; things do not remain the same. Provided that we allow sufficient time for the boundaries to be realigned, knowledge will permit further development. Time also implies hope. If things can be different, they may also be better. However, by the use of phantasy we may attempt to stop time in its tracks. Without time there is no hope, but also no disappointment nor the fear that things might even get worse.

We can conclude that learning is a complicated and at times difficult task. The pleasure principle may dominate over the reality principle especially when the individual or group is presented with a difficult task. In this respect, we can recall Bion's basic assumption activities as an example of groups regressing from the reality principle. In such a case there will be a block to learning as opposed to progression and learning should that be desirable.

SUMMARY

What we perceive is limited by the threshold of our available means of perception. In other words, something only has meaning in relation to our current knowledge. Thus, as Piaget theorises, the response of

the individual (or group) is determined by the organism's own structure. This may also be linked to Bion's theory of a preconception
mating with sense data to produce a conception.

The individual forms boundaries to manage the relations between
inside and outside or between reality and phantasy, or, as Piaget
says, to maintain a 'state of dynamic equilibrium'. Such boundaries
are not static but are in a state of flux, constantly interacting with
new elements of the environment. Knowledge is therefore to be considered as an activity rather than a state. The subject and object are
indivisibly linked.

The process of 'accommodation' defines the object of knowledge,
and the process of 'assimilation' defines the subject of knowledge.
Perception is a form of accommodation. Assimilation activity transforms a given input into objects that correspond to the previous
current knowledge. Accommodation activity transforms the organism
according to the particular characteristics of the input. Thus we can
see that the process of learning is an activity that is governed by
the indivisible relationship of the subject and object. Not only is our
learning affected by the threshold of our perception but also by the
nature of the object. Should our preconceptions be too few or too
rigid, or should the nature of the object be new to our existing
reality, then the learning experience is likely to be difficult.

Bateson's 'Logical Categories of Learning' help us to make sense
of the complexities of our apperceptive habits. His theory that all
learning, other than Zero Learning, is in some degree stochastic
provides that processes of learning can be built upon a hierarchic
classification of the types of data which are to be apperceived in the
various learning processes. Linking Bateson's categories to Kuhn's
theory of paradigms sheds light and understanding on both theories.
It also shows how difficult the process of learning can be at the
'higher' levels. Furthermore, by demonstrating the open-ended nature
of learning we can better understand that context and paradigm also
act as bases of learning.

Learning is affected not only by the complexity of the data but
also by the type of learning. A distinction is drawn between 'knowing
about' – that is, cognitive knowledge – and 'knowledge of acquaintance', which is knowledge of human behaviour. The latter is a particularly difficult process because it acts directly on the personality
boundaries.

There will always be conflict between the demands of reality testing
and the more primitive qualities associated with the pleasure principle.
It should not be assumed that the reality principle will inevitably dominate. In this regard we will recall that boundaries were formed in the
first instance as defences against anxiety and as a means of reality
testing. Consequently, any disturbance of these boundaries, such as
may result from a difficult learning experience, may result in extreme
anxiety. In such circumstances, the learning process can create

resistance and blocks to learning may develop. Knowledge can be used as a property which, once acquired, brings closure. Reification is another block: to know the word is to possess control over concrete reality; to control the word is to control the thing.

A particular type of learning which may be considered most relevant to culture, is organisational socialisation. The experience of entering a culture is a unique opportunity to study both culture and to further our knowledge of learning. It is this aspect that I turn to next.

9

ORGANISATIONAL SOCIALISATION

As will be seen, organisational socialisation is an important area of study with regard to culture as it provides extremely relevant data. The fact that it involves movement from one social grouping to another permits a heightened awareness of at least one side of the equation, that is, from the perspective of the individual as opposed to that of the group. It also involves a process of learning the new culture. I shall begin with a description of my own experience and then relate that to a theoretical explanation.

A PERSONAL REFLECTION

In Chapter 7, I described how, on joining the police, I was confronted with a different – unfamiliar – language. This was also the case when I moved from one part of the organisation to another – from uniform to CID. What I was describing was the fact that the world of those I was joining, as represented by the language as symbols, was very different from the world of my then current experience. Here I shall take this explanation further by describing the effect that socialisation had on me.

Joining the police service was a new and difficult experience. I was confronted with new colleagues, new buildings, new working systems, a new public environment, new streets, new people and, above all, a new role. A new role which was, of course, very public, and one which carried over into 'off-duty'. A role which carried with it widely ranging expectations depending on the position of the perceiver. On the one hand, the 'non-law abiding' would view the role holder with discomfort and rage through to fear, whilst at times regarding him with respect and even reverence. On the other hand, the 'law abiding' would view the role holder with such high esteem that it might be to the point of embarrassment.

Nevertheless, every experience is relative; and joining the police from the Royal Air Force was not such a difficult 'conversion' as joining the Royal Air Force. That was an extremely stressful experience. From a work situation where I was expected to use my own initiative and was able to make decisions, I was thrown into a world where others had total control of my actions. If I can recall my feelings and attitude, it was at times frightening, disorienting, frustrating and degrading, and I would often feel lonely, afraid and frustrated. This experience was an affront to my then known world.

In Chapter 7 I also described my initial move from being a uniform officer to that of being a detective. In that situation, whilst the structure and surroundings remained the same, this was still a new experience. Attitudes and values of those I was joining were somewhat different from those of my uniform colleagues. This was also the case with regard to those non-law abiding members of the public that my new role was bringing me into contact with. The attitudes and values of the habitual criminal were somewhat different from the average offending motorist. Therefore this 'conversion' also had its problems.

During my police career I experienced several role changes. Most of them did not result in the same sort of feelings described above. I believe that the reason for this is that most changes, usually promotions, were in the same area, and, as Csikszentmihalyi (1975) explains, they were within my capabilities and were simply stimulating. In other words, all that changed was some of the boundaries, but most remained intact. However, I was eventually promoted into a position that I was not familiar with; as the uniform officer in charge of a division. This was again a difficult 'conversion'. Values, attitudes and structures had all been present in my close environment; however, with the heightened awareness that impacting with this new world brought, they took on a totally new meaning.

Other situations, such as a two-month-long work experience in West Africa, where I was investigating fraud, created similar, if slightly different problems. Prolonged educational courses, such as my MSc course, also created a need for readjustment. During the course the students were faced with the imposition of a tight schedule, of an impossibly heavy reading list, and of the assignment of problems which were likely to be the most difficult for them to solve. It had the effect of informing me (and the other students) that I was not so smart and that there were a lot of things to be learned. This, in turn, had the effect of destroying many aspects of my self-image.

From my various experiences referred to above, it seems that socialisation operates at various levels and degrees of intensity. These may usefully be related to Bateson's 'Logical Learning Categories' that were referred to in the last chapter and it will help briefly to apply them at this stage. At the level of Zero Learning we can move sideways into the same or a similar role and it is simply a matter of absorbing new facts. There is no new habituation as the pre-existing responses still operate. At the level of Learning One there are more cues to fit facts into; here we become aware of our familiar surroundings as a result of our heightened awareness.

At the level of Learning Two the contexts are totally different and it is necessary to see the facts in a new light. This means a considerable change. Certainly this was true of one such as the socialisation into the Royal Air Force and possibly that of entry into the police. With regard to the levels of Learning Three and Learning Four, I do not feel that these apply, though, I would suggest that socialisation into the Royal Air Force gets close to the religious conversion described as typical of this level by Bateson.

Further reference to Bateson's levels of learning will be made as appropriate throughout the chapter. However, it seems that there is another categorisation which may help us to understand the process of socialisation. These are the categories of 'reality shock', referred to by Louis (1980), and 'culture shock', referred to by various authors. In particular, I believe that these categories provide us with some idea of the degrees of complexity involved.

REALITY SHOCK

Louis defines organisational socialisation as 'the process by which an individual comes to appreciate the values, abilities, expected behaviours, and social knowledge essential for assuming an organisational role and for participating as an organisational member' (1980, p. 229). She describes how the experience is characterised by disorientation, foreignness and a kind of sensory overload. Schein (1988) defines it as the process of 'learning the ropes', the process of being indoctrinated and trained, the process of being taught what is important in an organisation or some part of it.

The first thing that comes to mind from these descriptions is that it is an extremely anxiety provoking experience. This is where Louis coins the term 'reality shock' to explain the situation. She explains that it is clear that the newcomer's senses are inundated with unfamiliar cues. It would seem that the term 'reality shock' might well be applied to many of my socialisation experiences, but not to those that were the most stressful. Louis also usefully relates to stages of socialisation. The first of these is that termed by Merton (1957) as 'anticipatory socialisation'. At this stage, recruits still outside the organisation anticipate their experiences in the organisation they are about to enter. When beginning work, the individual passes from outsider to newcomer and enters the encounter stage. Differences between anticipation and experiences become apparent and contribute to reality shock. Coping with such difficulties and learning the ropes of the new setting typically takes six to ten months on the job.

As to content, Louis says there are two basic kinds of content that can be distinguished in socialisation. The first is role related learning, and the second is a more general appreciation of the culture of an organisation. In this regard Schein says that socialisation refers to the process of learning the value system, the norms, and the required behaviour patterns of the organisation, or group that he is entering. Both authors basically agree that this usually involves the basic goals or mission of the organisation, the strategy or means of achieving organisational aims, the behaviour patterns that are required for effective performance in the role, and a set of rules or principles which pertain to the maintenance of the identity and integrity of the organisation.

From my own experience it seems reasonable to say that in most socialisation processes there will be varying degrees of anxiety. For example, Berger and Luckmann (1966) and Schein give the example of the extremes that organisations such as religious orders go to in the initiation rites of novitiates. As Schein reminds us, it may be comforting to think of activities like this as being characteristic of primitive tribes or total institutions such as the military, but closer examination reveals it happens to a lesser degree in all organisations. This will clearly not be the case with many socialisation experiences which will result merely in a ruffle to our boundaries. However, it is the anxiety provoking situations that we are most concerned with, and it is to the issue of 'culture shock' that I now turn.

CULTURE SHOCK

Others, such as sociologists and anthropologists, also face the problem of socialisation. Many writers refer to this experience as 'culture shock'. Hunt refers to culture shock as 'the experience of being a stranger in an alien and unfamiliar world' (1989, p. 33). She goes on to explain that immersion in an alien culture is an intense experience, and that most researchers report feeling some mixture of confusion, anxiety, excitement, frustration, depression and embarrassment, which all sounds very

similar to my own experiences. Hunt also describes how some researchers have compared this experience to dying and that others also report
frequent anxieties about body health. As was my experience, some of
the discomfort stems from the fact that the researchers have lost their
bearings, do not know how to communicate in the new setting, and
often feel like helpless children.

A further explanation of 'culture shock' is given by Berger and
Kellner, who state, 'All forms of culture shock are ipso facto relativ-
izing. Indeed, at the core of the shock is the insight that perceptions
and norms previously taken for granted are now revealed to be
highly relative in terms of space and time.' They then go on to
quote Pascal's famous words, 'What is truth on one side of the
Pyrenees is error on the other'. 'The implication is', they state, 'that
our own notions of truth and error are dependent on our location in
geography and history' (1981, p. 60): that is, where, out of the
continuity of time and geography, we have sought to draw artificial
boundaries as a means of making sense out of our particular world.
The 'shock' comes when we enter the world of another group of
people who have created different boundaries, or vice versa.

It seems clear that the reason for 'culture shock' is, in its simplest
terms, one of creating new boundaries. In order to gain a better
understanding we need to explain what is involved in this process.
As a convenient starting point it will be recalled that in every change
there is a loss of the currently known. As is well known the growing
child passes through a series of identifications, constantly changing
and shifting, creating out of bits of personalities of others the unique
mosaic of the self. But what occurs within that mosaic when one or
more of the crucial love objects on which it has been partially
patterned is irrevocably lost?

In the concluding paragraphs of his excellent book on bereavement,
Parkes spoke of the need to relate his findings to the whole range of life
changes. Indeed, he went further because he ends by saying that 'we can
no longer deny that research into the effects of change is an essential
area of study' (1972, p. 213). I am pleased to have the opportunity to
do precisely that, at least, in regard to organisational change. It is also
acknowledged that I shall rely heavily on the work of Parkes, and
Bowlby (1969) in looking at culture shock.

In Chapter 4, I referred to the process of integration. Here we
need to determine precisely what happens to the integrated personality when we go through the process of dramatic organisational
socialisation, such as what happened to that unique mosaic that is
my self when I joined the Royal Air Force or the police. Whatever it

was, the process is central to the issue of culture shock and I now need to refer to the process again in greater depth.

Klein (1940) was of the view that when the infant has advanced to the 'depressive position', this brings about the intrapsychic integration of 'good and bad objects'. Once the infant has solidly established his 'good objects' within himself, a sense of reliance and trust upon them will protect him from annihilatory guilt, arising out of separation from or abandonment of his loved objects. Erikson (1959) defined identity formation as a transforming dynamic concept, a lifelong, largely unconscious process, always in modification in accordance with the social reality of a given moment. Introjection and projection, he suggests, are the preceding steps for later childhood identification.

Jacobson (1964) describes a gradual evolvement of object relations, beginning with a symbiotic mother–child unit, in which fusion of object representations and self-representations exist and there is, therefore, a blurring of ego boundaries. Her schema of identity formations, like that of Erikson, is conceptualised as a dynamic process in a state of constant transformation. Kernberg (1966) describes a model that links the processes of internalisation of object relations with the vicissitudes of instinctual drive derivatives, on the one hand, and, on the other hand, the building up of intrapsychic structures. Introjection, identification, and ego identity constitute, he suggests, three different sequential levels, in that order, in the process of internalisation of object relations.

For Kernberg, ego identity represents the highest level of organisation in this sequence of the development of the 'identification systems'. Whereas introjections and identifications are structures of the psychic apparatus at large, ego identity is a structure specific to the ego which evolves out of its synthesising functions. Ego identity as a final consolidated organisation is characterised by the following three aspects: (a) an awareness of a sense of 'continuity' of the self; (b) a sense of 'consistency' between the external representational world of objects in relation to the concept of the self, and vice versa; and (c) a sense of 'confirmation' – that is, a corroboration of one's own identity in interaction with the environment and the individual sensing of this environmental recognition.

There are several themes which run through the above views, not least the structuring of the ego as a dynamic process and the shared nature of ego development. Parkes (1972) has most helpfully described this process in greater depth. He starts from the position of asking, who is the real me? Am I the person I believe myself to be or the person the world believes me to be? Is there an essential unalterable me? He then goes on to describe how many of the possessions, attributions and characteristics that we term ours are ours only by consent. That is, they are part of a shared reality.

How then, asks Parkes (1972), does someone come to recognise this self, see themselves as an individual separate and different from their fellow human beings? The being that each of us infers from observing our own organism and behaviour and comparing it with that of others is what we call the 'self'. For example, following Parkes, I see myself as a consultant, ex-policeman, husband, commuter and academic — each of these aspects of my identity stems from my roles. I am also identified by my bodily characteristics — tall, white, male and balding, and by my behaviour — punctual, even-tempered and dog-loving. Finally, I have the attributes of my English nationality. Each of these characteristics defines both similarities and differences from other people. They enable me to be identified and they indicate to the world and to me that I have a certain status, certain powers and responsibilities, and certain possessions that are essentially my own.

That I require the continuity, consistency and confirmation of my world that Kernberg (1966) refers to, is without doubt, but Parkes (1972) reminds us that many of the tools by which I act upon that world, 'my hands', 'my language', 'my motor car', span the boundary between my 'self' and 'others'. He then poses the further question, 'Since I can share many of these "possessions", what is the boundary of me?' If the possessions and the roles by which we gain our continuity, consistency and confirmation are shared, then we can assume that if I lose my ability to predict and to act appropriately, my world begins to crumble, and since my view of myself is inextricably bound up with my view of the world, that too will begin to crumble. If I have relied upon other people or possessions to predict and act in many ways as an extension to myself then the loss of those people or possessions can be expected to have the same effect upon my view of myself as if I had lost a part of myself.

As Parkes reminds us, 'once again we are forced to realise that the skin is not the only boundary around the self and that the home we live in and the people to whom we are attached are, in some sense ours — they are parts of ourselves' (1972, p. 210). He also explains that there are several published accounts of the way in which people who have lost a home often try to build another in the same place and manner. Similarly immigrants in an alien culture commonly attempt to re-create around them the culture they have lost. It is clearly not possible for a person to identify with a lost home in the same way that one can identify with a lost person, but the loss of multiple loved objects resulting from a career change might be every bit as stressful.

What Parkes (1972) did not refer to, and what I believe was the further research that he was encouraging, was the fact that the loss of a group, while not as painful as that of an individual, can nevertheless be painful and result in the same processes of bereavement. Chapter 4 explained how the group acted 'as if' it were an individual and displayed precisely the same behaviours. For the members of the group, the group exists as an 'idea held in the mind' or as a necessary 'group illusion'. Whichever terminology we choose to use, the proposition is that groups and organisations are experienced as a 'group self' – a group with a common skin. This is a fact made clearer by Parkes' explanation.

Group relations training provides further support for this proposition. As has been well documented, and experienced by me, the closure of a conference brings with it a clear sense of mourning. If this is the experience after the relatively short period of a week or two then we can be sure that this will be magnified over a longer period of perhaps years. In all the situations described, I was faced with the need to give up one mode of life and accept another. In varying degrees I was saddened at the loss of my previous group, I missed going to work in the same place and with the same people and performing the same tasks.

Parkes is of the view that if those involved in change identify it as a gain, acceptance may not be hard, but when they see it as a loss or a 'mixed blessing' they will do their best to resist the change. It is his belief that 'resistance to change, the reluctance to give up possessions, people, status, expectations, is the basis of grief' (1972, p. 31). He then asserts that how someone copes with the challenge of change in their life will determine not only their view of the world but their view of themselves. He then points out that it is not an exaggeration to assert that personality is both a resultant and a determinant of change.

In Chapter 4 I also made reference to the fact that although organisations are no more than 'an idea held in the mind' or a 'group illusion', they are nevertheless experienced and regarded by their members as real. As such, organisations provide their members with the continuity, consistency and confirmation that Kernberg referred to. An organisation becomes for its members a universal truth – it is 'as if' this is the way of the world and that no other way exists. One of the effects of culture shock is to destroy that fantasy and thus discredit much of what was previously considered to be reality. The effect is to leave the individual with a limited means of reality testing. This may be seen as the state of chaos which

Winnicott described as disintegration and which was related to children in hospital by Menzies Lyth (1988).

From the moment of birth a child is related to the world around him, and the roles that a person performs in life are made up of a complex series of focal action patterns which constitute a repertoire of problem solutions. This repertoire, because it is based on experience, assumes that reasonable expectations of the world will be fulfilled. As time goes by, the individual's stock of 'solutions for all eventualities' grows greater, and novel solutions become rarer. Parkes (1972) explains that nearly all these roles, bodily characteristics, powers and possessions may be affected by a major loss such as a bereavement. It is my view that any major change in life will have this effect and this includes organisational socialisation involving culture shock. In such a case, the change not only alters expectations at the level of the local action patterns but also alters the overall plans and roles of which these form a part.

In order that we may fully understand the impact of such a major loss it will help to take a further look at the processes of introjection, projection and identification. According to Klein (1959):

> Introjection means that the outer world, its impact, the situations the infant lives through, and the objects he encounters, are not only expressed as external but are taken into the self and become part of his inner life. Inner life cannot be evaluated even in the adult without these additions to the personality that derive from continuous introjection. Projection, which goes on simultaneously, implies that there is a capacity in the child to attribute to other people around him feelings of various kinds, predominantly love and hate. (p. 250)

Jacobson (1964) takes the view that while becoming more and more subtle and refined, projection and introjection continue to play an essential part in the processes of identification and in the advance from primitive fusions to those selective identifications on which ego and super-ego development rests. More significantly she claims that:

> The adult ego will make extensive use of introjection and projection mechanisms, based on such fusion between self and object images, for the special purpose of establishing feeling and fantasy identification at any level, not only with our love objects but with our whole environment. Our subtle, empathetic understanding of others, especially those we love, depends on such temporary — either short lived or more lasting — identifications. (p. 40)

Explained in this way, we can see that the loss experienced in culture shock results in not only those introjected loved objects but also those familiar objects that we have come to use for projection: that is, for attributing to other people around us feelings of love and hate. In such a situation we are left with no such receptacle for our projections; furthermore, we are left to take back our projections. We are left with those parts of our feelings that we wished to get rid of, thus causing us further discomfort.

Such a change is a huge upheaval, and one which will very likely result in disintegration. Parkes has described how the world of the bereaved is in chaos. The individual joining a group may well be in the same state, if all the objects that provided his continuity, consistency and confirmation are no longer present he will also be in a state of chaos, or disintegration. In regard to this state, Parkes (1972) explains that in bereavement the first stage is one of numbness, which gives place to pining, and pining to disorganisation and despair, and it is only after the stage of disorganisation that recovery occurs. The process he is describing is that of mourning as referred to by Freud (1917).

MOURNING

It is to the process of mourning that I now turn. Here, Bowlby's (1969) view of this phenomenon as an adaptational process is most valuable. He describes the process of mourning as having three phases. Phase one is characterised by the urge to recover the lost object. Phase two is one of disorganisation: behaviour that was organised in synchronicity to the lost object, now, lacking it, becomes disorganised. The third phase is that of reorganisation: the acceptance of the objects lost and readiness to accept new objects; here discrimination between inappropriate behavioural patterns oriented toward the lost object and appropriate striving toward new objects takes place. I shall use Bowlby's three phases as a loose structure for describing the process of culture shock.

Phase 1: Urge to recover lost object

At phase one the process is characterised by the urge to recover the lost object, or more accurately, the lost objects. Garza-Guerrero classifies this stage as the 'encounter stage', because, he says, 'this is the phase that indeed deserves the name "culture shock", for shock implies a sense of suddenness, acuteness, abruptness' (1974, p. 418). This is the phase where Parkes suggested a state of numbness that gave place to pining. Exposed to this new reality, the newcomer's interaction with it fails relatively and temporarily to provide the basic elements upon which his own identity is solidly maintained.

Reflecting on my experience on entering the Royal Air Force, all previous knowledge was of little or no use to me. The previous experiences out of which I had constructed my unique self provided me with few clues as to how I should cope. My whole world was in relative chaos, I did not know how to react to this new environment. No doubt I spent many a night yearning to recover that which was lost, the multiple lost objects of my previous existence. My status, powers, responsibilities and possessions were all affected by the loss of my known reality. My sense of continuity, consistency, and confirmation, to use Kernberg's (1966) terms, were in danger in this phase of culture shock.

Both Parkes (1972) and Garza-Guerrero (1974) refer to the use of identification as a defence at this stage. The latter describes how mechanisms of identification are geared to recovering what was lost by alleviating both mourning and the menace to identity. Parkes is of the view that 'most of the phenomena that are referred to as defences have an important function in helping to regulate the quantity of novel, unorganised, or in other respects disabling information' (1972, p. 90). This is in accord with the view expressed in Chapter 4 where secondary identification was seen as part of the normal development process, yet also served as a defence to reduce the hostility between the self and object enabling separation from it to be denied.

In order to buy time the individual must defend himself against the complete realisation of his loss. Identification with the internal world of good objects, those past good objects that once resulted in integration, can be seen as part of the process of coming to grips with the new situation in a relatively safe way. By literally clinging to those good aspects of our past provides us with the strength, support and time to handle this chaotic situation. In a previous chapter I posed the question, 'How do we erase previous thinking in regard to change?' It would appear that the sensible consultant would answer, 'Not in a hurry.'

Phase 2: Disorganisation

For Parkes (1972) this is a period when a bereaved person reacts to both loss and deprivation. Deprivation implies the absence of a necessary person or thing as opposed to loss of that person or thing. We are told by Parkes that this reaction is what is termed 'grief'. When this starts to diminish there seems to follow a period of uncertainty, aimlessness, and apathy which Bowlby has called the phase not only of disorganisation but also despair. Here the characteristic emotion is one of depression. This period of depression is not a clear-cut period of grief but occurs again and again in one context or another.

Phase 3: Reorganisation

For Garza-Guerrero (1974) this is his second phase. Here, he describes how, once the initial shock of the cultural encounter is over, a gradual acceptance of the new culture develops. As has been said before, every change involves a loss and a gain. This phase is very similar to Winnicott's transitional space in as much as there is a transition from disintegration to integration, from loss to gain. Furthermore, there is the process of taking in new transitional objects and of learning new symbols. In Bateson's terms, an organisational socialisation process that resulted in severe culture shock would be learning at the level of Learning Two. The individual has to learn in a completely new way, the context itself has changed.

This phase encompasses the working through of the process of mourning described earlier and the subsequent intrapsychic reorganisation. Successful interactions will gradually reinforce disengagement with the past culture. Mourning with its adherence to the past and resistance to indiscriminately accepting the new culture, allows for a process of reorganisation to take place. Thus, the mourning process refers to a 'reshaping' of internalised object relations under the influence of the new reality. The individual gradually returns to secondary process activities and an integrated personality on the basis of reaffirmation and reintegration of his own identity in interaction with the new culture.

This leads to what is termed by Parkes as 'a new identity'. This is also the case with Garza-Guerrero, who uses this title for his third phase. However, he clarifies this statement when he observes that the new identity refers neither to a total engulfment in the new culture nor to the mere sum of bicultural endowments. Neither does new identity mean a stable achievement, but rather, as has been stated by Erikson (1950), it denotes a continually re-edited process: it is a dynamic, ever-changing process. Nevertheless, at this stage the new object relations have become introjected into the individual to the extent that the ego identity comprises a stable and integrated concept of the new self. Or, to use Piaget's terminology, to reach this stage the new objects will have needed to be accommodated into our structure in order for them to become assimilable objects.

What began as a threat to identity, mourning, and low self-esteem ends in a confirmation of both ego identity and self-esteem. Subjectively, the experience of this phase could be depicted as a gradual feeling of 'belonging' to the new reality, a comfortable growing sensation of fitness reflected in interpersonal interaction with the new world. Even in the least stressful experiences of organisational socialisation this is a slow process. In those career changes that I referred to which did not cause me great anxiety, it nevertheless took me some six to ten months to 'learn the ropes'.

'Learning the ropes' differed in intensity in regard to the circumstances. For example, following the period of basic training in the Royal Air Force we had developed ways of dealing with the anxieties, largely by learning to conform to the requirements, and had built our own social structures, our own boundaries, which provided us with a defence to our anxieties. The academic experience was similar as we also developed a peer culture, a kind of banding together of the students as a defence against the anxiety posed by the College and as a problem-solving device to develop norms of what and how to study. In both these instances, the experience was shared by a number of individuals. In other situations, such as joining the police, I was very much on my own and could not rely upon mutual support.

As with so many aspects of culture, the response of the individual will be influenced by subjective and objective factors. Using Piaget's (1951) terms, should the knowledge which I am confronted with be not so different from my current knowledge, I shall be able to 'assimilate' that knowledge. That is, I can absorb it into my own viewpoint, which will not have changed very much in consequence. However, should the knowledge be very different from my own, I shall have to 'accommodate' my point of view to the other. This will involve substantially changing my own viewpoint. In either case, I shall see the world differently after the experience. Here we can see how individuals and groups are constantly changing.

SUMMARY

Organisational socialisation can be a chaotic experience resulting in a considerable degree of disintegration. Personal reflection and views of others shows the painful nature of the process. Culture shock can be a stressful, anxiety provoking situation, a violent encounter – one which puts the newcomer's personality functioning to the test, thus challenging the stability of his psychic organisation. It is accompanied by a process of mourning brought about by the individual's gigantic loss of a variety of his loved objects in the abandoned culture.

Organisational socialisation is a valuable area of study as the process provides a deep insight into the processes of change. In examining the relative ease or difficulty associated with socialisation processes of different complexity we are afforded an insight into the various degrees of learning required in change. What is more, it provides information in regard to the effect that such changes have on individuals.

At the simplest level, change can be stimulating and have little if any effect on our personal boundaries. Slightly more difficult changes will be associated with what may be termed 'reality shock'. Here there will be a need for some adjustment to the individual's personal boundaries, in the nature of Bateson's Learning One level. However, it is when the change is of such a nature that the unique mosaic which is the self is utterly and totally confronted and found to be inadequate for dealing with the new reality, that we experience the more serious process, that of 'culture shock'. In this situation, the continuity, consistency and confirmation of the individual can no longer be relied upon.

The skin around the self is not the only boundary that we need to protect. Group and psychological boundaries or 'skins' are equally important to the process of reality testing. Many of these boundaries are shared by others who are then within that particular 'skin'. From birth, continuing through life, an individual is related to the world around him. It is this shared world that provides for the continuity, consistency and confirmation required of reality testing.

All change involves a loss and a gain. When the loss is of such a nature as to be totally chaotic it will most likely result in the experience that we have previously referred to as disintegration. In the first instance this will result in the process of mourning. There seems to be general agreement that mourning is a reaction to a real loss of a loved object – or perhaps more accurately to the loss of multiple loved objects. In this respect, we can imagine that if an individual's identity is so painfully threatened by mourning related to an individual single object loss, then the vicissitudes of the mourner's identity in a mourning following a multiple object loss, as in the case of culture shock, is also likely to be considerable but not, of course, as great.

The painful yearning to recover what was lost is reminiscent, affectively and adaptively, of earlier infantile object loss or separations. In like manner the individual uses the defence of identification with internal good objects which provides time to adjust to the change. Thus defence mechanisms may be seen not to have a single purpose of protection from anxiety but also a secondary purpose of providing time for the individual to adjust to the 'conversion' process. Eventually, the individual may come to terms with the new reality by adapting to a new identity. This will be a slow process which will possibly take some six to twelve months.

Thus we have seen that culture shock is a violent encounter – one which puts the newcomer's personality functioning to the test, thereby challenging the stability of his psychic organisation. It is accompanied by a process of mourning brought about by the individual's gigantic loss of a variety of his loved objects in the abandoned culture. As such it provides valuable information about the process of defence mechanisms and about the process of change, which will be dealt with in a later chapter.

10

'CREATIVITY'

In 'Beyond the Pleasure Principle' (1920) Freud postulated the existence of a conservative instinct. That there is much to support this view is well demonstrated by the manner in which we seek to form and create boundaries. We also, quite paradoxically, appear to have an exploratory or creative instinct. Indeed, the history of man could be seen as supporting such an idea. In this chapter I shall be looking at the relationship of these seemingly paradoxical instincts in an attempt to explain what is meant by 'creativity'. Creativity is highly relevant to culture and change, as it is largely through creativity that growth can occur. Creativity, as we shall see, is about reality testing and the drive to create is one of the factors that results in the dynamic nature of culture.

I shall commence with a substantial review of other writers, and, in order to provide some structure, I shall group those views according to the main categories that those other writers have used to explain the phenomenon. These are: viewing creativity as a mystical process; as an instinct or perhaps more accurately as a drive; as being similar to play; as requiring an holistic view; as resulting in something new; and as involving imagination in bringing about this something new. I shall then put my own interpretation of the process, referring back to other views where appropriate.

CATEGORIES USED TO EXPLAIN 'CREATIVITY'

A Mystical Process
An example of a mystical explanation is shown in this extract from Jung:

> The experience that furnishes the material for artistic expression is no longer familiar. It is a strange something that derives its existence from the hinterland of man's mind – that suggests the abyss of time separating us from pre-human ages, or evokes a super-human world of contrasting light

and darkness. It arises from timeless depths; it is foreign and cold, many sided, demonic and grotesque. A grimly ridiculous sample of the eternal chaos – it bursts asunder our human standards of value and aesthetic form. The disturbing vision of monstrous and meaningless happenings that in every way exceed the grasp of human feeling and comprehension makes quite other demands upon the powers of the artist than do the experiences of the foreground of life. (1961, p. 180)

I agree with Weisberg (1986) that we should jettison the persistent myths that we use to explain the phenomenon of creativity. In view of the difficult nature of the subject matter it is easy to understand why people look for a mythical solution. If something does not easily fit into our known categories we have to find some way to explain it and myth is an easy option. But, as the scientist Peter Medawar stated (in Evans and Deehan, 1988), 'That "creativity" is beyond analysis is a romantic illusion that we must now outgrow' (p. 14). This is the position taken here, and one which I hope to fulfil.

A Drive

A more useful way of looking at the phenomenon is to view it in the way that Miller (1983) has done, that is, as a drive. That there is such a drive appears to have been accepted by several writers. But it is variously seen as a reproductive instinct, a creative instinct or an exploratory drive, as the following selection of views shows. For example, Fromm (1955, 1962) observed that man can create life, a miraculous quality which he shares with all living beings, but with the difference that he alone is aware of being created and of being a creator. Man, or, more correctly, man and woman, can create by planting seeds, by producing material objects, by creating art, by creating ideas and by loving one another. Life itself is seen to be a creative process elaborating and maintaining order out of the randomness of matter.

Much the same is said by others, such as Maslow (1970), who was of the view that we are dealing with a fundamental characteristic, inherent in human nature, a potentiality given to all or most human beings at birth, which most often is lost or buried or inhibited as the person gets enculturated. This is also the view of Henry (1991), who observes that the capacity for creative action seems to be a basic feature of life, and of May (1975), who feels that we express our being by creating, and that creativity is a necessary sequel to being.

Koestler (1964) refers to an exploratory drive. However, it would appear that he means the same thing when he observes that satisfaction presupposes the existence of a need or appetite. Intellectual curiosity, the desire to understand, is derived from an urge as basic as hunger or sex; the exploratory drive. This, feels Koestler, is the prime mover behind human exploration and research. Quite apart from the views referred to above, we should not need too much convincing of the existence of a process that we would relate to as a creative drive.

Storr (1972) reminds us of Freud's remark that psycho-analysis could throw no light upon the technique or the gift of the artist. Yet Freud would have been the first to agree that artists are, like the rest of us, only human and that the same conflicts and the same disappointments afflict the artist as plague us all. In agreeing with Storr, I feel that it is important to extend his argument from artists to everybody. If indeed there is such a thing as a creative drive, it seems that it must be available to all and not just a select few.

In my view, this means that we are literally referring to everybody. Again Storr helpfully reminds us that creativity is more closely bound up with what might be called a 'dynamic of the normal' than with psychopathology. This is partially recognised by Pruyser (1979), who is of the view that the moment we consider including more ethereal products of the human mind in a list of creative entities, the way is open for a complete tilting of the customary perspective on creativity. We should not be arguing from specimens of creative work but should be attributing a potential or actual creativity to everybody and then to spot creative features in any and all of their activities. This is precisely what Maslow has done.

Maslow (1970) discovered that he had, like most other people, been thinking of creativeness in terms of products, and that he had unconsciously confined creativeness only to certain conventional areas of human endeavour. That is, he had unconsciously assumed that any painter was leading a creative life, as was any poet, any composer. Furthermore, theorists, artists, scientists, inventors, writers could be creative, but not others. His unresearched view was that you were in or you were out, all or none, as if creativeness were the sole prerogative of certain professionals. Following his research, however, he was of a contrary view – all were creative.

I believe this to be an important point. Creativity is not limited to a special class of people or to special products or to special circumstances, as some have argued. Rather, creativity is a drive possessed by all. As Storr (1972) points out, it is a perfectly normal activity for perfectly normal people. The interesting point may be why some are more 'creative' than others, why some of us may find that the rules that govern our reality are such as to prevent us from moving to other realities. This is a point that I will refer to again later.

Similar to Play

Another way of looking at the process and one which is perhaps the most frequent, is to liken it to the play of children. Many other writers have referred to play, and the following is only a selection. For example, Maslow (1970) made the link when he observed that creativeness in self-actualised people was in many respects like the creativeness of all happy and creative children. It was spontaneous, effortless, innocent, easy; a kind of freedom from stereotypes and clichés. For him it seemed to be made up largely of 'innocent' freedom of perception and 'innocent' uninhibited spontaneity and expressiveness. Commenting on his research involving creative people he was of the view that it was in this child-like sense that the subjects were creative.

This is also the case with Pruyser, who proposed that the primordially creative human act is analogical to what children think and do when they say to each other, 'Come on, let's play'; this call being an invitation to leave temporarily the realistic world and move into the world of illusion where the individual submits himself to new, super-imposed rules. A less direct view is put by Csikszentmihalyi (1975), when he observes that man at play is at the peak of his freedom and dignity. Davis and Wallbridge (1987) introduce us to the most important work of Winnicott when they remind us that the preoccupational playing of young children was seen by Winnicott as a further step in a sequence of activities in the area of illusion or the potential space between the inner self and the environment that leads to a mature capacity for participation in and contribution to the world's cultural fertility.

Thouless (1958) felt that play could be seen as a rehearsal of activities which would later be put to use in the serious business of life. On its psychological side, play in itself is enjoyable, but playful activity is also one which is a rehearsal of an instinctive activity, and it is an activity which is undertaken for its own sake, and not with the conscious aim of rehearsing useful activities. To support his view he provides the examples of analytic play – pulling things to pieces, and of synthetic play – building up new things. Of these he observes that they look like rehearsals of the adult behaviour of curiosity and of construction respectively. This is something which Storr agrees with. He feels that one of the biological functions of play is to teach young animals how to ritualise their primitive impulses of aggression in such a way that they can fit into a social group, whilst at the same time preserving their capabilities for serious fight in reality should the occasion call for it.

A different view of play is taken by Bohm and Peat (1991), when they explain that new thoughts generally arise with a play of the mind, and that the failure to appreciate this is one of the major blocks to creativity. Thought is generally considered to be a sober and weighty business. But here it is being suggested that creative play is an essential element in forming new hypotheses and ideas. Their view is that thought which tries to avoid play is in fact playing false with itself. On this view it appears that play is of the very essence of thought, or, as Henry (1991) explains, creative ideas flow where new ideas and challenges are welcomed and where people are encouraged to play.

Erikson (1977) refers to the fact that the adult plays for recreation. He steps out of his reality into imaginary realities for which he has made up arbitrary but nonetheless binding rules. But an adult rarely gets away with being a playboy. Social norms dictate that only he who works shall play. Games are formalised and therefore non-creative; they are transformations of (defences against the open-endedness of) play. Erikson also explains how the content of infantile play often proves to be the infantile way of thinking over difficult experiences and of restoring a sense of mastery, this is comparable to the way in which we repeat, in ruminations and endless talk, in daydreams and in dreams, experiences that have been too much for us.

Pruyser took the view that there were what he referred to as an 'austistic world', an 'illusionistic world' and a 'realistic world'. For him, play was located in the 'illusionistic world'. In formulating this view Pruyser has relied on Winnicott's writings to develop his own original view of creativity. Pruyser claims that:

> If one accentuates Winnicott's terms object and sphere and follow his speculation that the child's transitional activities are the origins of art and religion, one is bound to infer that Winnicott envisaged a perennial human penchant for seeking special relations with special objects in a special atmosphere over and beyond the 'subjective nonsense' of autism and the 'cold hard facts' of realistic sense perceptions. I have interpreted Winnicott's intentions in the latter sense and have made bold to speak of a 'third world', trying to define the relationships, objects, and atmosphere that prevail in it. (1979, p. 322)

Winnicott also expressed some significant views on play which I feel is captured in the following: 'It is in playing and only in playing that the child or adult is able to be creative and use the whole personality, and it is only in being creative that the individual discovers the self' (1971, p. 62). And, to conclude this short look at play it is interesting to note that in 'Instincts and Their Vicissitudes' (1915), Freud asked the question, 'What instincts should we suppose there are, and how many?' In answer to his own question he stated, 'No objection can be made to anyone's employing the concept of an instinct of play' (p. 120). There are many important points that have been raised in regard to play that provide us with useful information regarding the process of creativity. Not least, it suggests a sort of freedom from 'normal' constraints.

Requiring a Holistic View

A further view frequently put is that regarding the intensity of the experience. For May (1975), this is a matter of total awareness and he describes the intensity of the encounter as one of absorption, or being caught up in, wholly involved and so on. The encounter is with the world of the creator, that is, the pattern of meaningful relations in which a person exists and in the design of which he or she participates. Following this line of thought, May defines 'creativity' as the encounter of the intensively conscious human being with his or her world.

In describing how to identify creativity, Csikszentmihalyi observed that it required an holistic approach which took into account a person's goals and abilities and his subjective evaluation of the external situation. Pruyser took the view that a creative work is something called into being, something with a holistically unique character that transcends the ingredients from which it is made. Koestler refers to a sort of total awareness when he observes that full consciousness must be regarded as the upper limit of a continuous gradient from focal awareness to total awareness of an event. Awareness is a matter of degree, and, as has been previously stated, only a fraction of our multi-levelled activities at any moment enters the beam of focal consciousness.

The intensity of the experience is described in yet another way by Jaques (1970), who uses the ancient Greek concept of 'nous', that is, mind comprising both heart and soul, intellect and feeling, thought and impulse. On these views, to achieve contact with our creative source in this holistic manner is no easy task, as is explained by Fromm (1962) who asserts that this can only be achieved if we recognise that we are unable to focus our attention on the particulars of a whole without diminishing our comprehension of the whole; conversely we can focus on the whole only by diminishing our comprehension of the particulars which constitute the whole.

Resulting in Something New

Another of the essential elements of creativity is that something new is created. Again, there is general agreement from a wide range of writers on this point. For example, Evans and Deehan (1988) inform us that first of all, we certainly expect something new to result from creativity and that we expect the world to be different as a result of the process. Henry (1991) observes that creativity is concerned with developing new ideas, and that to do this we need to see the problem from a fresh perspective, which involves escaping from old ideas. In this respect we are reminded that there is a loss and a gain.

This is added to by Pozzi, who provides us with a definition when he writes, 'Let us take a brief look at the word "creativity". Its most commonly accepted meaning is "something that did not exist before is made to be"' (1990, p. 150). This is also the case with Storr, who has defined creativity simply and concisely as 'the ability to bring some-thing new into existence' (1972, p. 11). What this does not imply is that the 'something new' need not be new to everyone, or, indeed, new to anyone else save the person who creates it.

That creativity does produce something new, be it a new product, a new theory, a new work of art or whatever, can hardly be in doubt. However, the very act of bringing something new into being brings its own difficulties. It would seem that coming to terms with something totally new and different is not a simple matter and this raises the issue of anxiety. May (1975) referred to this when he wrote of the experience of encounter which brought with it anxiety. It is interesting that he uses the word 'encounter' in the same way that it was used in regard to culture shock. The anxiety referred to here is a result of the shaking of the self-world relationship that occurs in the encounter when our sense of identity is threatened. As a result of this encounter the world is not as we experienced it before, and since self and world are always correlated, we no longer are what we were before.

In this regard, May describes how the creative instinct comes into conflict with the conservative instinct. The conservative instinct de-mands order in our world – that our sense of identity, our world of reality, remain the same – whereas the creative drive demands that something must change in order for the new to come into being. This would appear to be the essence of the dynamic process that is life. The past, present and future form a new Gestalt, a new reality. The anxiety that we experience is a temporary rootlessness, disorientation, or, as May says, the 'anxiety of nothingness' because order comes out of disorder, form out of chaos. Paradoxically, ordering is disordering as it involves the destruction of pre-existing notions of reality.

In terms of creating something new we need to consider whether it is something new for the individual or something new for society. Miller (1983) points out that the socially defined categories of sin, disloyalty, crime and craziness, and the social sanctions against deviants guilty of such acts, provide a mechanism whereby the individual can split off and disown uncomfortable parts of himself and not have to judge on his own what is creative and what is destructive. The social categories vary from society to society or, as Miller states, 'A flower in one man's garden is a weed in another' (p. 7). Where there is a new reality for the individual, this will shake his self-world but he can take his own authority for that change. Where the change affects others, however, it also affects their authority and will therefore be much more difficult.

Involving Imagination

Pruyser (1979), examines three worlds: the autistic world of the infant, the realistic world of the adult, and the illusionistic or transitional world of the 'creator'. From the psycho-analytic concepts of transitional objects and pre-conscious spheres of mental activity, he constructs an illusionistic world which is not delusion, hallucination or phantasy, but is, rather, a world in which the person mentally interacts with and partakes of both the real and the unreal.

This is very similar to the concept put forward by Storr (1988) who considered that we all possess an inner world of phantasy which is part of man's biological endowment, and that it is the inevitable discrepancy between this inner world and the outer world that compels men to become inventive and imaginative. He asserts that there are good biological reasons for accepting the fact that man is so constituted that he possesses an inner world of the imagination which is different from, though connected to, the world of external reality. It is the discrepancy between the two worlds which motivates creative imagination. It is from phantasies which originate in the imagination and then connect with the external world that new ways are developed which illuminate the external world and make it more comprehensible.

At this stage, I believe that I have gone far enough in my review of other writers to provide a useful backcloth for formulating my own views on the process of creativity. Before doing so, however, it may be useful to summarise the foregoing. First, there does appear to be a clear drive to create: if this were not the case human nature would not be the dynamic process that it is. We can also say that the process has some sort of relationship to the play of children. It is a complex process that requires total awareness to come into being. It has been said that in order to achieve this it requires that we take an holistic approach. The process is about bringing something new into being, that is, order out of formlessness. Furthermore, this something new is the result of some sort of imagination, illusion or phantasy.

RELATIONSHIP TO SYMBOLISM

Thus far I have not referred to symbolism in regard to creativity, yet it will be recalled that in Chapter 6 such a relationship was stressed. A brief review will remind us that symbolism, albeit not using true symbols but symbolic equations, commences when the infant is still influenced by the primary process. Fenichel (1946) considers that original symbolic thinking is directed by the primary process. It being not only a method of distortion but also part of the primal pre-logical thinking. Klein considers that symbolism flows from iden- tification. Anxiety sets going the mechanism of identification and this contributes to make the infant equate the bodily organs in question with other things. From here there is a gradual development from symbolic gestures to speech symbolism.

The development of true symbols occurs with the development of play which we have seen is most relevant to creativity. Winnicott tells us that when we witness the infant's first employment of a transitional object, the first 'not me' possession, we are witnessing both the child's first use of a symbol and the first experience of play. Klein then describes how the child constantly advances from his original primitive symbols, games and activities, so that we find symbols at work in increasingly complicated inventions, leaving the former ones behind. For Klein symbolism is the foundation of all sublimation and every talent.

Highly relevant to creativity is the fact that speech symbols allow us to form concepts, so that once we have a piece of 'reality' we can play with it, think about it, and, most importantly, relate it to other pieces. The benefit lies in the fact that symbolic experience can yield the possibility of prospect and retrospect. What is fixed in consciousness is there to go back to: a prediction, an expectation, is formulated by reference back. What is more important in terms of creativity is the fact that we may opt out of the handling of reality for a time and improvise to our own satisfaction upon our represented world. That is, we may operate directly upon the representation itself; in other words, we may use our imagination to create.

Words and language used as symbols will have a considerable effect on our ability to create. For an experience to come into awareness, it must be comprehensible in accordance with the categories in which conscious thought is organised. Thus the concept of a discovery will have meaning only in relation to the knowledge available to the discoverer at the time. By penetrating into unknown territory with revolutionary changes such as Kuhn's paradigms, there will be disturbing consequences for previously settled opinions. This will be commented on again later.

THE PROCESS OF 'CREATIVITY'

In formulating my own view I shall follow the sequence of categories in the above summary. However, in order to get a proper understanding of what is involved, it will require considerable explanation over and above what has already been discussed. I have not found it easy to document this explanation. Nevertheless, I consider the process of creativity to be a key element in coming to an understanding of culture and therefore it will be worthwhile.

That there is something in the order of a creative drive is not difficult to accept. The difficulty lies in the paradoxical nature of the conservative instinct to the creative instinct. That they exist side by side is explained by Allport (1955), who points out that nothing could be more evident than the fact that the conservative instinct represents demands for tension reduction. However, while we certainly learn habitual modes for reducing tension, this is only half the problem. We also come to regard many of our past satisfactions to be worthless, because although we want stability, we also want variety. While we learn dependable modes of reducing tension we also abandon old habits and take risks in searching out new courses of conduct. It is only through this risk taking and variation that growth can occur. Storr (1988) agrees and asserts that (societal) survival cannot be ensured unless intelligence and imagination take over from innate patterns in making provision for basic needs.

In previous chapters we have referred to these innate patterns as the world of reality, or the world as perceived by the individual. This world is constantly reality tested against the social milieu in which the individual exists. And while this is a changing, dynamic world, we should not forget that the loss of part or parts of that

world can cause disintegration. It is against this background that we
need to view the process of creativity. It is not this aspect that we
need to explain; rather it is that of risk taking or imagination
referred to above. The important point is that we do not forget that
it is taking place in the context of our world of reality.

The views of other writers have been valuable in describing the
similarity of the process of creativity with that of play. What they do
not do is to provide an explanation for the process, which is what I
shall now do. It will be recalled that both Winnicott and Klein
described symbolism as the basis of all creative endeavours. It therefore seems appropriate to return to the views of Winnicott who also
stated that creative experience begins with creative living first manifested in play. Of play, Freud (1908) wrote that every child at play
behaves like a creative writer. That is, he creates a world of his own
by rearranging things in a new way which links things of the real
world in a way which pleases him. This linking, said Freud, is all
that differentiates the child's play from 'phantasying'.

This linking, as Freud called it, is taking place in what Winnicott
has referred to as the 'transitional space' – the potential space
between the individual and the environment. Winnicott (1971)
informs us that the special feature of the potential space is that it
depends for its existence on living experiences, not on inherited
tendencies. The tangible and visual things to which Freud referred
may also be termed 'transitional objects'. These transitional objects
are a link between the inner and outer worlds, belonging wholly to
neither, yet clearly pertaining to both. Consequently, they may be
presumed to be an advance upon phantasy which has no relation at
all to the world outside the object.

This advance on phantasy is what has been termed 'imagination'. In
regard to imagination, Erikson (1977) shows that the growing child's
play is the training ground for the experience of a leeway of imaginative
choices within an existence governed and guided by roles and visions.
The use of transitional objects suggests that the process of imagination
begins very early in life. Sinnott (1959) terms it 'the great gift of
imagination', which he describes as man's most distinctive trait, for it
makes possible his creativeness. New experiences could not have
appeared unless there had been someone who could imagine a situation
never yet experienced, who could picture in his mind something he had
not seen or discover a new way of looking at what is already there.

We know that the potential space is concerned with symbols –
with the complex matter of the meaning of meaning. It is the place
where symbols are used for the different concepts of experience.

These concepts of experience include both conscious and unconscious processes – primary and secondary processes. Therefore, using symbols is a way of being in touch with the inner psychic reality – of discovering the self – and is an aspect of what Winnicott calls 'creative apperception'. The ability to form and use symbols, then, brings meaning to the world of both imagination and the world of shared reality. Creative apperception depends upon linking subjective and objective, upon colouring the external world with the warm hues of the imagination.

Primary and Secondary Processes

I believe that it is here that we begin to understand the process of imagination and subsequently that of creativity. By reference to the two types of mental functioning – the primary and secondary processes we have the genesis of an explanation. By nature, one provides the origination, the other the rational basis of living. Primary process thought is unconscious and it operates outside the bounds of logic and reality. Secondary process thought operates consciously and it is subject to all the controls imposed by our conscious minds.

In the primary process we are oblivious to the categories of space and time. The id has no organisation, produces no collective will, the logical laws of thought do not apply, contrary impulses exist side by side without cancelling each other out. There is nothing in the id that corresponds to the idea of time. Freud considered that the pleasure principle was only gradually replaced by the reality principle. Since no mental content is ever completely expunged, traces of the pleasure principle lingered on and could, so Freud believed, be detected not only in dreams, but also in play. Rycroft (1981) reminds us that Darwin and Richter emphasise the imagination's independence of the will. A similarity between dreams and products of the waking imagination is that this production is independent of the will.

I agree with Storr when he asserts that Freud was right in linking play and phantasy, but that he was wrong in believing that play and phantasy should be abandoned in favour of rationality. Storr was also of the view that there are good biological reasons for accepting the fact that man is so constituted that he possesses an inner world of the imagination which is different from, though connected to, the world of the primary process. It is this activity that resembles play, it is this spontaneous, uninhibited, and innocent activity that is free of the 'normal' constraints.

This is where the views regarding the intensity of the experience come in, because the primary process is only available through the means of total awareness described earlier. It is only by means of an holistic approach that we can gain access to this world of imagination. Rogers (1954) explains that in order to gain access to this inner world, it means there must be a lack of rigidity and permeability of boundaries in concepts, beliefs, perceptions and hypothesis. It also means a tolerance for ambiguity where ambiguity exists. In a person who is open to experience, each stimulus is freely relayed through the nervous system, without being distorted by any process of defensiveness. This means that instead of perceiving in predetermined categories, the individual is aware of all of the experiences in his world imaginary and shared.

Should we have any doubts that the primary process is still available to us all we need only refer to its role in dreams. Or, perhaps more accurately, to give due regard to Rycroft's views, to primary process-like activity. For Rycroft, dreaming is an imaginative activity and all imaginative activity, waking or sleeping, is independent of the will. Coming at it from the opposite direction, Sinnott (1959) observes that creative imagination is especially active at the mind's unconscious level. Here, he says, mental work is being done. Here, quite without mental participation (that is, of the secondary process type) choices are being made and ideas fitted together into patterns. Thus the unconscious mind is able to solve problems and to lay at least the foundation for creative activity.

On this view, the living system here is exercising its ability to integrate and organise a pattern out of formlessness, an achievement which rational thought, being somewhat removed from its primitive living source and bound with habit and convention, may be incapable of doing. In other words this is not secondary process activity which would apply all sorts of limitations, but primary process activity which is not inhibited by the restrictions of shared reality. Thus the process of imagination is a primary process activity. The creation of something new occurs originally in primary process activity.

This tends to be supported by the experience reported by many authors where a creative notion, or 'discovery', has come into being on waking in the morning or earlier. Indeed, I can recall several occasions in the process of writing this book where this has been the case. This is associated with another experience. Here, despite the importance of the 'discovery', it has been lost to awareness unless committed to paper or tape quickly. This tends to suggest that there might be a different part of the mental process involved, one that does not operate the process of memory: however, this is speculation. Another reason may be that on achieving consciousness the secondary process takes over, that process not being independent of the will. The result may be anxiety which is dealt with by a denial of the 'discovery'.

LEFT BRAIN AND RIGHT BRAIN

This calls to mind Ornstein's (1977) theory of left brain and right brain activity. Here it is considered that the left brain is predominantly involved with analytic, logical thinking, especially in verbal and mathematical functions. In contrast, the right brain seems specialised for holistic mentation and artistic endeavour. This point of view is supported by Jung (1956), who asserted that we have two kinds of thinking: directed thinking, and dreaming or fantasy thinking. The former operates with speech elements for the purpose of communication, and is difficult and exhausting; the latter is effortless, working as it were spontaneously, with the contents ready to hand, and guarded by unconscious motives. The one produces innovation and adaptation, copies reality, and tries to act upon it; the other turns away from reality, sets free subjective tendencies, and, as regards adaptation, is unproductive.

ANXIETY AND GUILT

It is here that I depart from the views of others. The anxiety associated with creativity is seldom mentioned, it is far more likely that there will be references to play as I have shown above. While not dismissing the relationship to play, I believe that where creativity is viewed solely from the perspective of play and without reference to the extreme anxieties that may occur in the process, we are only viewing one half of the picture. To be creative requires the courage to overcome the inevitable guilt that will be associated with the process. I can perhaps explain this best by personal example. While working on a paper for my MSc I came to the conclusion that a particular phenomenon did not exist. In myself I was quite confident, until I started to consider what the tutor would say. I suffered considerable feelings of guilt that I ought not to be expressing such a view because it was contrary to established belief.

In common with Rogers I do not believe that many significantly creative products are formed without the feeling, 'I am alone.' That 'no one has ever done just this before'. That 'I have ventured into territory where no one has been.' 'Perhaps I am foolish, or wrong, or

lost, or abnormal.' A highly appropriate example is the creative activity of Bion which involved his taking very considerable personal risks
with regard to his professional reputation. Trist describes how 'Bion
asked if he was a bit mad to be giving serious consideration to such
ideas?' Trist replied that 'he had to have the courage of his own
logic'. 'Freud', he went on to say, 'must have given himself some
bad frights when he found the key concepts of psycho-analysis
arising in his head for the first time' (1985, p. 33).

While we create in the imaginary world of the primary process we
exist and bring our creations into being in the world of reality which is
governed by the secondary process, a world that includes the super-ego.
According to Abraham (1979), the super-ego takes on those functions
of criticising the behaviour of the ego which form the individual into a
social being. Of those functions, the one we call conscience interests us
most at present. The super-ego instructs the ego by means of that
function as to what it may do or not do, in the same way as the
persons in authority over it used formerly to do. Toward the end of his
life, Freud extended his view in regard to persons in authority when he
stated that what is operating in the super-ego 'is not only the personal
qualities of the parents but also everything that had a determining effect
on themselves, the tastes and standards of the social class in which they
lived and the innate dispositions and traditions of the race from which
they sprang' (1940b, p. 378).

Thus the conscience that is instructing us what we may do or
not do is developed from the world of our reality. Consequently,
to create something radically new will almost certainly result in
conflict with our conscience which will be instructing us how we
ought to behave. That is, in a manner consistent with the known
reality. In this regard, Rank (1945) points out that we see in the
creative impulse not only the highest form of individual will affirmation, but also the most mighty will conquest of the individual
will over the will of his society. For Rank this explains the guilt
which the creative process necessarily produces. It is this going
beyond the limits set by the world of reality to which the ego
reacts with guilt. Guilt is experienced in regard to those others
that he opposes through his 'discovery', new paradigm, or whatever
we choose to call it. Guilt is also experienced in regard to himself,
as was explained above, for daring to step 'out of line'.

According to Allport (1955) guilt is a 'poignant suffering' that we
experience when decisions are made which we feel are inappropriate.
Thus to be creative requires a good deal of courage. A resilient pioneering courage and single-mindedness are necessary if new ideas are to be

spread – the sort of courage that is able to override the conscience, one which is able to handle the feelings of guilt. This is where we come back to the conservative instinct: in order to have the necessary courage to create we need to be secure. It is the secure infant who later exhibits the greatest interest in toys and other impersonal objects in the environment. It is also here that knowledge can be used as a stimulus to approach the 'not knowing', allowing us to put up with ignorance as a basic condition for achieving mental development.

NEED FOR A 'BASIC TRUST'

The secure infant is one who has, in Winnicott's terms, a basic trust in his mother. Winnicott says of this trust, 'The word trust in this context shows an understanding of what I mean by the building up of confidence based on experience, at the time of maximal dependence, before the enjoyment and employment of separation and independence' (1988, p. 120). To achieve this position of trust the mother needs to hold the infant unanxiously while the infant is itself anxious. The function of holding in psychological terms is to provide ego-support, in particular, at the stage of absolute dependence before integration of the ego has become established. Or, to use Bion's terminology, the mother acts as a 'container' for the anxieties of the infant and as such, the infant introjects the maternal object as a container capable of containing anxiety and conflict.

As Segal (1981) reminds us, independence is never absolute. The healthy individual does not become isolated, but becomes related to the environment in such a way that the individual and environment can be said to be interdependent. In my view there is not one holding environment that occurs during infancy but a succession of holding environments throughout life; this being a lifelong activity of differentiation and integration. The creating of the object, a process of differentiation, is followed by our relating to it, a process of integration.

It seems clear that if we are to create there must be a sufficient trust based on our experience. Such experience is to be found in the environment of the creator. Should the organisational holding environment be such as to provide trust it will permit creativity, whereas, should the contrary pertain, it is unlikely that we will have the confidence to do so. When we speak of differentiation or creativity it seems important to bear in mind that we are not usually speaking of sensational 'discoveries'. More likely, we shall be referring to small, relatively inconsequential developments which are, nevertheless, all part of the dynamic process of life.

The reader may well ask, What about rebelliousness? Where does this fit in? The first point that I should make is that creativity does not have to be task related, it may equally be anti-task. Similarly, it does not have to follow social controls: for example, there are many examples of creative behaviour that have been considered to be criminal and have been deliberately antisocial. Where individuals or groups perceive themselves to be marginalised they do not consider themselves subject to the social controls pertaining to either an organisation or to society in general. They will experience no guilt in regard to violating what for others are regarded as social controls. Consequently, while these marginalised individuals or groups may appear rebellious from the reality existing for others, from their own reality they are not. So they have greater freedom to be creative.

'CREATIVITY' IN GROUPS

Thus far I have related creativity to the individual, but I would point out that the conditions that enable or inhibit individual creativity also apply to groups or organisations. In the same way that I referred to the interrelatedness of the individual with the organisation holding environment, so the same applies to groups. If they, like individuals, have developed a basic trust and perceive their holding environment as good enough there is a likelihood that they can be creative. Where the reverse applies then they are unlikely to be encouraged to be creative.

I say 'likely' because much will also depend on creative pairing with individuals and groups of other sizes. Where there are individuals with a 'resilient pioneering courage' able to override their conscience and to handle their inevitable feelings of guilt, this will encourage creativity. Trist (1985) provides a good example of this when he describes how Bion used him and others in creative pairings when he was developing his highly creative views on groups. In like manner, while completing my PhD I had the much appreciated benefit of creative pairing with my adviser, tutor and fellow students. The process of verbalising and discussing concepts, of sharing them with someone else acts to reduce anxiety by making known the unknown. The anxiety arises from the fact that the reaction of others to the concepts is unknown and thus I am left with fears that they may be considered nonsense. I should add that the reverse of creative pairing is also likely: where others do not have the same pioneering courage they may deter and suppress creativity.

The example of creative pairing referred to above may also be seen as a situation where the other person or persons provide a holding environment for the individual's creativity. There is also the situation where out of a creative pairing something new may be produced as in the act of reproduction. This creative pairing differs from the previous example by virtue that it is a fusion of imaginative thoughts that results in the new product.

In Chapter 8 I referred to the fact that learning was 'an indissociable subject-object relationship', and in Chapter 9 I made extensive reference to the loss involved in change. In terms of loss, there can be no creating of a new object without the loss of an existing object; in any learning there must be an unlearning of much that one thought one knew – even, in exceptional situations, of almost returning to the ignorance of the child. In terms of learning, this can present problems because if the language of the new concept cannot be understood, if there is no shared categorical framework, then the concept of intersubjective communication will be null.

From the foregoing it seems clear that there are considerable barriers to the process of creativity. As if the difficulties of conscience and guilt are not enough there is still the problem that learning anything new must involve some unlearning. Our knowledge and understanding forms a consistent whole which must undergo some modification, however slight, when incorporating something new. Creation cannot be achieved without death: integration is not possible without some fragmentation of the previous, incomplete, or incorrect, integration of a level, or set of informational levels. Eros and Thanatos are twin brothers, inseparable. Thus we see a similar situation with regard to socialisation, save that, in this case, the change is self-imposed and not imposed by outside forces.

SUMMARY

The views of other writers may be summarised as follows: there does appear to be a clear drive to create; if this were not the case human nature would not be the dynamic process that it is. The process has some sort of relationship to the play of children. It is a complex process that requires total awareness or full consciousness to come into being. It has been said that in order to achieve creativity it is necessary that a holistic approach is taken. The process is about bringing something new into being, that is, order out of formlessness. Furthermore, this something new is the result of some sort of imagination, illusion or phantasy.

The drive to create operates alongside the conservative instinct. Thus creativity takes place in the context of our world of reality. Creative experience is first manifested in play. In play the infant links his imagined objects with the real world, a process to be distinguished from phantasy which has no relation to the external world. This linking is what has been termed imagination, which develops from early in life and takes place in the transitional space. The transitional space is concerned with symbols and is the place where symbols are used for the different concepts of experience – the primary and secondary processes.

It is through these two processes that we begin to understand the processes of imagination and hence creativity. It is from this point that my original view of creativity is developed. My view is that the inner world of imagination is the world of the primary process. It is here that we have the freedom to create and it is this activity that resembles play. However, to be in touch with the primary process requires a total awareness or a holistic approach. The primary process has the ability to organise patterns out of formlessness; being unconscious activity, it is not restricted by the limitations imposed on secondary process activity. The difficulty arises when the 'creation' is brought into consciousness, here secondary process activity becomes dominant. This may result in anxiety arising from feelings about being wrong or mad, or whatever, which may in turn result in denial, for example.

Anxiety is seldom mentioned in regard to creativity but here it is regarded as an important consideration. Our conscience that is instructing us what we may or may not do is developed from the world of our reality. Consequently, the process of creativity may well result in conflict with our conscience which will be instructing us how we ought to behave. Such conflict will inevitably be experienced as the poignant suffering that we know as guilt.

Thus to be creative we need a good deal of courage but, above all, we need to be secure. This means, to use Winnicott's term, there must be a good enough 'holding environment'. The view taken here is that there is not only a succession of holding environments throughout life but that we all belong to multiple holding environments. Whether they are good enough to provide the 'basic trust' required will determine if creativity will occur. Finally, the process of creativity is a difficult process that may be inhibited by or result in guilt and anxiety; it will also inevitably result in loss as well as gain.

These concepts will be further developed in the next chapter when I return to and develop the psycho-dynamic explanation of organisational culture.

11

A PSYCHO-DYNAMIC EXPLANATION OF ORGANISATIONAL CULTURE II

The previous chapters in this section have provided the reader with an understanding of some of the fundamental concepts concerned with human behaviour that is necessary if we are to begin to understand organisational culture. In this chapter these concepts will be further developed and applied to the theory first outlined in Chapter 3 to provide a fuller and more technical explanation of a psychodynamic explanation of organisational culture.

Where better to start with any detailed explanation of psychodynamic phenomena than with Freud (1921), who asserted at the very beginning of his 'Group Psychology and the Analysis of the Ego' that there was no real difference between individual and group psychology. There can be little doubt, as Bion (1961) has stated, that the interrelatedness of the individual and the group is a key concept. Indeed, the overview of the very first relationship, that of the infant with the mother, provides vital information regarding culture.

THE MATERNAL HOLDING ENVIRONMENT

In order to provide the right context for what follows I shall need to return briefly to some of the aspects of infant development previously referred to. I shall start with the notion that to understand how culture develops, we first need to consider the most basic of all relationships – the aspect of holding. This relationship characterises the merged state when the baby and mother are not yet separated out in the baby's rudimentary mind. It is through this relationship that the infant experiences a sense of being. The infant's sense of being relies on the capacity of the mother (who is a part of the infant) to be someone 'who is' and not someone 'who does', until the infant is ready to initiate the doing. Out of these primitive beginnings comes object relating in terms of the infant's creation of the mother and the mother's care, made possible by the mother doing the right things at the right time – that is, when the infant is ready for it.

Holding is 'the basis for what gradually becomes a self-experiencing being'. The very young infant does not recognise his mother as a distinct entity. He nevertheless forms particular expectations in respect to that element in his environment that succours him. Winnicott found a particular need to emphasize the actual nature of the concrete environment, especially at the stage of absolute dependence. The importance of 'good enough' holding is shown by the fact that there is no emotional or physical survival of an infant minus environment. The baby's use of the non-human environment depends upon the previous use of a human environment.

When Winnicott says there is never just an infant, he does not mean only that someone has to attend to and take care of this small creature. He means that if there is a thriving infant he or she comes 'attached to' another person. As Bowlby (1969) has so clearly shown in the successful attachment of baby and mother, one sees that the baby is endowed with a host of abilities that seduce the mother – the baby's grasp of the mother's garment, his orientation to her eyes – and that the mother is able to attend to this beguiling and is won over. Here we have clear data to support a two-way process. It is not a case of the mother acting as an autonomous holding agent, it is, even at this stage, an interrelationship. As Winnicott pointed out, the infant creates the mother.

Bion's (1963) formulations of these processes are also valuable. His view of this interrelationship is of the mother seen as a container who can contain what the baby projects and work with it, her capacity for what he calls 'reverie' being crucial. Bion also discussed the role of the mother in helping the baby develop his own capacity for thinking and so become more able to deal with these situations himself. Of this, he pointed out that the prior experience is of having thoughts particularly provoked by maternal absence and frustration and thinking is a development forced on the psyche by the necessity for dealing with thoughts. He also observed that if this process does not take place effectively the baby tends to introject not a comforting, progressive experience but what he called a nameless dread, severe contentless anxiety.

Very important in these interactions is the mother's capacity to feel what the baby feels and respond appropriately. This implies that she should have enough capacity to take in the baby's massive projections of intense feelings and phantasies, to accept them without undue diminishment through denials or other defences, and not be physically overwhelmed by them as the baby feels he will be. The 'good enough' mother values and respects the reality of his feelings while making a more reality-based assessment of their phantasy content.

The aspect of 'good enough' holding is important to both personality development, and, as we have seen in Chapter 3, to the development of culture. The issue of holding can be examined with respect not only to the fundamental question as to whether the infant is held, but to the question of how the infant is held. How the child is held or 'hosted' may raise questions not of whether he will continue to function but of how he will. Among these questions one of the most important might be how the child comes to experience anxiety. Or, more specifically, how does the mother respond to the infant's anxiety? Is the response essentially to the anxiety or to the person who is feeling anxious? Response to the anxiety will be experienced by the infant to come from himself, whereas response to the infant may result in continuing dependency.

How the infant is held will also depend on the infant, as is pointed out by Winnicott. The capacity to form images and to use these constructively by recombination into new patterns is dependent on the individual's ability to trust. The word 'trust' in this context shows an understanding by the building up of confidence based on experience, before the enjoyment and employment of separation and independence. The potential space between baby and mother, between child and family, between individual and society or the world, depends on experience which leads to trust. That is to say, there is a mutuality of experience or an overlap of potential spaces. Where there is not a basic trust it may not be possible to develop or maintain a capacity to experience a relationship to external reality.

Menzies Lyth (1988) has explained, although not explicitly, that children in hospital need a holding environment that can contain them. In her research she identified the need for close spatial boundaries in hospital, something comprehensible for the infant to identify with as 'my' place or 'our' place. She found that if the boundaries are drawn too wide or there are no boundaries the children are not able to identify with the holding environment. Small children need this holding together within a bounded space but also by attached people in terms of consistency in modes of response. Consistent testing of reality helps to build an effective identity.

The self-system is thus structured by the internalisation of the relationship with mother and child, undifferentiated at the start then progressively separated throughout the long period of human dependence. Individual and environment are structured by, and within, each other. Early structuring of the personality is inevitably dominated by the physical closeness in which the mother's attitudes are communicated through innumerable signals in her whole handling of, and responses to, her child. The emotional experiences are gradually cohered by consistent reliable mothering into a 'primary or central self' reference. This integration is a labile process with threats to it producing at times intense anxiety and aggression.

Another process that comes into being during the period of maternal holding is that of identification. It will be recalled that Freud referred to identification as the earliest expression of an emotional tie with another person, and that it is by identifying with the parents that the child adopts their standards and values. Identification brings into play such functions as adaptation to reality, reality testing, sense of reality, the self-concept (with its self and object representations) and the capacity to form object relations.

Moving rapidly on we have seen how the growing child passes through a series of identifications, constantly changing and shifting, creating out of bits of personalities of others the unique mosaic of the self. The individual is part of a group from earliest infancy – initially a group of two, the mother–infant dyad; then a group of three or more as the existence of father and siblings have to be accommodated; later a series of overlapping family and social groups. These coexist in external reality and the developing individual's internal world.

Many of the possessions of his world are part of a shared reality. The infant relies on other people and possessions to be predictable and act in many ways as an extension of himself. Fairbairn has described how, from the outset, the self-system is structured by the internalisation of the relationship with mother and child. Thus we can see how the child originally internalises the relationship with the mother, including the language, and then as he matures and learns to communicate with his elders and his peers he learns certain modes and manners of expressing himself and fulfilling his requirements, and he also learns to expect consistent behaviour from others. In other words, he requires the continuity, consistency and confirmation of his world that Kernberg (1966) refers to.

In order to ensure the healthy development in the individual in terms of the continuity, consistency and confirmation required, there is a need for the establishment of firm boundaries for the self and others across which realistic and effective relationships and transactions can take place and within which one's own identity can be established. In order to achieve this the individual needs to develop a categorical framework, as it is only in this way that it is possible for him to produce anything of his own that is intelligible to others. Organised life is organised in the minds of all who participate in it and this organisation takes place by means of a conceptual framework, even though they may not be aware of the framework. Through learning the language we learn the local customs and assumptions, so the programming with which our identity is constituted is in effect our linguistic programming, our induction into the network of human associations.

Erikson spoke of ego identity as 'a sense that the ego is learning effective steps toward a tangible collective future, that it is developing into a defined ego within a social reality' (1959, p. 22). Learning the language and hence the conceptual framework of that social reality provides us with the necessary continuity for a tangible collective future. This is important because the sense of an ego identity is based on the common perception of an individual's self sameness and continuity in time, together with the perception that meaningful people recognise this self sameness and continuity. This is not to deny the fact that identity is constantly being negotiated, but we should not forget Jacobson's concept of 'the capacity to remain the same in the midst of change' (1964, p. 23).

Soon the process of learning brings with it a high regard for possessions, for loved objects, and later, for ideal causes and loyalties. We are speaking here of whatever objects a person calls 'mine'. As we grow older we identify with groups, neighbourhood and nation, as well as with possessions, clothes, home. They become matters of importance to us in a sense that other people's families, nations or possessions are not. The ego, according to Freud, has the task of keeping the organism as a whole in touch with reality, of mediating between unconscious impulses and the outer world.

To summarise, we can now better understand why Bion stated that the human individual was a group animal (albeit at war with his own 'groupishness'), the study of whom one needed binocular vision: that the individual is required to be looked at from the position of the group and the group from the position of the individual; that there was a 'socio-' and a 'psycho-' perspective; and that they were interdependent. The postulated situation where the person at the personal or psychological level could be viewed as an organism perpetually requiring, and seeking, personal relationships for his development and maintenance. Of this relationship of the individual with the group Bion agrees with Freud that a group 'instinct' is not primitive and that much of his groupishness originates in his upbringing within the family.

ORGANISATIONAL HOLDING ENVIRONMENTS

Much of the foregoing has necessarily been in regard to the development of the individual. I now want to refer to organisations. The 'nature of organisations' was fully dealt with in Chapter 4; however, it is perhaps important that we recall some of the more significant aspects. Freud spoke of intense identification of group members with both the leader and the group as a whole. In his view this resulted in a 'psychic cement', which, although operating outside awareness, often leads to a common ideal. Identity with a group entity goes beyond the mere perception of it and the investing of it with some emotional meaning, for identification in this sense also contains an element of responding or, more specifically, an element of individual commitment. To belong to or to feel part of a group (some people have used the term ego involved) also implies a more or less transitory giving up of some aspect of the individual's self (or self-schema) to the group as a group.

Group identification has been defined as a set of pre-conscious and unconscious attitudes which incline each member to apperceive the group as an extension of himself and impel him to remain in direct contact with the other members and to adhere to the group standards. The result of an individual's group identification is that he reacts to the attributes of the group as if these attributes were also his own. While the belief in the group is a powerful belief on the part of its members, it is important to recall that it is only a perceived object or an illusion. For Anzieu (1984) the group illusion corresponds to the founding moment in which the group is formed. It becomes a group when it is gripped with the collective imaginative belief that the group exists, as a reality that is both immanent and transcends each of them.

I now want to add to this previous discussion by building on the concept of an organisation as a holding environment. Erikson (1959) provides us with an indication of the way that organisations are used for reality testing when he illustrates how the synthesising function of the group constantly works on subsuming fewer and fewer images, thus making it possible that the whole frightening world of infinite variability becomes manageable and bearable. In synthesising, the group employs mechanisms of condensation and pictorial representation which characterise the products of collective imagery. This is reinforced by the universal trend of groups towards some form of uniformity including literally special uniforms or distinctive clothing through which incomplete self-certainty, for a time, can hide in a group certainty.

The close link between personality and culture is illustrated by several writers. For example, Schindler (1952) refers to group formation as the development of a 'group personality'. He thought that this 'common denominator' of the individual group member's characteristics could be divided into a group id, ego and super-ego. For Schindler the group id pertains to common needs such as security or pleasure. The super-ego refers to perceptions of the father leader and mother group, while the ego 'registers' the id and the super-ego functions and judges whether or not they serve the group's purposes.

Relating to group relations training, Schindler observes that the personalities of group members construct a group first around a common agency, for example, the id, ego or super-ego; then they do so around an organising unconscious phantasy or imago. He points out that this agency and this organisation may or may not be appropriate for realising the goals ascribed to or assumed by the group. Other factors affecting the group's destiny include the composition of the group, its educational level and the degree of contact between members, as well as the attitudes of other groups and the overall social context. These are matters that will be commented on again shortly.

Anzieu (1984) notes that regression provoked by the group often goes beyond the Oedipal structure on which Freud based his application of psycho-analysis to culture. He noted that this situation mobilises archaic persecutory and depressive anxieties linked to the dual relation to the mother. The group illusion in this regressive situation is precisely the counterpart of these archaic anxieties, just as for the infant, the phantasy of fusion with the good mother is the counterpart of the phantasies of the bad breast and the bad object. 'We are all good objects in the womb of the good mother and we all love one another in her as she loves and gives birth to, feeds and cares for us' (1984, p. 153). The group elicits the phantasy that participants are equal at the all-powerful and self-sufficient breast of the mother experienced as part object.

The problem of the individual coming to terms with the emotional life of the group was likened by Bion to that of the infant in its first relationship, viz, with the breast-mother. The group identity can become for the individual the symbolic representation of a nurturing mother. Terms such as mother earth and motherland and even Alma Mater are of relevance here. In a broader sense the hypothesis can be advanced that the universal need to belong, to establish a state of psychological unity with others, represents a covert wish for restoring an earlier state of unconflicted well being inherent in the exclusive union with mother.

Money-Kyrle (1950) was the first to introduce the perception of a mother image in group formation. That the need and yearning for a 'good' mother exists in the very core of our being has been posited above. As has also been said, there is a similar need and yearning for a father figure and for siblings, and, consequently, for the family as a group. It seems perfectly reasonable to conclude that the early holding environments are clearly very influential in our development and that they will subsequently affect our adult behaviour.

I now want to look at the relatedness of the group to the holding environment. In much the same way that the infant relates to the maternal holding environment, so the members of an organisation relate to the organisational holding environment. If the holding environment is 'good enough', that is (in simple terms), if the primary task is clear enough and achievable, the culture that develops will be task supportive. However, where, for any one of a variety of reasons, the holding environment is not 'good enough' there may be regression or an anti-task culture.

Provided that there is a good enough holding environment, the anxiety of venturing into the unknown, the process by which maturation provokes change, is not fundamentally disruptive. The anxiety can be dominated, just because the thread of continuity has not been broken, and can always be given a reassuring tug. Conceived in this way, the idea of growth does not contradict the assumption of a conservative impulse. If there is a hierarchy of needs, and the urge to explore new kinds of satisfaction is only released when we feel confident that more basic needs are assured, then spontaneous growth follows from the consolidation of familiar patterns of expectation. The reactions of conservatism are latent, because no threat to the established structure of meaning provokes them.

In situations where the group members perceive the organisational holding environment to be good enough and to have basic trust in it, we shall have progression. Progression means not just differentiation but differentiation and reintegration, a process which is essentially that of adaptation: a differentiation from that which was the very subject of my personal organisation and which becomes thereby the object of a new organisation on behalf of a new subjectivity that co-ordinates it. We are vulnerable every time to a qualitatively new kind of separation anxiety. Paradoxically, we have the fear of being completely unseparate, of being swallowed up and taken over; and the fear of being totally separate, of being utterly alone, abandoned and remote beyond recall.

Recurring issues of differentiation and integration throughout life come to be understood as the consequence or reflections of the

earliest period. Subject-object relations emerge out of a lifelong process of development: a succession of qualitative differentiations of the
self from the world, with a qualitatively more extensive object with
which to be in relation created each time. These processes are highly
significant in regard to the development and, more particularly, the
perpetuation of culture and will be referred to in greater detail later
in this chapter.

Group relations training provides valuable information in regard
to the interrelatedness of the group and the holding environment.
Scheidlinger (1980) tells us that there always develops rapidly an
underlying common group problem, a common group tension of
which the group is not aware, but which determines its behaviour.
This common group tension seems to represent what he calls the
common denominator of the dominant unconscious fantasies of all
members. He describes how a remark made by one member is often
not taken up by anybody, apparently because nobody can fit it into
what is unconsciously at the back of his mind, then gradually a
subject catches on and becomes the unconsciously determined topic
of the group until the next interpretation produces closure of this
particular phase of the session.

Although he does not specifically state it as being so, what
Scheidlinger is describing is the formation of the group culture: the
development of the culture out of the relatedness to the holding
environment. Especially useful here is Bion's idea that the individual in
some sense always reflects the needs of the group. At least during some
periods it is as if the group was speaking through many voices and the
particular individual whose vocal chords are thus utilised may be functioning primarily on behalf of the group. Every group member takes up
a particular role characteristic for his personality structure, because of
the particular unconscious fantasy of group relations he entertains in his
mind and which he tries to solve through appropriate behaviour in the
group. Furthermore, every group requires and gets certain people to act
as containers for its conservative wishes on the one hand and its
progressive wishes on the other hand.

Bion (1961) has described how a certain group culture puts pressure on different individuals to take a certain role; for example, the
fight group requires a fighting leader. Building on this view,
Armelius and Armelius (1985) believe (as did Schindler) that the
individual group composition may be considered as a resource that
the group has for creating different group cultures. In turn, the
group culture that actually develops in the group will influence the
behaviour of each individual member in the group. Some people are

more likely to act in a pairing culture than others, and these people will contribute more to that culture than the others, who may merely support the culture by their passive acceptance. The individual thus influences and is influenced by the group culture.

In some respects this is correct: that is, the culture will be affected by the composition of the group. However, what is not said is that the composition alone does not create the culture. It seems clear that the composition of the group could change, yet this would not result in a corresponding change to the culture. The culture is created by the interrelatedness of the group of individuals (of whatever composition) and the organisational holding environment. The result of that interrelatedness is the group or organisational culture.

This relatedness is perhaps best demonstrated by further references to group relations training. Regression in such groups is triggered by a lack of structure; the group leader refuses to act like a chairman, and since norms of behaviour in a meeting require a chairman to act in a way consonant with them, the group leader's behaviour makes them inoperative. The group is then perceived as an unstructured and therefore confluent global object, which comes to represent the mother of a very small child who is so much bigger than her baby. This kind of transference activates a state of the self in each of the group's members (or lack thereof) which, to a certain extent, corresponds to the state of self of a baby.

The concept of relatedness to the holding environment also provides clarification of Bion's basic assumption activities. Where the holding environment is perceived by the members, at that time, as not being good enough, I believe that they regress to a temporary position where they behave 'as if' they were in the maternal holding environment. It is the interrelatedness of the group with the holding environment that produces what Bion (1961) has called the basic assumption culture. This is made clearer by Sutherland (1985) who describes how the group dominated by an assumption evolves an appropriate culture to express it: for example, the dependent group establishes a leader who is felt to be helpful in supplying what it wants. Moreover the assumptions can be strong enough for members to be controlled by them to the extent of their thinking and behaviour becoming almost totally unrealistic in relation to the work task.

The group is then for each member an undifferentiated whole into which he is pressed inexorably to conform and in which each has lost his independent individuality. It will be recalled that when a group is operating in a basic assumption mode it is using concrete symbols or symbolic equations; it is not able to use true symbols.

This is an indication that there is a regression to the paranoid-schizoid position as indicated by Bion above. In this position the child is highly dependent on the maternal holding environment. Thus we can view the three basic assumption activities in that light. Bion himself pointed out that the basic assumptions in the group crystallised for him replicas of the emotions with which the infant related to the mother and, later, the family.

BASIC ASSUMPTION 'CULTURES'

I feel that it is important to distinguish basic assumption activity, in general, from the underlying group or organisational culture. Sutherland (1985) informs us that the function of basic assumptions is to defend the group against anxieties of primitive fantasies becoming too intense. In this respect they are basic underlying defences available to be mobilized at any time. They do not conflict with each other; rather, they change from one to another and the fact that conflict only occurs between them and the work group serves to emphasise the point.

I totally accept that under certain conditions an organisation culture may be dominated by and be characterised by one or other of the basic assumption activities, but I consider that it is misleading to refer to basic assumption activities in general terms as 'cultures'. The temporary nature of such activities is apparent by the fact that by showing the group how it is using basic assumption activity to avoid its task, it can become more task orientated. In this regard, and to distinguish both processes, I prefer to refer to basic assumption activities as 'temporary cultures' or, better still, simply as 'activities'.

'NOT GOOD ENOUGH' HOLDING ENVIRONMENTS

I now want to look at some examples of the effects of relatedness of groups with holding environments that are 'not good enough'. The phenomena described – for example, scapegoating – are not in any way new. However, looked at in the light of the explanation of culture provided here, I believe this sheds new light on these known phenomena. Furthermore, it provides additional support for the view being put forward.

It was mentioned above that progression means differentiation and reintegration. Integration without differentiation solidifies but does not lead to group formation. The forming of larger aggregates, with loss of function of the components and rigidity of structure as a whole, is not integration but aggregation. We see this phenomenon before our eyes every day in bureaucracy and institutionalisation. The bureaucratic organisation disintegrates into fragments when what little information it can transmit to its various levels, due to its low degree of integration, blocks up the channels of transmission. In a mature situation (which will be described shortly), group formation increases differentiation and allows its participants greater freedom within the group than they have as separate individuals: all integration is based upon this fact. It provides greater opportunities for mutuality of experience and overlapping of potential spaces which will lead to progression.

In this situation we can see the effects of a not good enough holding environment that we choose to call a bureaucracy. Because of its fragmentary nature and lack of communication it does not provide the basic trust required of a good enough holding environment. The result is that there is no progression; the interrelatedness of the members of the organisation with the holding environment results in a regressive or concrete culture.

A further example is where frustration at the lack of a good enough holding environment engenders aggression, and when it cannot be discharged against the frustrating object – namely, the leader. It is redirected (displaced) toward substitutes. In addition to people, inanimate objects, particularly those associated in some way with the frustrating agents, may be used. Thus the destruction of property, such as furniture, walls, floors and appliances, is quite often the result of displaced aggression originally intended for one or more persons or even to institutions – such as government – which one feels impotent to influence. Here is an example of adults behaving in almost the same manner as children who are frustrated by the maternal holding environment. The perceived view of the members of the organisation is that the holding environment is not good enough; they do not have basic trust and become frustrated. In infantile terms they throw a tantrum.

Similarly, the phenomenon of scapegoat formation is a manifestation of the displacement of aggressive impulses upon an individual or a group. It occurs most often when the expression of these impulses against the substitute object seems less fraught with imagined or real danger than their direct expression. We can see here similarities with the infant who uses splitting to project the bad part object. Again, the perception of the group is that the holding environment is not good enough and thus they resort to less mature, infantile behaviour.

Freud (1921) made some interesting observations about the disintegration of a group through panic. Contrary to the assumption of others, he asserted that the primary factor here was not the degree of outside danger or conflict confronting the group, but rather the breakdown of libidinal ties within it. It is of the very essence of panic that it bears no relation to the danger that threatens, and often breaks out upon the most trivial occasions. According to Freud, such primarily egocentric demeanour – self-love instead of love for others – can be observed in groups which are in the process of disintegration, where the state of the group is such that they do not perceive the existence of a holding environment; where they feel, in infantile terms, that the mother has deserted them. As has been so vividly demonstrated in the former Yugoslavia, it seems that panic is an entirely natural response to such a situation.

As Menzies Lyth (1988) points out, unfortunately for task performance, members of institutions are also likely to seek satisfaction of personal needs that are anti-task; very often they need to mitigate the stresses and strains of the task itself and of confrontation with the human material on which the task is focused. She also informs us that members try to establish a 'social system that also acts as a defence against anxiety', both personal anxiety and that evoked by institutional membership. Jaques (1955) has referred to a 'socially structured defence system'. This will appear in all aspects of the institution, both formal and informal; in attitudes and interpersonal relations, in customs and conventions; and also, very importantly, in the actual formal social structure of the organisation and its management system. The danger, according to Menzies Lyth, is that since the anxieties defended against are primitive and violent, defences will also be primitive.

What Menzies Lyth, and for that matter Jaques, are describing here is a situation where the interrelatedness of the group members and the holding environment is such that it is perceived with anxiety. The response to this anxiety results in a culture that will allay the fears of the group. The fact that this is anti-task is not a concern for the members. The logic is not in the supporting of the organisational task but in developing a culture that defends against the anxiety. The function of culture is to enable the members of the organisation to produce forms of behaviour which will be advantageous to them under the conditions imposed by their environment.

As well as creative and happy moments, some of the team meetings and seminars of the police internal consultants experienced tensions, crises and ruptures. I came to the conclusion that what was occurring was a notion of 'phantasies of break-up', this being the specifically group version of the hateful envy conceptualised by Melanie Klein. The anxiety aroused by breaking-apart phantasies can perhaps be best understood if we look at the situation of the infant.

At a pre-genital level, it is a separation anxiety. The child who grows up resents his dependence on his mother and projects on to her his wish to be rid of her; he phantasises a bad mother who rejects her children as a bad object or lets them kill one another. What is broken apart here is the symbiotic bond between mother and child. In other words, there is a lack of basic trust in the maternal holding environment. In like manner, there was a lack of basic trust in the holding environment of the internal consultants.

Change is inevitably to some extent an excursion into the unknown. It implies a commitment to future events that are not entirely predictable and to their consequences, and inevitably provokes doubt and anxiety. Any significant change within a social system implies changes in existing social relationships and social structure. It therefore implies a change in the culture. The social system, the holding environment, which was previously related to by the group members, is now threatening to exist (or is now existing) in a different form. In maternal holding environment terms, this would be the same as losing or changing our mother, or the no less anxiety-provoking thought that she suddenly changed in some way.

All changes are encounters with circumstances, sensations and emotions, for which our previous life experience cannot fully have prepared us. According to Rycroft:

> Anxiety is the expectation of something as yet unknown. Since the unknown for human beings includes alienated unconscious parts of themselves, this as-yet-unknown may be either inside or outside themselves and the same emotion, anxiety, may be evoked by either subjective or objective occurrences. The fact that anxiety is evoked by the as-yet-unknown means that all novel experiences tend to be preceded by anxiety, regardless of whether we anticipate that the experience will be pleasant or distressing. (1968a, p. 15)

Having covered much ground it may be useful to try to pull together some of the more pertinent points. In the same way that Winnicott would say that 'there is not just an infant' we can say that 'there is not just a group'. The group and the environment are structured by and within each other. It is a dynamic process that is constantly changing at both the cultural and holding environment levels. It is through the interrelatedness of the group members and the organisational holding environment that the members develop the group culture. How the culture develops will depend on the way in which the holding environment is perceived.

PERPETUATION OF CULTURE

I want now to look at the issue of how culture is perpetuated. The first point I should stress is that culture (like personality) is a process rather than a thing, it is constantly evolving into new forms. The next point is that without some system of reducing our experiences to familiar form we should be imprisoned in the uniqueness of the here and now. Thus we see that, on the one hand, culture is dynamic and changing, but, on the other hand, there is a need for some system of making sense out of total chaos. In effect, we are talking about the processes of differentiation and integration which were referred to earlier.

I have referred previously to the fact that the main characteristic of object relations when the depressive position has been reached is that the object is felt as a whole object. In connection with this there is a greater degree of awareness of differentiation and of the separateness of the ego and the object. Here I want to expand on this part of the developmental process to provide a background to understanding how culture is perpetuated.

According to Fairbairn: 'Ego development is characterised by a process whereby an original state of infantile dependence based upon primary identification with the object is abandoned in favour of adult or mature dependence based upon differentiation of the object from the self.' He further explains this as follows:

> It would not be wrong to say that psychologically speaking, identification with the object and infantile dependence are but two aspects of the same phenomenon. On the other hand, mature dependence involves a relationship between two independent individuals, who are completely differentiated from one another as mutual objects. The more mature a relationship is, the less it is characterised by primary identification; for what such identification essentially represents is failure to differentiate the object. (1952, p. 163)

It is correct to speak here of mature dependence, rather than independence, since a relationship implies dependence of some sort. Fairbairn points out that what distinguished mature dependence from infantile dependence is that it is characterised neither by a one-sided attitude of incorporation nor by an attitude of primary emotional identification. On the contrary it is characterised by a capacity on the part of a differentiated individual for co-operative relationships with differentiated objects. That is, a relationship involving evenly matched giving and taking between two differentiated individuals who are mutually dependent, and between whom there is no disparity of dependence. This may be an ideal picture but it is one which is never completely realised.

Emotional maturity, like physical maturity, is an extremely complex matter. Winnicott (1988) makes the important point that the psyche becomes something that has a position from which to become related to external reality, becomes a thing with a capacity to create and perceive external reality, a qualitatively enriched being able to go further than can be explained by environmental influences, and able not only to adapt but also to refuse to adapt, and becomes a creature with what feels like a capacity for choice. According to Winnicott: 'Maturity means, among other things, a capacity for tolerating ideas, and parents need this capacity which at its best is part of a social maturity. A mature social system (while making certain demands in regard to action) allows freedom of ideas and the free expression of them' (1988, p. 59). This is a slow process and the child only gradually reaches the ability to distinguish between dream and reality. In maturity environment is something to which the individual contributes and for which the individual man or woman takes responsibility.

Much, however, can occur during the process of maternal holding that will affect the process of movement from infantile dependence to mature dependence. Winnicott reminds us that in the development of the psyche there is a possibility of failure at every point, and indeed there can be no such thing as growth without distortion due to some degree of failure of environmental adaptation. He observes that if organised defences against anxiety are more in evidence than the instincts and their conscious control and influence on action and imagination, then the clinical picture is of psycho-neurosis rather than of health. In like manner, Fairbairn points out that the persistence of a preponderating schizoid or depressive tendency arising during the stage of infantile dependency is reflected by (a) the schizoid (introvert), and (b) the depressive (extrovert).

For the infant there are fears of being completely unseparate, of being swallowed up and taken over: and conversely, the fear of being totally separate, of being utterly alone, abandoned and remote beyond recall. Should the maternal holding environment not provide the necessary basic trust the infant is unlikely to progress satisfactorily to adult dependence. The mother's ability to aid her child in this process is determined by the extent to which she can remain open to all responses from her child, whether she feels them to be bad or good. The ideal mother, of course, does not exist. Fortunately, however, our growth to maturity as individuals does not depend upon having perfect mothers: they only have to be good enough. The good enough mother responds automatically in a complex manner.

According to Symington (1986) a mother cannot find out what to do from books or from anyone else when her baby spontaneously reaches out towards her in gesture and action, especially at certain moments. A mother can be taught a lot; she can be shown how to hold the baby, how to feed the baby, how to wind the baby and how to bath the baby. However, only she can know how to respond when the baby gives her that strange look, makes a peculiar noise, suddenly throws his hand in the air or starts to look intently at some object in the room.

Faced with such a difficult situation the parents may not provide a good enough holding environment, and Winnicott's view that there is a possibility of failure at every point seems to be perfectly under-standable. Where, however, the maternal and later the family holding environments are perceived by the infant to be good enough, where there is basic trust, the infant will satisfactorily progress to mature dependence. Such trust will strongly influence the perception of the holding environment, and that trust will be based on the life experi-ences of the infant. Thus we return to the point that the individual and the environment are structured by and within each other.

It is not possible to state precisely what is a good enough holding environment, but we can say that it is made possible by the mother doing the right thing at the right time: that is, when the baby is ready for it. She provides the context in which development takes place. There is never complete integration – the individual and the environment are interdependent. There is no emotional or physical survival of an infant without environment, reliable holding has to be a feature of the environment if the child is to survive. Ego support continues in adult life, especially when there is anxiety. In the same way we cannot say precisely what is not a good enough holding environment but we do know that if this process does not take place effectively, the baby tends to introject not a comforting, progressive experience but – as has been said before – what Bion called a nameless dread, severe contentless anxiety.

In the same way that the maternal holding environment affects the development of adult maturity in the infant, so the organisational holding environment will affect the existence or otherwise of mature dependence in the group. Where the members of an organisation, or part of an organisation, have a basic trust and perceive the holding environment as good enough, there will exist a state of mature dependence. Where, however, the reverse applies, there may exist a state akin to infantile dependence. For ease of reference, and in typical categorising fashion, I shall henceforth refer to these situations as mature and immature.

In the mature situation the members of the organisation will be able to differentiate objects from the self and be able to take part in co-operative relationships with differentiated objects. In an immature situation, on the other hand, the members of the organisation will not be able to differentiate between themselves and objects, there will be a one-sided attitude of incorporation and an attitude of primary emotional identification. As change involves the very creating of new objects (a process of differentiation) as well as our relating to them (a process of integration), it is essential that a mature situation exists.

Where an immature situation exists there can be little or no progression. Differentiation not being possible, the culture will be perpetuated in the same form until such time as a mature situation exists. Where, however, a mature situation exists, the culture will provide for co-operative relationships between the members of the organisation and the organisational holding environment. Here the view of Jacobson is most applicable to the mature organisation: 'the capacity to remain the same in the midst of change' (1964, p. 23). We can thus see that in a mature organisation the culture will be perpetuated and characterised by gradual and smooth change because of the ability of the members to differentiate and to adapt to change. In the immature organisation the culture will be perpetuated with little or no change because the members are unable to differentiate and adapt – that is, until such time as the members develop an adult dependence.

Before I leave this discussion on perpetuation of culture I should like to refer back to Bion's basic assumption activities. Sutherland describes the situation of group members as follows: 'The group is for each member an undifferentiated whole into which he is pressed inexorably to conform and in which each has lost his independent individuality' (1985, p. 59). What is being described here is none other than what was described by Fairbairn as infantile dependency. This further convinces me that in the 'normal' use of the terminology we are referring to a temporary culture: it is a temporary regression from mature dependence by the use of the defence of infantile dependency, used in the way that Parkes described as providing not only a defence to the immediate anxiety but also time to adapt to the new reality.

REPRESENTATION OF CULTURE

I want now to look at how culture is represented. Much of what I have to say has already been referred to in the Chapter 6. However, there are still a few points to make. If we start from the position that the function of culture as a whole is to enable the members of the organisation, or part of the organisation, to produce forms of behaviour that will be advantageous to them under the conditions imposed by the environment, we can appreciate that there is a need to develop a categorical framework to represent those forms of behaviour. It is only in this way that the members of the group will be able to produce anything of their own which is intelligible to others.

Organised life is organised in the minds of all who participate in it and this organisation takes place by means of a conceptual framework even though they may not be aware of the framework. The world we respond to, or the world towards which we direct our behaviour, is the world as we symbolise it, or represent it to ourselves. Thus each group comes to have its own unique language, its own 'private language' or idiom. As Erikson reminds us, the synthesising function of the group constantly works on subsuming fewer and fewer images by employing mechanisms of condensation and pictorial representation.

Referring back to our discussion of perpetuation of culture it seems that where an immature situation exists and little progression is taking place, the opportunity exists to synthesise and develop a more and more private form of language. Where there is a mature situation the opportunities for adaptability and differentiation will result in a less concrete private language. The other point that needs restating in this context, is the point regarding concrete symbols or symbolic equations. Where there is regression to the paranoid-schizoid position there will not be progression: words will not be used as true symbols.

SOME PRACTICAL APPLICATIONS

I shall conclude this chapter with a brief look at how this knowledge can be used to look at organisational problems. Two similar cases show the benefit of such knowledge. The first is a well publicised situation of a city police crime squad; the other concerns a problem with a division of a conglomerate. In both cases the relevant part of the organisation was seen by the ruling coalition to be not performing well or, to put it more strongly, dysfunctional. They were seen to be 'out of line' with the main organisation. The view of those at the top was that the members of those parts of the organisation were the cause of the dysfunctional behaviour.

From our knowledge of how culture develops this does not seem a very helpful view as it does not take us any further than what we know. Simply allocating blame to those groups as if they were the cause without recognising that a deeper problem exists does not provide an explanation. By using the knowledge that the culture develops through the interrelatedness of the members with the holding environment, from their perception of the holding environment, it will be possible to analyse the cause more accurately. The sort of questions we need to ask are 'How did the division of the conglomerate and the city crime squad perceive their respective holding environments?', and, 'Why did they perceive them in this way?' The sort of answers that we might reasonably expect would be in the nature of: 'They don't care about us'; 'They don't understand us'; 'They don't even know we exist'; or, 'They don't care what we do.'

The answers to these sorts of questions will provide an answer to why those parts of the organisations were dysfunctional. It will provide us with not just an effect but, much more importantly, the cause. Armed with such information organisations may be able to prevent such occurrences happening again. On a general note, any organisation wishing to develop a task culture should pay particular attention to the holding environment, or, more particularly, to how the members perceive the holding environment, and any organisation wishing to positively influence the culture should aim to ensure that a mature situation exists.

We need to bear in mind, however, that organisational culture is influenced by unconscious feelings and fantasies and that the way to understand this is through deliberate intervention and the deciphering of the response. The way in which the consultant is used and experienced and also the feelings evoked in him may offer evidence of the underlying and unstated issues and feelings in the client system. By interacting with the organisation the consultant can gain an understanding of the unconscious level and hence the culture of the organisation. This is a matter that will be referred to in greater detail in the next chapter.

SUMMARY

Culture, like personality, is less a finished product than a transitive process. Both the process and the product are unique. Each culture is an idiom unto itself which develops in its own particular context and that context must be understood in order to comprehend the idiom. It is not possible to produce cultures to order, they are dynamic continua and the whole is more important than any of the parts. The important thing is to discover the processes by which they develop, grow and change.

The view taken here is that these processes are similar to those concerned with infant development. In particular, it is postulated that if we want to understand how culture develops we first need to consider the most basic of all relationships – the aspect of maternal holding.

The initial social reality is the maternal holding environment. Here the establishment of integration and the development of ego related-ness both rely upon good enough holding. Independence is never abso-lute; the healthy individual continues to be related to the environment in such a way that the individual and environment can be seen to be interdependent. Thus integration is never total or perfect and the environment constantly provides ego support and permits an adapta-tion to reality, reality testing, and a sense of reality which are just as important to the adult as to the infant. From here we develop the important view that several holding environments may exist at any given time. In the same way that the maternal holding environment influences the personality of the infant, so the organisational holding environment influences the culture.

Organisational culture develops out of the interrelatedness of the members of the group and the organisational holding environment. The characteristics of organisational culture are:

1. it is a psycho-social process;
2. it is a dynamic process;
3. it is evidenced by sameness and continuity;
4. it is unique to every organisation and part of an organisation;
5. it is influenced by conscious and unconscious processes;
6. it is such as will enable the members to produce forms of behaviour that will be advantageous to them under the conditions imposed by the environment.

Reliable holding is as vital to the members of an organisation as it is to the infant. Therefore to understand culture we need to understand the most basic of all relationships – the aspect of holding. Good enough holding is not to be seen purely in terms of the mother's actions, rather, it should be seen as an interrelationship between mother and infant. On the infant's side this will depend on trust based on his experience of the holding environment. Thus individual and environment are structured by, and within, each other. The individual is a group animal that is required to be looked at from the position of the group, and the group from the position of the individual.

On becoming an adult many of the holding environments will be organisational holding environments of varying kinds. The close link between personality and culture is illustrated by several writers who variously refer to a 'group personality', and groups are also linked to maternal or family holding environments. This may not be surprising as group members relate to the organisational holding environment in much the same way that infants relate to the maternal holding environment, and it is out of this interrelatedness that culture develops. Where the holding environment is perceived by the members of the organisation as good enough the anxiety of change will not be fundamentally disruptive. Where the holding environment is not perceived as good enough the resulting culture will more likely be characterised by infant-like behaviour, such as splitting resulting in scapegoating, and panic resulting in disintegration. In these circumstances the culture is likely to be anti-task.

A particular type of infant-like behaviour is the basic assumption activities described by Bion. These have also been referred to as 'cultures', which, it is suggested, is misleading. Consequently, these activities need to be distinguished from what is being described in this book as organisational culture. They do develop as a result of the interrelatedness of the members of the organisation with the holding environment as perceived at that time but will not normally be identical to the underlying culture of the organisation. In this regard, and to distinguish both processes, I refer to basic assumption activities as 'temporary cultures' or, better still, simply as 'activities'.

Ego development is characterised by a process whereby an original state of infantile dependence based on primary identification with the object is abandoned in favour of adult or mature dependence based upon differentiation of the object from the self. Infantile dependence is characterised by a one-sided attitude of incorporation and an attitude of primary emotional identification. Mature dependence is characterised by a capacity on the part of a differentiated individual for co-operative relationships with differentiated objects – by a relationship between two differentiated individuals who are mutually dependent and between whom there is no disparity of dependence.

Emotional maturity, just the same as physical maturity, is a complex matter: it means a capacity for tolerating ideas and for not only being able to adapt but also to choose not to adapt. In maturity, environment is something to which the individual contributes and for which he takes responsibility. Much, however, can occur during the process of maternal holding that will affect the process of movement from infantile dependence to mature dependence. It is not possible to specify what is good enough holding or, for that matter, what is not a good enough holding environment, but we do know that where there is not good enough holding it can result in psycho-neurosis rather than health.

In the same way that the maternal holding environment affects the development of mature dependence in the infant, so the organisational holding environment will affect the existence or otherwise of mature dependence in the group. In the mature situation the culture will be perpetuated and characterised by gradual and smooth change because of the ability of the members to differentiate and to adapt to change. In the immature situation the culture will be perpetuated with little or no change because the members are unable to differentiate and adapt. As change involves the very creating of new objects (a process of differentiation) as well as our relating to them (a process of integration) it is essential that a mature situation exists.

Representation of culture is chiefly by the use of words and language used as symbols. Each culture is represented by its own unique language, its own private language or idiom. Where an immature situation exists there is more opportunity to synthesise and develop a more and more private form of language. Mechanisms of condensation and pictorial representation are more likely in view of the lack of adaptability. In the mature situation the opportunities for adaptability and differentiation will result in a less concrete private language.

Knowledge of how culture develops provides the opportunity to analyse the cause of organisational problems more accurately. We need to bear in mind, however, that culture is influenced by unconscious feelings and fantasies and that the way to understanding is through deliberate intervention and the deciphering of the responses. These are matters that will be dealt with in the next part which will build on the theoretical explanations provided in this, by applying the various concepts to the management of change.

PART III

APPLICATION OF THE CONCEPT OF ORGANISATIONAL CULTURE TO THE MANAGEMENT OF CHANGE

This book is essentially about two interrelated areas of research. The first is the development of an explanation of the concept of organisational culture, which was mainly dealt with in Part I. The second is the application of the concept of organisational culture to the management of change, which is the main topic of this part. However, it will be appreciated that these matters are interrelated and cannot be treated in isolation. This is also the case in this part, in which I apply the theory, as developed, first to managing organisational change, and, second, to a case study.

In Chapter 12 the developed theory is applied to managing organisational change in a theoretical manner. Here I look at how it can be seen to affect learning, symbolism, creativity, boundaries, and socialisation. I also look at the role of the consultant and his relation to culture. Here there is a further development and explanation of the proposition, first referred to in Chapter 2, that it is not possible to establish both the conscious and unconscious aspects of the culture without deliberate intervention and the deciphering of the responses to the consultant. Seen from the perspective of personality, this seems an obvious remark. We could no more determine the personality of an individual merely by observing him than we could determine the nature of an organisation merely by observing it. It is only when there is a direct intervention that we can determine either personality or culture.

The psycho-dynamic model provides us with a means of examining the transference and counter-transference within the relationship between consultant and clients. Action research provides the opportunity to engage the client system in a manner which provides similar results to personal psycho-analysis. So that the manner in which the consultant is used and experienced will provide the consultant with important information in regard to unconscious processes.

This and the previous findings are then applied to an organisational case study. In Chapter 13 I describe my findings in regard to culture when working in the capacity of internal consultant, carrying out an action research project in the Metropolitan Police Service. This project involved working with several different groups over a period of more than a year. The findings provide valuable data not only on the process of managing change but also on the nature of police culture.

12

MANAGING
ORGANISATIONAL CHANGE

By way of introduction to this chapter I want to add a further clarification regarding culture. In referring to how culture develops I noted the interrelatedness of the individual members of the organisation with their holding environment. The members of the organisation (or group) are, of course, inseparable from the holding environment. The group and the holding environment are structured by and within each other. However, the culture and the holding environment must be distinguished from each other. In like manner, the culture is inseparable from the personality; the culture and personality are structured by and within each other, but they are conceptually distinct. Despite their interrelatedness, the personality is no more identical to the culture than the culture is to the holding environment. Thus, we can perhaps better understand the unique nature of culture.

This clarification leads to the inference that in many ways the culture can be seen 'as if' it were the 'personality of the organisation'. The effect of culture on members of the group is comparable to the effect of personality on the individual. For example, where the individual has experienced his holding environment as good enough his personality may develop to the extent that he is capable of progression. Where, however, the holding environment is not experienced as good enough his personality may lack the confidence for progression, or at least for rapid progression.

Because we are all unique we all react to experiences in different ways. Some of us would find that we could not easily adapt to the culture shock of a difficult socialisation experience, or withstand the anxieties of third-level learning (Learning Two), or have the courage to be creative, whereas others might take all of these activities in their stride and with a minimum of anxiety. In other words, some will have developed satisfactorily from infantile dependence to mature dependence while others may have done so less satisfactorily. In the same manner, there are organisations which, as noted in the last chapter, may be classed as mature and others as immature, both of which have developed corresponding cultures.

In this respect, we can also regard culture 'as if it were the personality of the organisation. What we are concerned with in regard to managing change is whether the culture is mature or immature and this will depend on whether the members of the organisation experience the holding environment as good enough or not. In general, we may say that where they experience it to be good enough the culture that develops will be mature, thus permitting progression, but where the contrary exists it will be immature and be inclined to regression.

The difficulty that we have is in establishing the degree of maturity in either a personality or a culture. On the face of things, an individual or a group may, at a conscious level, espouse their willingness and ability to be adaptable. However, we need to be aware that aspects of ourselves may be denied, suppressed or disowned and become more or less unconscious. Ideas may be unconscious because they are repressed owing to their unthinkable nature deriving from a memory, thought or feeling which conflicts with our view of ourselves and what is acceptable. Thus we can see that on the face of things an organisation, or part of an organisation, may appear to be mature but, when examined at the unconscious level, it may prove to be immature.

One other introductory point I should make is that when we refer to culture we refer to the group as a whole. Individuals in a culture take on the roles that are imposed by the culture and an individual may speak for the membership as a whole. The group may perceive the holding environment in many different ways: for example, as a warm loving mother, a stern and strict father, or a highly competitive family. The way the group relates to the consultant will provide data in regard to how they relate to the holding environment, that is, it will provide data in regard to the culture. Culture is as deep-seated and all-pervading in regard to the members of the organisation (or group) as personality is in regard to the individual. In looking at the effects of culture in regard to managing change I shall particularly consider how it affects learning, symbolism, creativity, boundaries and socialisation. I shall also look at the role of the consultant and his relation to the culture. But I shall start by looking at the effect of culture on different types of change.

THE EFFECTS OF DIFFERENT TYPES OF CHANGE

In discriminating between different kinds of change, we can say that at one end of the spectrum there are those changes which are incremental or substitutional and where the culture is not disrupted. The change is routine, in the sense that the reorganisation seems compatible with the established meaning of life, and adds or subtracts very little. Whatever needs to be learned can be assimilated easily. Here we are talking about change that involves a level of learning akin to Bateson's Zero Learning. In theory this sort of change should not be difficult in most cultures. However, where there is an immature situation, and the anxiety is exceptionally high, the organisation is likely to regress even in such circumstances.

From this simple type of change, there is a range of changes right through to the most complicated or disruptive at the other end of the spectrum where the effect of the change is that the continuity of the culture is totally broken. In these circumstances, even where the most mature of cultures exists there will be a likelihood of regression unless the change is managed with considerable skill. In view of the potential difficulties in managing such changes, it is this kind of change that I shall mainly refer to in this chapter.

Change is inevitably to some extent an excursion into the unknown. Even the simplest change described above implies a commitment to future events that are not entirely predictable and may well provoke doubt and anxiety. Menzies Lyth informs us that, 'any significant change within a social system implies changes in existing social relationships and social structure' (1988, p. 62). Bearing in mind the all-pervading nature of culture, it follows that any significant social or structural change implies a change in the culture. Despite the many popular accounts of culture, or perhaps because of them, it is not always recognised by consultants or organisations that in almost every change we must take account of the culture.

One of the consequences of ignoring the culture is that a simplistic approach is taken. As Menzies Lyth (1988) has pointed out, they get some kind of experts in who have a look at the situation and draw up a blueprint of what needs to be done, and then they leave the organisation to get on with it, but of course the blueprints don't normally take because they don't allow for the other side. The blueprint deals with structure and role but it doesn't deal with change in attitudes and cultures. A further consequence is that the wrong problems are addressed. Because they are only dealing with problems at face value they frequently end up dealing with the wrong problem. This may be particularly so where the consultant lacks a psycho-analytic orientation as he may well confine himself to role and structure without having sufficient understanding of the contribution of unconscious content and dynamics. He may well suggest changes in role and structure without the backing of the requisite changes in work culture.

These, then, are some of the problems of dealing with the complicated processes involved. I believe that what was referred to by Menzies Lyth is a common problem in many organisations where there is a reliance on a structure, a technology, a new leader or a new system such as MBO or TQM, which is seen as the magic to solve their problems. We should not be surprised that nothing effective happens; that the change effort fails to have any significant effect. The problem which is causing difficulty for the organisation has not been identified and has therefore been avoided.

An example of this sort of behaviour occurred while this research was being conducted. An external consultant identified the need for greater corporacy and shared purpose throughout the Metropolitan Police. What was clearly required was an organisational change that dealt with the cultural issues of the lack of corporacy. Although the culture was frequently referred to, in the event the main decision was to provide a new structure for decision making, the setting up of various executive meetings. Other decisions included inputs on leadership and total quality, both purely cognitive and neither recognising the cultural aspect.

BOUNDARIES AND CHANGE

The type of change is also worth looking at in terms of the likely effect on the organisation. Some changes will only impact on a few of the groups' boundaries and will thus not be very threatening. This is not the case with something like a major strategic change where the nature of the change is such as to impact on most, if not all, of the boundaries created by the groups in the organisation. The nature of strategy or purpose is to question the very existence of the organisation. Such typical questions as, 'Why are we in business?' and 'What business are we in?', go right to the heart of the reason for existing. As such, it could easily result in feelings of disintegration.

Faced with a passion for form, the danger is that organisations that experience the anxiety of making a difficult decision, regarding strategy, for example, are liable to look for an alternative magical solution. The real issue then, is how to deal with the situation, how to keep organisations in a learning mode where rational thinking predominates. Menzies Lyth relates to this problem when she states, 'Major institutional change cannot be effected by decision making alone, or even mainly: it inevitably involves a slow, gradual and often painful evolutionary process. This process is in many ways akin to analytical forms of psychotherapy and has some of the same difficulties and rewards' (1988, p. 150). In situations of major organisational change it requires that account must be taken of the culture.

The all-pervading nature of culture is such that there is interaction between all parts of the organisation which makes each process dependent on the other. This means that any changes to one part of the organisation will cause and again be influenced by changes in the others. The disruption to the organised whole may be viewed as a highly threatening experience. In developing a culture the members of an organisation develop a structure of meaning. Any change is liable to undermine the very structure of meaning on which it has come to rely for its sense of continuity, consistency and confirmation. To give up those known ways of behaviour and embark on the unknown would be experienced as nothing less than social chaos and individual breakdown. The effects of change make more sense if we bear in mind that culture is developed as a result of the group producing forms of behaviour that are advantageous to them under the conditions imposed by their holding environment.

Rice describes what happens during change when he points out that, 'If chaos is defined as uncertainty about boundary definition, or more colloquially, as not knowing who, or what belongs where, then every transaction is potentially chaotic' (1976, p. 34). In these circumstances it is hardly surprising that organisations look for simplistic or magical solutions to their problems. Alternatively, they may, in order to avoid the anxiety, try to avoid change wherever possible. This is what happened in the health service, as reported by Menzies Lyth, who says they would avoid change – almost, one might say, at all costs – and tend to cling to the familiar even when the familiar had obviously ceased to be appropriate or relevant. The appropriate or the relevant needs to be seen in terms of the culture. Logic should be measured in terms of the development of the culture, not by an outsider's rationality. To the members of the organisation the familiar is both appropriate and relevant.

This is not to deny the paradoxical nature of the regularity that culture imposes on us. On the one hand disruption is likely to bring the chaos referred to above; on the other hand we need the sound base on which to develop. This is important, as many organisational changes will involve development in a wide range of areas. We need, then, to consider the relationship between culture and learning. In Piaget's terms assimilation depends upon the pre-existence of organising structure sufficiently developed to incorporate the experience. The process of assimilation may lead to modifications of structure (accommodation), but only within limits of continuity.

LEARNING AND CHANGE

According to Piaget, knowledge is an activity rather than a state. However, should our preconceptions be too few or too rigid – should the culture be immature – this activity is likely to be very limited. It will also be affected by the type of learning: where the knowledge is, to use James's term, 'knowledge about', it may be assimilated in most cultures (see p. 102). Where the knowledge is 'knowledge of acquaintance', however, there are likely to be difficulties in most cultures other than those that are mature. In this regard Fairbairn points out that, 'If a mature individual loses an object, however important, he still has some objects remaining. His eggs are not all in one basket. Further he has a choice of objects and can desert one for another. The infant, on the other hand, has no choice. The infant is completely dependent on his object' (1952, p. 47). The same may be said to apply to members of organisations that are immature.

Learning at the lowest levels of Bateson's hierarchy of learning levels should not cause difficulties in most cultures. Learning at the higher levels or on the scale of Khun's paradigm change requires a very mature culture. These types of learning will impact on most or all of the group or individual boundaries. Thus, to attempt such learning may be a very threatening experience, one which threatens the harmony and integration with feelings of disintegration. Equally, of course, it can also feel exciting and challenging when it is felt to be within one's capacity. Unless the culture is extremely mature, such changes will create anxiety and this will prevent learning.

Even taking a far less difficult situation than a paradigm change, such as computer learning by the computer illiterate, there will be no purpose in immediately talking in terms of hardware, software, bytes or other much more complicated matters. There is no point in asking someone to see what they cannot see. If a paradigm is not within the perceived reality of those concerned, they will not be able to understand it without some explanation: it would be like asking a blind man to see. It is only after they have, figuratively speaking, 'opened their eyes' that they can begin to see the new concept. To proceed without this assistance will only serve to create anxiety and prevent learning.

SOCIALISATION AND CHANGE

A different form of learning is experienced in 'culture shock'. Here, though, the stress in the first instance is not on learning but on loss. If grieving is a response to loss of meaning, then it should be provoked by all situations of loss, including organisational change, where the ability to make sense of life is severely disrupted. It will be recalled that the defences used in 'culture shock' served a double purpose, that of defence as such and also the provision of time to reintegrate. So wherever major organisational changes are involved we need to allow some kind of moratorium on other business, so that people can give their minds to repairing their attachments and reintegrating the culture.

This experience of loss can be most difficult, as I have described with regard to my own experience and that of others in the process of socialisation. In the first instance this will result in mourning for the loss of the loved objects. Where the change results in a massive loss of shared loved objects the vicissitudes of the mourners' identities are likely to be similar but not equal to that experienced by the loss of a close relative. In this respect I am reminded of some of the comments of those involved in major organisational change referred to earlier which had distinct connotations of human loss.

According to Marris (1974): 'When we argue about the need for social change, we tend to explain conservatism away as ignorance, a failure of nerve, the obstinate protection of untenable privileges – as if the resistance could be broken by exposing its irrationality' (p. 6). Yet the conservative instinct is as necessary for survival as adaptability: and indeed adaptability itself depends upon it. The ability to learn from experience relies upon the stability of the interpretations by which we predict the pattern of events. We assimilate new experiences by placing them in the context of a familiar, reliable construction of reality. This structure in turn rests not only on the regularity of events themselves, but on the continuity of their meaning. In terms of the organisation this structure is the culture. However, in making the foregoing points I should not wish to present a picture of culture as being unitary. In practice some individuals are more socialised, others less so and therefore more marginally committed.

CREATIVITY AND CHANGE

The will to adapt to change has to overcome an impulse to restore the past which is equally universal. Despite the anxiety of venturing into the unknown, the process by which maturation provokes change is disruptive, but not fundamentally so. Progression is made possible by the existence of a good enough holding environment. Conceived in this way, the idea of creativity does not contradict the assumption of a conservative impulse. Change in one area of our lives is possible only if other areas remain stable. In this situation the defensive reactions of conservatism are latent, because we are able to deal with the threat to the established structure of meaning. We can see, then, that an organisation will only be creative if the holding environment is perceived as good enough by the members who, in turn, develop a mature culture. It will be recalled that it takes considerable courage to create, there has to be a freedom from anxiety and a confidence to overcome the inevitable guilt associated with such activity. Above all, the members of the organisation must feel secure; they must perceive their holding environment as good enough.

LANGUAGE AND CHANGE

In discussing learning I referred to the proposition that before a new paradigm can be conceptualised, it must be explained. The way that we explain this is by language used as symbols. Therefore, before a group can begin to conceptualise they must have time to understand the symbols. In some cases, the relevant 'private language' may easily be understood and the consultant will be able to proceed in a relatively short time. However, where the 'private language' is more complex, such as computerisation for the computer illiterate (to use the previous example), it may be a considerably longer period before the consultant can gain understanding and proceed in a meaningful manner.

The predictability of behaviour is therefore profoundly important. It depends not only on some shared sense of the meaning of relationships but on conventions of expressing this meaning. Each culture will develop its own 'private language', its own form of expression peculiar to that language, its own idiom. As Marris points out, 'Each symbolic grammar is a language to express the meaning of relationships – their purposes, expected patterns of interaction, the framework of assumptions about the world into which they fit' (1974, p. 7). This may bring problems for both the consultant and the group.

In many change processes those involved will understand the language being used, and will be able freely to create symbols. They will be able to mate their preconceptions with sense data in order to create new conceptions. Referring back to the view of Szmidla and Khaleelee (1975), under the conditions where the position of the clients (the object inline) is very different from that of those seeking to implement change (the subject inline), there is likely to be some difficulty in reconciling both horizons (inlines). Nevertheless, they will at least be able to work with the same symbols and will at least be able to communicate.

In these circumstances the task of the consultant may by no means be easy, but it is possible. What, though, of the situation where those involved do not understand the symbols that are being used? It seems obvious that if I were to travel to, say, Denmark, I would not be able to create symbols that were understandable to those in an organisation. I should therefore be of little value as a consultant. It may not be so obvious but should I go into any new organisation I will need to take account of the cultural influence on language. I will need to appreciate the uniqueness of the symbols. Before either the consultant or the members of the organisation can be expected to begin to address the issues they need to be able to use and understand the same symbols. Creating a shared language – that is, a language shared by consultant and client – is often an important function for the consultant.

In this context it is perhaps of interest to recall that the derivation of the word 'symbolic', as explained by Segal, is that the word comes from the Greek, meaning 'throwing together or bringing together'. Rollo May (1975) also makes the same point, but adds that the antonym of 'symbolic' is 'diabolic', meaning 'pulling apart'. In terms of the consultant not understanding the particular language of the culture, or the members of the organisation not understanding the language of the change, it seems likely that anxiety may be provoked. In the circumstances it seems fair to say that this may be truly diabolical in both the academic and metaphorical senses.

Should the consultant not attend to the understanding of the symbols needed to communicate with all concerned the result may be extreme anxiety, and instead of the desired progression the result may be regression. This would appear to be at the heart of the problem of managing change. Should the anxiety be such as to cause the individual or group to resort to the use of defence mechanisms, such as projective identification, the result will be a reversion to symbolic equations. The symbolic substitute will be felt to be the original object. The individual will be 'blocked' in his approach to the task. According to Jaques (1970):

> If the discrepancy between reality and symbolic aspects is too great, lack of interest or hatred is aroused, and loss of incentive ensues. This hatred may be intensified by violent splitting and fragmentation, the incomplete objective being concretely introjected and identified with destroyed and persecuting internal objects. The objective itself then becomes increasingly persecutory through violent projection and concrete symbol formation. (p. 87).

Jaques observes that if the depressive position has been sufficiently worked through the symbolic content of work will be connected mainly with reparation. He explains, 'The more reality content of the work is consistent with the unconscious symbolic reparation activities, the greater will be the love for the task' (p. 87). This again seems most pertinent to the process of change. If the level of anxiety is kept down by virtue of the reality of the task being consistent with the objectives of the individual, the 'greater will be the love for the task'. If, on the other hand, there is a disparity between the individual's objectives and his task, the result will be anxiety and the formation of concrete symbols.

It may be helpful at this stage to provide a short explanation of what we mean by the notion of the 'individual's objectives'. Jaques helpfully informs us that 'An objective is an object-to-be – one which has to be brought into being, to be created' (1970, p. 86). The objective may be allocated to the individual as part of his job or it may be worked for to achieve some personal satisfaction, such as those described in Maslow's Hierarchy of Needs. As to the amount of effort applied to a task Vroom's Expectancy Theory asserts that this will depend on the individual's belief that his effort will increase the probability of his achieving the reward. Such reward may of course be intrinsic or extrinsic. Individuals will pursue their own objectives. Where they can achieve them by doing what the organisation requires, then organisation objectives are likely to be achieved as well. Work is most satisfying where both the individual and organisation objectives are in concert. It is when they are not that problems such as those described above are likely to occur.

I have emphasised the need for the consultant to understand the language of the objects of change. When I was an internal consultant, I found that on most occasions I was speaking the same language as my client group. However, there were still many 'private' variations of that language which I had to learn. Every group has its own distinctive version of the language, which sometimes results in the same symbols having different meanings. An equally valid point is the private language developed by consultants; we also have our holding environments from which we develop our culture which is expressed in our own private language, and we must be careful that we do not take it into a different culture.

As is frequently the case, Anzieu provides an interesting view of symbols when he states: 'In "The Ego and the Id" Freud wrote in an elliptical way that the superego derives from acoustic roots: this means that the orders, injunctions and threats that the child has heard uttered are at the origin of the superego – in short parental voices.' He continues, 'the child learns not only words, but rules. Speaking means putting sounds and then words into a certain order that makes them take on a meaning.' Anzieu then concludes: 'The superego derives from an acoustic origin: it forms with the acquisition of speech' (1990, p. 62). Thus in the early stages the super-ego is influenced by the parents, but later it is influenced by the social milieu. This being the case, it would appear that where, for example, there are constant demands on police for more accountability, this may have a considerable effect on the collective super-ego of the police, as will be described in the next chapter. This, in turn, will also affect the organisational culture.

THE ROLE OF THE CONSULTANT

I should now like to turn to a more specific consideration of the role of the consultant. If the change presents a problem that the group does not know how to cope with, then the consultant has the task of both dealing with the tendency of the group members to regress as well as enabling them to see that they have the ability to effect the change. Menzies Lyth (1989) makes the important point that the consultant's responsibility lies in helping insights to develop, freeing thinking about problems, helping the client to get away from unhelpful methods of thinking and behaving, facilitating the evolution of ideas for change, and then helping him to bear the anxiety and uncertainty of the change.

Here Bion's (1963) concept of the mother seen as a container who can contain what the baby projects and work with it is extremely valuable. As, of course, is Winnicott's concept of a good enough holding environment. Bion discusses the role of the mother in helping the baby develop his own capacity for thinking and so become more able to deal himself with these situations. Winnicott talks of the subtle co-operation that mothers can give, which supports yet does not dominate. Menzies Lyth and others have suggested that the consultant should act as a container for a group undergoing change. In keeping with my view of culture I prefer to consider the role of consultant as one who is acting as a substitute or temporary holding environment throughout the change process.

In any extensive change process the culture and the holding environment will be severely disrupted. The consultant can assist the client by providing a substitute for that holding environment until it and the culture have reintegrated. By supporting yet not dominating, the consultant can reduce the anxiety and provide the confidence for progression. The members of the organisation need a consistent picture of themselves as reflected by the others if they are to reintegrate their culture. The consultant can provide the consistency in modes of communication and response that are important if the members of the organisation are to learn to interpret responses meaningfully and benefit from them.

The requirements of the members of an organisation may be described in a similar manner to those of a baby or young child. The need is for a containing person who respects and values the child's anxiety and depression, assesses appropriately their content and conveys understanding, security and the tolerability of such experience: someone who can mourn with the baby for his losses, which may indeed coincide with her own – for example, at weaning – and set a pattern of normality for such experiences. These relationships and processes are difficult and painful for both mother and baby, although rewarding when they are seen to be resolvable by the pair and set in context of the directly gratifying aspects of the relationship (Menzies Lyth, 1988).

Some of the difficulties and pain of the mother are also experienced by the consultant. It will involve being subject to and taking in the group's massive projections of intense feelings and phantasies, accepting them without undue diminishment through denials or other defences, and not being overwhelmed by them. Being a 'good enough' holding environment means keeping your head while all others about you are losing theirs. It means gaining people's co-operation before you move them forward, just as Winnicott says that the mother needs to do before lifting the child. By his reactions the consultant conveys back to the members an appropriately modified version of what they have projected. The consultant may also sometimes be the receptacle for the system's hostility, thereby facilitating informed co-operation in the task of change.

It is a major task, then, for the consultant to keep himself in a state where he is receptive to the phenomena he must work with. Freud (1911) recommends 'evenly suspended attention', not directing one's attention to anything in particular, not making a premature selection or prejudgement about what is significant. Bion (1970) recommends eschewing memory and desire, not consciously summoning up memories about the patient or what has previously happened. Bain (1982) also stresses the value of ignorance and adds that even if one is not ignorant, a 'cultivated ignorance' is essential to the role of social consultant. Menzies Lyth (1989) talks about the need to take a fresh look at the situation, to set aside habitual ways of looking at things, to blind oneself to the obvious, to think again. The rationale for all these views is to free the consultant's mind to be receptive to the here and now and in this way to allow the evolution of understanding, and also importing and carrying confusion – avoiding the defence of premature interpretation.

According to Menzies Lyth (1989), if the consultant can hold on to ignorance and evenly suspended attention, meaning will probably emerge and one will experience the reward of at least one mystery or part of a mystery solved, uncertainty and doubt dispersed. However, by way of exception she also points out that the consultant may need to give a good deal of support to the client to go along with the process, especially a client who is accustomed to using the 'expert' and expects him to produce a definitive answer quickly. The problem being that if the consultant resists the pressure, he or she may be bitterly attacked as though they are delinquently withholding that to which the client is entitled. Failing that, the client clutches at straws and magical unrealistic answers.

In terms of culture, if the interrelatedness of the group with the holding environment produces a culture that is highly dependent it must be treated as such. There is no point in trying to deal with such an organisation in a totally unstructured way. All that this will do is to create anxiety, an anxiety that develops from a fear of being alone without support. In the first instance, then, the response of the consultant must be in keeping with the current culture.

As Menzies Lyth (1989) points out, 'the strain of this way of working is considerable for the consultant'. She adds that, 'One exists most of the time in a state of partially self imposed ignorance which may feel profound, frightening and painful' (1989, p. 32).

Seen in the light of personal boundaries, this is quite understandable. What is being asked is that the consultant ignore, albeit temporarily, all of the boundaries that he has created for his own development. This will undoubtedly result in temporary feelings of disintegration.

In major organisational change two or more consultants working together are more likely to deal with these painful feelings. Indeed, this will be an advantage with any change, and where a person is working alone he needs his own consultant to come home to. He needs the support of being able to talk things through away from the problems of the consultancy. With regard to transference and countertransference, which I shall refer to next, two people can be very useful in helping each other to sort out, check and recheck them and disentangle each other from relationships that interfere with work or from attitudes inconsistent with consultancy.

TRANSFERENCE AND COUNTER-TRANSFERENCE

As Hunt informs us, introspection is particularly important, because, 'The roles that researchers assume in fieldwork often mobilise transferences as a result of their link to unconscious phantasies.' She reminds us that this is a two-way process when she states, 'Both researcher and subject continually impose archaic images onto the person of the other' (1989, p. 61). While we may eschew all memory and desire (or at least, try to do so), it will still not stop this unconscious process. However, provided that we are sufficiently aware of it, this will be of benefit, as the same clues that analysts employ to help them recognise counter-transferences in the analytic setting may be used by the researcher. Strong emotions of anger, anxiety, love or shame, boredom or annoyance may all indicate the presence of transference.

Transference phenomena are things that all of us show every moment of our lives to varying degrees. Freud pointed out: 'Transference arises spontaneously in all human relationships just as it does between the patient and the physician' (1910, p. 83). Our particular interpretations, and even distortions, of the external environment, whether physical or social, are influenced by our particular unconscious need systems. Our behaviour is therefore governed not only by conscious needs and environmental demands but also by unconscious needs.

According to Greenson (1965):

Transference is the experiencing of feelings, drives, attitudes, fantasies, and defences toward a person in the present which are inappropriate to that person and are a repetition, a displacement of reactions originating in regard to significant persons in early childhood. I emphasise that for a reaction to be considered transference, it must have two characteristics: it must be a repetition of the past and it must be inappropriate to the present (p. 171).

Thus a person (subject) exhibiting transference in a relationship experiences the other (object) in a way that is not representative of the actual object and which cannot be accounted for on the basis of the current situation alone but is based on previous interpersonal experience.

Starting from this point, and following Scheidlinger (1980), the consultant needs to ask, 'What makes this client behave (speak or act) toward me in this particular way at this moment?' In other words, what role does he unconsciously try to push me into, what sort of relationship is he unconsciously trying to establish between us? A working hypothesis is that answers to these questions will enable the consultant to establish contact with the unconscious level of the organisation, which is essential if we are to understand the culture. Lacan (1977) informs us that 'the transference is the enaction of the unconscious' – an enaction which, in the group, is very often a way forward or, as Lacan terms it, a 'passage l'acte'.

PROJECTIVE IDENTIFICATION

In Chapter 6 I referred to 'projective identification'; I now need to refer to it again in greater depth. This primitive defence mechanism was first identified by Melanie Klein (1948) in her studies of infant development but it has since been found to be a universal phenomenon. Horwitz (1985) informs us that, unlike projection, projective identification is not limited to ridding oneself of unwanted impulses – wishes to dominate, control and devalue are also among the motives. It is when we refer to the use of projective identification in groups, however, that we realise the significance for culture and change. Bion (1961) believed that the group aroused primitive feelings in its members and that this resulted in their using the defence of projective identification.

Although the process starts with a person projecting a part of his self on to and into one or more persons, it is the impact on the other person that is of greatest interest. A phantasy is created which is a wishful one – that is, it has behind it a pressure toward gratification or fulfilment. The member of a group tries to actualise the unconscious wishful transference fantasies, to make them real, to experience them as part of reality. The other person undergoes an identification or a fusion with the projected content and its unconscious meanings and has the experience of being manipulated into a particular role.

Sandler (1987) informs us that projective identification provides an added dimension to transference, in that transference need not be regarded as simply a repetition of the past. It can also be a reflection of fantasies about the relation to the analyst created in the present by projective identification. In trying to actualise his unconscious wishful phantasy the patient – or, more appropriately, the member of a group – will externalise the wish into the person of the consultant. This may evoke a counter-transference response which can be meaningful to the consultant.

The valuable information to be found in transference and counter-transference can be the crucial clue to what is going on. According to Miller: 'The way in which the consultant is used and experienced, and also the feelings evoked in him, may offer evidence of underlying and unstated issues and feelings in the client system: that which is repressed by the client may be expressed by the consultant' (1990, p. 171). For the understanding of culture, transference and counter-transference are essential. It is only by the consultant interacting with the client system that he can gain an understanding of the unconscious level and hence the culture of the organisation.

SUMMARY

In many ways the culture can be seen as 'the personality of the organisation'. In the same way that the maternal holding environment affects the development of personality, so the organisational holding environment affects the culture. Both culture and personality are unique and both can usefully be viewed from the perspective of mature or immature. The degree of maturity of culture will affect the response of members of the organisation to change. Being deep-seated and all-pervading the culture will affect every organisational change.

Different types of change, be it in terms of complexity or in depth of learning, will impact on the culture in different ways. The most critical factor, however, is the culture itself. Any change will cause some sort of disruption to the culture: the more immature that the culture is the greater will be the anxiety and regression. Likely results are that the wrong problem or a lesser problem will be dealt with, or the need for change will be totally denied. In any event the problems of the organisation will not be dealt with. It helps if the consultant has a psychoanalytic orientation; however, the relevant point is that the consultant takes heed of both the conscious level and, more importantly, the unconscious level of maturity in the organisation.

Every major organisational change will affect the culture. The culture is developed by the members of the organisation producing forms of behaviour that are most advantageous to them under the conditions imposed by their holding environment. With this in mind, any change that affects the culture will be potentially chaotic. Where the culture tends toward being mature this will provide the necessary base for even the most complex learning and creativity.

All changes to organisational culture will involve a loss – a loss experienced not as badly as, but with similar results to the loss of a relative. This is true of both mature and immature situations. The difference is in how the loss is worked with. In the same way that defences are used in bereavement not only as defences but also to provide time for reintegration, so must organisational members be given time and support in order that they may reintegrate their culture.

The culture of an organisation is represented by the language. Each culture will have its own 'private language'. Dangers arise when consultants believe they understand this 'private language' but are not aware of differences of meaning. Use of inappropriate or 'foreign' language will impact directly on the culture and may cause anxiety. Consequently, creating a shared language – that is, a language shared by consultant and client – is often a necessary condition for the consultant. Should there be regression, the symbols used will not be true symbols that allow for progression, but symbolic equations or concrete symbols.

The consultant has the responsibility for relating to the emotional and cognitive state of the group. A helpful approach is to see the consultant as a container, similar to Bion's view of the mother. My view is that the consultant should be seen as a temporary or substitute holding environment. He should temporarily replace the disrupted organisational holding environment and provide a substitute holding environment for the members to interrelate with until they have reintegrated their new culture. To fully understand what is going on in the group he should as far as possible remain in what has variously been termed a state of 'evenly suspended attention'. This is a demanding role which can be frightening and painful. It is desirable that the consultant should have a partner to provide support and help in sorting out the transference and counter-transference.

An understanding of transference and counter-transference is highly relevant both to culture and to the management of organisational change. The way in which the consultant is used and experienced, and also the feelings evoked in him, may offer evidence of underlying and unstated issues and feelings in the client system. By interacting with the client system the consultant can gain an understanding of the unconscious level and hence the culture of the organisation.

In the next chapter many of the concepts related to will be applied to change and culture in the Metropolitan Police Service.

13

A CASE STUDY

In this chapter I shall be applying the explanation of culture to the management of a particular change. In doing so, I shall be writing from the perspective of my previous role as an internal consultant in the Metropolitan Police Service. This role in itself raises some interesting dynamics which will be referred to briefly. First, I need to give some descriptive data on the Metropolitan Police.

The Metropolitan Police Service is Britain's largest police service with a staff of around 45,000, which consists of some 28,000 police officers and 17,000 civilian employees. The Service has its headquarters at New Scotland Yard in Central London which is also the location of the ruling coalition, the Commissioner and his Policy Committee of senior police and civilian employees. The Met provides policing for a geographic area of some 799 square miles, a population of 6.5 million with a further 2 million daily commuters, and it operates from 1943 different buildings. For operational purposes it is divided into eight geographic units known as Areas and these are again divided into smaller geographic units known as Divisions.

There are several differences between police and civilian employees: for example, different career structure, ranks as opposed to grades, different pay structure and rates of pay, and different conditions of employment. In the main, civilians are employed centrally in headquarters functions, such as transport, engineers, computers, finance and, of course, clerical duties. Although there are exceptions, civilians are not generally employed at the interface with the public. One or two headquarters functions, especially personnel, are joint police and civilian departments.

The main point of interface with the public is at the divisional level which is mainly staffed by police personnel. Most of the officers employed at this level are posted to units called Reliefs which have responsibility for policing that geographic area over the twenty-four-hour period. In addition there is a group of officers at each division, known as home beat officers, who have specific responsibility for a small geographic area known as a Beat. There are also a number of detectives attached to each division. Detectives are also employed at the Area and headquarters levels. At headquarters there are a number of operational units, such as the Company Fraud Squad, the Central Drugs Squad, the Flying Squad and the Serious Crime Squad. At the Area level there are also drug squads, domestic violence units and juvenile offenders units. These officers also interface with the public but the segment of the public that they interface with is, generally speaking, the non-law abiding.

In terms of the nature of organisations and from this brief description it will be seen that there are several obvious groups of people. As might be expected, there are also countless others, too numerous to mention, but reasonably easily identifiable. Each of these groups is itself differentiated by the various roles performed: for example, civilians are categorised into computer people, engineers, or finance people, while police are differentiated into uniformed officers and detective officers which can again be categorised into, for example, fraud squad detectives or flying squad detectives.

Most employees are posted to many different roles throughout their service, yet they quickly perceive themselves as a finance person or a personnel person or a uniform person or a detective person, or whatever. It quickly becomes an idea held in the mind of the members that the group exists. The finance group, for example, is a perceived object of those employed in that group and for those outside the boundary. All of these groups are artificial creations but all involved treat them as if they exist. From time to time new groups are created either on a temporary basis, such as a murder squad, or to meet an identified need of a more permanent nature, such as domestic violence. In these cases a 'group illusion' (to use Anzieu's term) quickly develops at the moment that there is a collective belief that the group exists.

In hierarchical terms there are eleven different police ranks from police constable through to Commissioner. All but one, or arguably two, of these ranks are seen as managerial roles. The number of civilian grades and managerial levels is slightly more complicated but is roughly similar to police. In the terms described by Mintzberg (1988) the Met is a typical bureaucracy and has all the attributes that he describes in connection with such an organisation: that is, many levels of rank, a proliferation of rules, regulations, and formalised communication throughout the organisation, and a large operating core which is the officer on the beat.

The importance of the need for attachment and for social relatedness (Bion's 'groupishness'), leads to the development of groups which in time provide the certainty without which their members could not survive. In their own way, each of these groups establishes the necessary firm boundaries for itself and others across which realistic and effective relationships and transactions can take place and within which their identity can be established.

The foregoing is all valuable information to any organisational consultant, as would be other information regarding such matters as task, technology or strategy. Analyses of these and other aspects of organisations are important to our understanding, but they do not tell us anything about the unconscious processes of culture. Most of this type of information can be obtained by a passive observer. However, if we want to learn more deeply about the culture it is necessary to take an active participation in the lives of the subjects of the culture. This being the main purpose of this chapter, I shall be dealing with this in depth. First, however, I want briefly to explain my role as an internal consultant.

THE INTERNAL CONSULTANT ROLE

I write from the perspective of being a member of and having served in the Metropolitan Police both as a detective and as a uniformed officer and, for the period described, as an internal consultant still with the status of Chief Superintendent. It has taken a long time to develop some of the knowledge and skills required to understand organisational culture; a process which continues, sometimes painfully. Since becoming a consultant I have frequently come to the conclusion that just when I think I know something I suddenly discover that I know nothing.

Being a police officer, a Chief Superintendent, and an internal consultant, inevitably created situations where there were mismatches of identity. To refer once again to Szmidla's (1975) concept of 'inline' and 'outline', here we had a situation where me, my inline, could be somewhat different from the other person's outline of me; where the identity others conferred on me and the identity I claimed for myself clearly differed. In terms of junior officers there could be issues of dependency, whereas, with senior officers, there were more likely to be issues of counter-dependency. As to being a police officer, it is interesting that even after seven years as an internal consultant I could still be perceived in a prior role such as detective. Indeed, while engaged on this research an officer commented with words to the effect, 'and you, a detective officer, have done all this'.

This may be seen as an example of how different people see different worlds, of how reality is within the current knowledge of those concerned. Nevertheless, it comes as something of a shock when one has come to be, and to know oneself as, a consultant only to find that this is not reflected back by certain others. The very essence of identity is, albeit momentarily, challenged. This serves to make the point that every relationship involves a negotiation of identities.

As an internal consultant and part of the organisation, I was undoubtedly also part of the organisation culture. However, it is equally clear that different groups within the same holding environment perceive that holding environment in different ways. Thus, the same holding environment can produce variations on the same culture. This is just as true for detectives, home beat officers or engineers, as it is for the group of internal consultants. It would be impossible not to be part of the culture, but the knowledge and skill of developing a 'cultivated ignorance' or of setting aside habitual ways of thinking does allow a view of the organisation that is less contaminated by the culture.

Nevis (1987) refers to another difficulty, the need for affiliation. This is a problem for an internal consultant, especially when some of his clients are previous work colleagues. Remaining at or near the boundary and not becoming engulfed by affiliation needs can be a difficult process. In the early days of my consultancy experience this was indeed a most difficult problem, but time and experience creates an awareness that if you are to succeed in helping people there is a need to stay at the boundary and not become involved. Needless to say, there must be other means of satisfying affiliation needs and this is where the role of a working partner becomes significant.

Returning to the organisation, it may assist at this stage if I apply the concept of a 'holding environment' to the Met. The external holding environment of the Met includes all those external social objects referred to earlier: for example, the ruling coalition, the private language, the attitudes and beliefs, multiple organisational tasks, and multiple organisational roles. Being an open system the external holding environment is particularly influenced by external social objects in the external environment, such as Home Office (the police authority of the Met), the Crown Prosecution Service, the judiciary, the Independent Complaints Authority, and the news media. The internalised – psychological and unconscious – holding environment, is developed from the phantasised views of the members of the Met partially based on their perception of the external holding environment. Precisely what this is will become clearer from the ensuing discussion.

THE 'MET' CULTURE

Both Freud and Bion recognised that certain organisations were liable to be affected in specific ways. Freud referred to 'artificial groups' – namely, the church and the army – about which he said, 'A certain external force is employed to prevent them from disintegrating and to check alterations to their structure' (1921, p. 122). Bion (1955) referred to these same organisations as 'specialised groups'. In regard to these he pointed out that the task of these organisations is particularly prone to stimulate the activity of one or other of the basic assumptions. A church is liable to influence from the dependent group phenomena, and indeed takes some of the burden of that basic assumption on behalf of the wider society. The army suffers a similar liability from fight/flight phenomena. He also suggested that the aristocracy may be a specialised group that fulfils the same function for the pairing group.

Kets De Vries and Miller (1987) showed that various organisations reflect the attitude and character of the leaders. However, I am not so much concerned here with the effects that seem to emanate from within the organisation, or perhaps more accurately, from the members of the organisation. I am far more concerned with the view of Freud that 'external force' has an effect on an organisation. He referred to this as 'preventing disintegration' and 'checking alternatives in their structure', about which he said, 'Any attempt at leaving it is usually met with persecution or with severe punishment, or has quite definite conditions attached to it' (1921, p. 122).

What Freud appears to be saying is that in the case of both the church and the army there is a control over the members which prevents them from leaving. In the case of the church this results in an anxiety arising from a fear of a phantasy authority, while in the army the anxiety is in regard to the actual authority. In both cases, the authority acts in a super-ego manner in regard to the members of the organisation. As Freud (1926) explained, the super-ego is the vehicle of the phenomenon that we call conscience.

This was referred to earlier, but just what is meant by the term super-ego is well explained by Bettelheim, who states, 'Conscience, or the super-ego, is essentially a set of rules one has internalised by making them one's own without knowing where they come from. To then break such a rule is to experience guilt' (1969, p. 125). It would appear, then, that while we are not aware of the fact, we are nevertheless introjecting a set of rules which are influenced not only by our parents but also by the family, racial and national traditions handed on through them, as well as the demands of the individual's immediate social milieu.

The Metropolitan Police is an open system as are all other organisations. Indeed, it may be considered that it is more open than many others by virtue of the fact that it is a public service – a result is that there is a lack of control over impingements from the environment. Other than spatial boundaries that mark the geographic extent of the area policed, the organisation boundaries have, of necessity, to be reasonably open. The provision of a twenty-four-hour a day, every day of the year, service of 'helping people', makes it extremely difficult to define task boundaries. Being such an open system, the external force, in the shape of public opinion (usually represented by pressure groups), can have a considerable influence on the organisation.

When we have a group of individuals who closely identify with each other, as in a police service, it seems perfectly logical that they should introject the same set of rules, that they should share what might be called a collective super-ego. This is supported by Bettelheim (1969) who points out that a collective super-ego is derived from collective demands instead of uniquely personal ones. It is still an inner voice that echoes an original external equivalent. Only, it is not a voice that shouts to me in particular 'Thou shalt not' but rather a chorus of many voices shouting 'You [plural] must not.' Explaining that this is even more powerful than an individual conscience he states, 'Such a voice is more inescapable. We can try to hide from a parent, even from God ... but we can never hide from a control system of which we are quite consciously a part' (Bettelheim 1969, p. 126). This has great significance in regard to an organisation such as the police which is subject to the 'collective demands' of the various segments of the public. It would appear to be rather like a process of osmosis whereby the collective demands are gradually diffused into the collective conscience and the unconscious, until they form part of the rules – which also, of course, include explicit official rules: these presumably shape and are shaped by the underlying rules.

This leads to a consideration of environmental factors: for example, the needs of the general public, as evidenced in the old saying, 'If you want to know the time ask a policeman', the expectation being that he or she will be right. Similarly, the adversarial judicial system requires that police are right or wrong, with the result that police are not allowed to be wrong. There are also, most pertinently, calls for accountability, which again demand that police be right. In such circumstances there is a need to be in control, police need to make sure that they do not make mistakes. That means that they do not take chances, they follow the rules, some of which are, as stated, statutory rules.

I feel certain that these 'collective demands' of the public play a considerable part in the formation of the collective conscience of the police. In addition to these usual collective demands, however, there have been exceptional demands throughout the 1970s and into the 1980s. Following accusations of corruption, brutality and racism, as well as riots, there were long and powerful collective demands for 'accountability'. These reached a high point with the introduction of the Police and Criminal Evidence Act 1984, which introduced several measures to make the police more accountable. This served to reinforce the collective conscience and imposed an even greater control over the members of the force. The situation has changed little since that date with further allegations of corruption, racism and brutality.

These 'collective demands' impact on all members of the organisation, police and civilian employees alike; however, for ease of reference, from now on I shall simply refer to police. One of the results is that police cannot hide from the control system of which they are a part, and this, associated with the lack of firm boundaries, in turn, results in anxiety. Difficult though the issue of defining task boundaries may be, senior management are not at this time accepting their responsibility for clear definition of such boundaries. The fact that they are also part of the culture means that they too need to ensure that they do not make mistakes – that they are always right and do not take risks – and this prevents them from making the decisions that would permit the necessary boundaries. The effect on the members is one of considerable ambiguity. Where the ambiguity prevents continuity, consistency and confirmation, where the world is perceived as unfamiliar, vague, mysterious and unpredictable, then it is apt to be threatening. Such a lack of boundaries limits reality testing. The result for the members of the organisation is that they do not perceive the holding environment as good enough. In their interrelatedness with this not good enough environment the members seek to produce a culture that will be advantageous to them under the conditions imposed by the environment. The result is a culture dominated by conscience whereby being right is all important and taking chances is far too risky to contemplate.

The culture thus imposes a sort of control on the organisation which is manifested in a demand for a static and unchanging order and structure, the avoidance of change and the restriction to activities which police feel they are good at. This is a narrow world that can be a highly defended one where they feel they must be right if they pursue it. Unfortunately, the world is not static and unchanging and there are therefore continued threats to this culture. In this context, perhaps we should recall that the logic involved here is not one that should be viewed from a position of detached rationality but from the position of the culture. The effect is that greater openness and the responsiveness required generates greater anxiety, which in turn calls for more rigid defences, so that one of the most open organisations becomes in reality what can only be called a closed organisation.

From my various experiences of consultancy interventions the overwhelming impression that I have gained is of a culture that is evidenced by a considerable need for control on the part of all involved, the control being exercised to prevent the extreme anxiety arising from the feeling of guilt that the members experience when they have doubts about the correctness of their actions. A conscience that imposes a control on its members to ensure that they are always right and that they do not do anything that might be considered a risk. The result is that those in positions of authority frequently do not accept their responsibility on the basis that if you do not do anything you cannot be wrong, whereas if you do you could be wrong.

The result is that police have a serious lack of belief in themselves and low self-esteem. They seem unable to take the decisions that will begin to deal with their problems. Instead, they wait for someone else to take the decisions and tell them what to do. This is reflected in calls by various individuals and representative bodies for a Royal Commission into policing. Doubtless, if someone else makes the decision, police cannot be wrong. I am reminded of the title of the book by Rollo May, *The Courage To Create* (1975): in circumstances where the collective conscience is such as to impose a strict control on the members of the organisation, it requires immense courage to create.

I referred to the issue of guilt in regard to creativity but I feel that it may now be of benefit to expand on that. Freud (1926) explained that the unconscious sense of guilt represents the super-ego's resistance. This is further explained by Melanie Klein when she states that, 'Freud approached the problem of guilt from two main angles. On the one hand, he left no doubt that anxiety and guilt are closely connected with each other. On the other hand, he came to the conclusion that the term "guilt" is only applicable in regard to manifestations of conscience which are the result of super-ego development' (1948, p. 33). We can therefore say that the collective demands leading to the collective conscience are extremely powerful because to act contrary to our conscience is to experience both guilt and anxiety. It follows therefore, that the collective demands of the public will have a considerable effect on the way the police behave. In this respect I am reminded of the saying, 'the public get the sort of police that they deserve'.

It will perhaps help to consider what produces the anxiety and what can be done to reduce it. As to what produces it, in general terms it seems quite clear: it is a fear of moving from a known and settled world to an unknown and uncertain one. This is in line with what Rycroft called the essence of anxiety when he stated, 'a problem, a danger, a test situation, or an opportunity has been encountered, but its precise nature is as yet unknown and no effective action can yet be taken'. However, what he goes on to say provides us with a clue as to what we can do to reduce the anxiety: 'the anxiety disappears the moment the situation is fully understood' (1968a, p. 12).

The process is more specifically explained by Anna Freud (1966) who points out that dread of the super-ego is the anxiety which sets the defensive process going. In this instance, then, the collective super-ego sets various defence processes in motion, as will be described later. When members of the organisation are asked to be creative, or to make decisions, defence mechanisms, such as denial, come into operation because the conscience says you will only do as you are told, you will not make your own decisions.

According to Racker (1968), 'Members have the problem of admitting that they have desires or phantasies and this is experienced with shame, with a sense of humiliation, or of contemptibility, with feelings of guilt, or in more general terms it is experienced with pain or anxiety' (p. 11). Knowing, from past experience, that to ignore the public censorship can be painful, the members oppose change by various means of resistance. That is, the different ways in which the ego achieves rejection are called the defence mechanisms, since in the last instance the purpose is to defend against a fantasied danger to the ego or to the object.

TRANSFERENCE AND COUNTER-TRANSFERENCE AS A MEANS TO UNDERSTANDING

In acting as a container, or a substitute holding environment, the 'bad' feelings are projected on to the consultant; the bits that the group wants to get rid of are evidenced in the transference. Transference was referred to in the last chapter but a further description by Symington

(1986) will add to our understanding. He describes transference as the process whereby the consultant is sucked into the outer personality structure of the client group. He also reminds us that it is not pleasant to be on the end of negative transference. It is not pleasant to be misrepresented because most of us have ideas about ourselves that we wish to cherish. If we are in the business of consultancy, we all like to see ourselves as efficient, helpful and caring. Consequently, if we are not aware of the dynamics we shall be most unlikely to successfully deal with the anxieties and move forward.

The transference will not only project on to the consultant (or another group member or the group as a whole) the present, repressed, unbearable reality, but also the important figures from the past as they related to the client, especially in childhood. The consultant becomes the bad object and becomes the recipient of the bad object's activity. This can, at times, be a very demanding experience for the consultant. An example of this type of transference will be referred to below. I shall also provide an example where the opposite applies, where the transference may be seen as positive and while in this case it can feel very pleasant, it may be too much so.

One of 'those demanding times' happened during a meeting with a group that occurred following a period where, for several days before it, I had been working very hard on a different project that had been proving particularly irksome. The result was that I attended the meeting feeling exceptionally tired and lacking in energy. The meeting had its share of negative transference which was not unduly expected. However, when one of the members made a particularly personal attack regarding my role my internal reaction was a strong feeling of anger. I have to admit that I needed a considerable amount of control not to communicate that feeling to the group. To have done so would of course have been very harmful to the process. To have moved from a position of being at or near the boundary to one of being totally within the boundary and engulfed by the emotions of the group, would have prevented me from helping the client. This example also serves to remind us that this is not a one-way process and that the consultant also takes himself into the room. 'Suspending all memory and desire' is sometimes easier than at others.

As I stated above the client can also project positive transferences on to the consultant. At first sight this may appear helpful, indeed it can be very seductive, but it can be equally difficult to deal with. A particular group meeting had been in progress for some time during which various members had been expressing their concerns and doubts about the way forward. All was well until one member strongly identified with the consultant (me) and 'laid down the law' that they should, in effect, get on with things, and warned against the consequences of not doing so! The result was that anxiety was raised even more rather than being contained as it was before that particular input.

The seductive nature of the input made it most difficult to deal with. On the face of things, it was intended to be helpful but a closer examination shows that this is not so. Referring back to the previous comment on control, in spite of the fact that it was not negative – on the contrary, it was in the guise of being collusive with the consultant – this may also nevertheless be seen as an attempt at control. It was rather like an elder sibling siding with mother or father saying to the younger sibling, 'you must eat your greens, or you will not grow up strong'. This was experienced in the transference as a feeling of being like a displaced parent.

What I have been referring to in the police culture is a typical immature situation, as described earlier: one in which there is little or no progression and where differentiation is not possible because there is not a sufficient basic trust in the organisational holding environment. Consequently police introject not a comforting progressive experience but the severe contentless anxiety that Bion referred to. The members are not able to differentiate between themselves and objects; there is, as Fairbairn describes, a one-sided attitude of incorporation and an attitude of primary emotional identification. The creation of new objects is not possible; identification is with existing objects; there is no capacity for tolerating or expressing new ideas, and they feel they have no choice.

This signifies that anxiety is high and the organisation itself is in a situation where the paranoid-schizoid mechanism predominates. There is a reliance on tight and rigid hierarchical roles and closely controlled tasks. There is a fear and a belief that mistakes will not be permitted and will not be admitted. The feelings of chaos experienced by the members of the organisation are disturbing in the extreme. The way that this is dealt with in the paranoid-schizoid position is to build in the systems of control, which are seen as 'good', and to project all of the 'bad' feelings on to anything which is likely to disturb those systems. This includes any proposed new system, and the consultants.

By deliberate intervention and deciphering the responses – that is, the way in which I, as consultant, was used and experienced and also the feelings evoked in me – it has been possible to gain an understanding of the unconscious level of the Met, that of the culture. Thus far I have largely addressed the subject by describing the nature of the culture, how it has come about, and the effects of such a culture on the organisation. I now want to show more specifically how the culture affects the management of change: how it was experienced by me in terms of the transference and counter-transference arising from the way I was used by the members of the organisation, and how the problems that it posed were dealt with. The following application will relate to one particular intervention which involved an action research project in a mixed police and civilian department.

The subject matter of this intervention is not really important for the purpose of this book; much more important is the process and above all the findings. Before commencing the project I arranged that I should have a partner whom I knew that I could rely on for mutual support. In any culture this is helpful, but in what I have referred to as an immature culture I believe it is essential. The early activities involved visiting the various branches concerned, which, in most cases, meant meeting the senior managers. In doing so, we had two objectives: first, to carry out a diagnosis of the current systems and practices, and, second, to build up a rapport and gain the confidence of our clients. Following this, we presented our findings and proposed way forward to the Head of Department, the principal client, for his approval before going through the same process with the managers of the branches concerned.

There were distinctions between each of the groups that we were working with and these were manifested in the 'private languages' used by the groups. One group in particular was isolated both physically, in terms of geographic location, and, to a degree, politically in terms of not often being involved in the decision-making process. The perception of the members of this group was, not surprisingly, one of feeling cut off, that the senior management in their holding environment did not care for them and did not provide for them. One of the results was an extreme lack of basic trust and a highly independent culture. In many respects it reminded me of the examples of the division of the conglomerate and the city police crime squad referred to at the end of Chapter 12.

The proposed way forward was a two-part process. The first involved three activities designed to increase cognitive knowledge: reading packs prepared by the consultants; proposed visits to other organisations where the process could be seen in action; and seminars where an academic expert would be able to explain further and add to their knowledge. The second part of the process involved workshops designed to develop the new system. The first was a two-day workshop for all involved to agree a system and individual group responsibilities for achieving it. This was to be followed by one-day workshops for each of the groups to help them develop their part of the new system.

In order to link the two parts we planned a series of meetings with each of the groups concerned where we aimed to provide as much support and containment as possible. In other words, we aimed to act as a substitute holding environment while their original holding environment was disrupted by the change process. The following describes some of the results of this intervention and provides an insight to the effects of the organisational culture.

On the face of it, it would appear that our attempt at cognitive development was important as a means of providing an understanding, thus giving those concerned the necessary confidence and thereby reducing the anxiety. However, this initially proved to be not as successful as hoped. The reason is as explained by Liddell, when he points out that: 'Anxiety accompanies intellectual activity, as its shadow' (1956, p. 12). By this he meant that knowledge has a habit of revealing unexpected areas of ignorance and this in turn tends to engender the very anxiety that it sets out to reduce. This was almost exactly what happened in this situation, basically because we provided too much too soon:

This was disappointing because, in a previous intervention, the sharing of written information had proved to be highly successful in gaining confidence by means of providing an in-depth understanding of the issues involved. It also ensured that those concerned knew and were talking the same language, thus permitting all to relate to each other. Such a process was felt equally important in regard to this intervention and despite the early anxiety I believe it eventually went a long way to achieving the objectives of change.

Control quickly became a feature of this intervention. There were clear signs that senior managers in each of the various branches sought to be in control by restricting access to information and decision making. Part of our objective as consultants was to involve as many personnel as possible so that they would all participate in, and own, the development of the new system. When this point was addressed it became clear that this was seen as threatening to the senior managers, as evidenced by remarks made in the absence of junior staff, such as: 'We tell them what to do'; and, 'They [junior personnel] could not contribute anything.' Or, when in the company of junior staff, the remarks were the same but were put as a joke as follows: 'You do as you are told don't you?' (accompanied by laughter).

Another of our objectives was to take the various clients through a process where they would devise the new system themselves. Despite mentioning this on almost every occasion that we came into contact with the groups, there seemed to be a denial that it would happen. Remarks such as, 'your system' were frequently used even though they were fully aware that workshops had been arranged for them to devise the future needs.

As a sort of knock-on from this denial, it also seemed that the need for control was resulting in a dependency mode. This expressed itself with remarks such as: 'Tell us what to do and we will do it', which seems to be rather like: 'The law says so, therefore we cannot be wrong.' They were in effect saying: 'If we devise this new system we may get it wrong; therefore we will let someone else get it wrong or we will do as we are told; either way we cannot be wrong.' At one particular meeting this was indicated by a strong impassioned plea for a framework, a need for someone to tell them where they were going. It was also indicated by a request to involve other 'experts' to join them – people who had more knowledge than they had – who would be able to tell them what to do. Again, the conclusion to be drawn was that if an 'expert' has said it is right 'we' must also be right.

The need for control was also evidenced by the lack of co-operation between the various branches. Despite the fact that there were fairly obvious needs for links between them in order to effectively carry out their respective tasks there were virtually none. There was a mutual lack of trust and a near 'bunker mentality' resulting from the need to be in control: the restriction to as narrow a world as they could possibly achieve so that it could be defended with certainty.

The fear of being out of control was shown in relation to another part of the process. As mentioned, one of the ways in which it was planned to achieve the necessary cognitive development of the personnel concerned was to arrange visits to other organisations to see the appropriate process in action. In discussing the need and requirement for such visits one of those involved suggested that the visits would be more useful after we had devised the new system. It would appear that there was a fear of visiting other organisations when not in possession of full knowledge of the subject matter – in other words, a fear of being out of control.

At one of the group meetings I had become aware that instructions were being formulated that would not be adequate for future needs and would subsequently need changing. When the issue was raised it was as though the possibility of a new system did not exist.

The talk was all about what we have to do 'at the present time' and any reference to the new system had little to do with them. At the same time, there was a clear recognition that they would need to change the instructions 'when the new system had been developed'. The outcome was that it was as if there was no link between the two events. It seems that by denying the implications of change, they were able to deny the unbearable reality of change itself.

The need for control, as described, is influenced by the culture of the Met as a defence against the extreme anxieties experienced and arising from the collective conscience. If we see the function of culture as a whole as being to enable the members of the organisation to produce behaviour which is advantageous under the conditions imposed by the environment, we can see that in doing so, they reach a level that is least anxiety-provoking for everyone. The problem is that the culture pervades almost every aspect of the organisation at this time and seriously interferes with attempts to carry out necessary change.

In order to make progress it was necessary to do everything possible to reduce the anxiety and to ensure that depressive mechanisms were available so that people would be able to relate to each other for at least part of the time in such a way that anxiety would be dealt with rather than shelved. At several of the group meetings this proved to be possible. However, this was only after a lot of hard work and a lot of containment of negative projections. All the pain described in the last chapter was present in these situations. The experience of the consultant was one of feeling rejected and of being used as a sort of dumping ground for all manner of moans and groans, of not being trusted. This was expressed in such terms as: 'What are you really trying to do?', or, 'When are you going to impose your grand idea?' This was hardly surprising as it was merely a reflection of a culture where you do not participate in decision making, you do as you are told.

The next important stage of this particular intervention was the workshops. The first was a two-day workshop for all involved – some sixty people. Having identified the need for a new system, the purpose of this workshop was for the members to participate in developing the particular system required, to identify the areas of responsibility within that system, and to establish what each of the branches would need in order to do their part and what they would in turn have to do for others. This workshop was then followed by a series of one-day workshops for each of the branches to help them plan how they could carry out their part of the system. The following paragraphs deal with the workshops.

At the outset, the most senior police officer present asked for guidance as to the status of the workshops in regard to whether it was permitted to make decisions or whether it was limited to making recommendations about decisions. This was followed by questions from others regarding the value of the workshop in view of a proposed structural change. There were also questions about whether others, such as senior departmental management and the Policy Committee, agreed with what we were doing. I sought to deal with the anxiety by making it clear that the heads of department concerned had agreed on the process and that the necessary authority had been given for them to make decisions. This sufficed in order to get the process of engaging with the primary task started. However, it was clear that there was a great deal of anxiety arising from the doubts of the members regarding the correctness of their actions.

This situation continued throughout the first day, with the result that few really addressed the primary task head-on. Instead they chose to skirt round it by dealing with other related matters and, in particular, strongly questioning the commitment of senior management. In fact, they went further than this in stating, on several occasions, that what was required was 'firm, or strong, leadership'. It would appear that they were making it quite clear that their perception of the holding environment was that it was not good enough and that they did not have a basic trust. There was just not the courage to create; the fear of being wrong was greater than any understanding of the need to change.

By the end of the first day my partner and I both felt extremely bruised and not a little discouraged. At this stage our fears and anxiety about the group staying in a regressed position and not acting in a progressive manner were very high and were seriously interfering with the process. Nevertheless, we managed to see through the fog of the counter-transference sufficiently to agree that we somehow needed to ensure a greater focus for the following day. We agreed that we would change the planned process and work for the first part of the day as a total group and that we would provide an outline structure of the new system that all of those present would be familiar with. We felt that a degree of structure was required in order to provide some sort of consistency, continuity and confirmation.

Later that evening, having got away from the situation and relaxed after my evening meal I was able to put things into a clearer perspective. I then began to relate the transference of the members to my previous knowledge of the culture. In the process of making sense of previous notes I began to get a real appreciation of what was happening in the transference and counter-transference, which I will return to shortly.

If anything, at the start of the next day there was even more anxiety than on the previous day. The result of the next session was very mixed. However, there was total support from the membership for the outline structure that had been posted up by us at the start of the day. I was also able to take something from each of the group presentations as being positive moves forward which I could use as the basis of the next session. The outline plan used to provide a structure was one which had been contained in the reading supplied to the members as part of the cognitive development process. It had also been referred to by the 'expert' at his seminars. It would appear that a primary reason for the acceptance of the outline plan was a direct result of the cognitive development. In accepting the plan, I can only assume that there was no feeling of risk on the part of the membership. Because of the seminars, presentations, and reading, they accepted that this system was right. It may also indicate that the posting up of the outline structure provided the members with an affirmation of a safe holding environment.

At the conclusion of the workshop I was able to show that we had broadly achieved our purpose sufficiently to proceed to the next stage. However, from one or two remarks made by the members and the quality of outcomes, my partner and I were left feeling quite despondent. In our view at that point it was difficult to see where we could plan to go forward when the culture was creating so much resistance. Here, again, personal reflection permitted a better understanding of the situation. It was not possible to do this when the event was taking place because of the vast amount of information, not to mention emotion, that was present at the time. However, getting clear of the immediate situation and being able to reflect on the events in a rational manner permitted me to consider again the impact of transference and counter-transference.

The starting point was that the membership were not simply awkward or stupid. Furthermore, they were not deliberately avoiding or denying the need for change – on the contrary. But the transference was further evidence that the common conscience was severely repressing the impulses of the members to be creative. The extreme control exercised by the common super-ego of those involved demanded that they not take a risk, they had to be sure that they were right. For the consultants this denial and task evasion was a very frustrating and annoying situation, which resulted in counter-transference. To be dominated by the counter-transference would be harmful to the progress of the project. To push for change, to chastise the members for lack of commitment, or to get angry because of lack of progress, would not deal with the members' anxiety. On the contrary, it would only serve to increase the anxiety exhibited in the transference. What was needed was some way to give them the confidence to be right.

In terms of providing a temporary holding environment it was important that a mature dependency existed between the consultants and the clients. In order to keep the level of anxiety as low as possible it was necessary to stay close to the existing culture, with its need for structure, yet to ensure that depressive mechanisms of differentiation were available so that people were able to relate to each other for at least part of the time, thus dealing with the anxiety instead of shelving it. Consequently, we planned to use the outline structure, which the clients had agreed, as the basis of the one-day workshops and to relate this to what they already did so that they could show where they would fit into a new system. This would be a reasonably safe activity which it would then be possible to build on in order to look at future needs. The other benefit of this approach was that they would all be talking to the same system and using the same language, so that they would all be able to relate to each other subsequently.

In the event the one-day workshops, structured as they were to deal with the culture of the organisation, proved constructive and progressive. Had they not been so constructed I have little doubt that they would have been regressive. An interesting point was that four of the five groups had few, if any, negative views about the two-day workshops; indeed, on the contrary, they expressed quite a lot of positive views. The fifth group, while not expressing many positive views, nevertheless expressed few negative views. I feel certain that knowledge of the culture and the structuring of events in a way that created minimum anxiety for such a culture was responsible for much of the success of these workshops. Nevertheless, in reflecting on this situation it seemed clear that many of the consultant views were founded on the feelings arising from the counter-transference – feelings of fear of failing in us as a result of the way that we were used and experienced.

Reference has already been made to transference and counter-transference in this chapter but it is felt that this is an appropriate point to provide a further explanation. Racker points out that, 'Transference is, firstly, an expression of the resistance, and secondly those feelings are a displaced repetition of older ones. The impulses and feelings (love or hate, desire or fear) directed towards the consultant were thus transferred from the original objects (usually the parents and siblings)' (1968, p. 44). In this case, the original objects from whom the impulses and feelings were transferred were those of the public.

According to Racker, 'The interpretation of the resistance must precede the interpretation of the repressed impulses or be linked with it' (1968, p. 44). By backtracking in this manner it will be possible to determine the original cause from which the resistance arose. However, this is only one half of the picture because, as has been discussed, Freud discovered that impulses and feelings towards the client also emerge in the consultant, that is, the phenomenon of counter-transference. Relating back to the workshops provides us with an example of this, in the situation where the membership reacted by not engaging the primary task. The spontaneous counter-transference reaction of myself and my partner was one of a certain anxiety and annoyance and, indeed, of discouragement. That this was no bad thing is described by Racker: 'This (counter-transference) can be used as a tool for understanding the transference. Why is the consultant the object of such transference?' (1968, p. 60). Thus the working through of the counter-transference can help to explain what is happening in the transference.

CONSULTANT 'KNOW THYSELF'

This raises the most interesting of all subjects for a consultant, the capacity to know himself. His capacity to perceive what his client has repeated from his unconscious is first dependent on the degree to which he is conscious of his own unconscious. In other words, he needs to be able to distinguish between what belongs to him and what belongs to the client. It also means that he should create a situation in which he is disposed to admit all possible thoughts and feelings in his unconscious. To achieve this means that the consultant must not fix his attention in any predetermined direction, it means 'suspending all memory, desire and understanding' (to use Bion's terminology). It also means staying at the boundary, being close enough to experience the feelings but not so close as to become flooded by the experience.

The consultant can act as a container for the anxieties of his clients only if he is conscious of his own unconscious. Although referring to analyst and patient, Racker explains, 'The analytic transformation process depends then, to a large extent, on the quantity and quality of Eros the analyst is able to put into action for his patient' (1968, p. 32). He also points out that the patient will only make use of the interpretation when he finds himself in a good affective relation to the analyst. If the consultant is not aware of his own personal proclivities, if he is not aware that the counter-transference feelings are his and not the client's, he is unlikely to have a good affective relationship with the client.

SUMMARY

The Metropolitan Police in common with other organisations is constantly evolving into what the members make it – and what the public make it. It consists of groups of people, some of which, such as the Fraud Squad, are well known and others less so; all are nevertheless perceived objects for those employed in the particular group and for those outside the boundary. Each may be an artificial creation, or an idea held in the mind, but they are still treated by their members as if they exist. Each group establishes its own boundaries across which reality testing and relationships can take place. In Mintzberg's terms, the Met is a typical bureaucracy. Valuable as this information may be, it does not tell us anything about the unconscious processes of the culture. To gain such an understanding requires that we take an active participation in the lives of the members of the Met. We need to deliberately intervene and decipher the responses to the intervention.

The development of consultancy skills is not only a lengthy process but at times a painful one, and one which never ends. The role of internal consultant while still a police officer of Chief Superintendent rank produces interesting dynamics. The rank sometimes creates dependency in junior officers and counter-dependency in senior officers. The fact that I was a police officer sometimes created role confusion which was threatening to the self-identity. Furthermore, the role of internal consultant sometimes creates problems as the consultant is also part of the organisational culture. The development of a 'cultivated ignorance' will allow the consultant to reduce the effect of the culture.

Freud and Bion recognised that certain organisations were particularly liable to be affected by the external environment by virtue of their reason for being. The influential factor in the situations that they describe is the role of authority acting in a super-ego manner, the super-ego being the vehicle for the phenomenon that we call conscience. Conscience is a set of rules which are internalised without one knowing where they come from. To break such a rule is to experience guilt. The Met is strongly influenced by the 'collective demands' of the public manifested in, for example, the adversarial judicial system and demands for accountability.

The lack of firm boundaries and the internalised 'collective conscience' limits reality testing and creates anxiety. The outcome is that the members view the Met holding environment as not good enough. In their interrelatedness with the holding environment the members seek to develop a culture that will be advantageous to them under the conditions imposed by the environment. The result is a culture dominated by conscience whereby being right is all-important and taking chances is not to be contemplated. Thus there is a demand for control, for static unchanging order and structure, the avoidance of change and pursuit of activities that police feel they are good at.

The all-pervading nature of culture is more fully realised when it is appreciated that the 'collective conscience' is part of all members of the Met and that it has developed over a long period of time as if it were water seeping through a wall, as in the process of osmosis. It becomes ingrained into the culture of the organisation and, therefore, any suggested change will be experienced with anxiety and guilt, as to do something new might not be right. The result is a lack of self-belief and low self-esteem which, in turn, means little progress and little meaningful change.

Dread of the super-ego sets various defence processes, such as denial, in motion. The anxiety also causes the members of the organisation to project their feelings on to others, such as a consultant. In this process of transference the consultant is 'sucked into the outer personality structure of the group'. The projection of negative transference can be a most unpleasant and demanding experience for the consultant. Positive transference may not be painful, but it is highly seductive and consequently can be equally dangerous for the consultant.

It may be necessary to provide a new language as part of the process of change. Cognitive development may also be relevant to the success of an intervention. However, as Liddell has pointed out, 'anxiety accompanies intellectual activity as its shadow' (1956, p. 12). Knowledge itself may reveal areas of ignorance and, in turn, engender anxiety. Care is therefore needed – in particular, care to relate to the culture in deciding how, when, how much and in what form the cognitive development should take place.

In a situation where anxiety levels are high and an organisation is in a position where the paranoid-schizoid mechanisms predominate it is necessary to do everything possible to reduce the anxiety and to ensure that depressive mechanisms are available so that people are able to relate to each other for at least part of the time. Once again, this requires a knowledge and understanding of the culture in order that the most appropriate responses may be planned.

Knowledge and understanding of the culture permit a more accurate analysis of the transference and counter-transference. Although it may not be possible to make such an analysis when the process is taking place because of the amount of information, not to mention emotion, present at the time. However, personal reflection after the event should permit a clearer understanding. Here the consultant needs to be able to distinguish between what belongs to the client and what belongs to him: that is, to distinguish between the transference and the counter-transference. To do so, the consultant must know himself, must be conscious of his own unconscious, must be aware of his own personal proclivities. Knowledge of self contributes to the awareness of the consultant, particularly in knowing what effect he is likely to have on his client.

AFTERWORD

In developing the ideas for this book it has been my intention to provide the reader with a different way of looking at organisational development and organisational behaviour, one which will provide consultants and managers with a deeper understanding of their organisations. A way of looking which will have provided them with an insight to things that they knew about in their organisations but could not previously fully understand. In this last brief comment I shall continue that process by reflecting and developing on the previous material.

In this uncertain field, one thing that I can say with some certainty is that this will not be the last or the final word on this complicated phenomenon. On the contrary, I would expect, and hope, that our knowledge and understanding will continue. The intention has not been to disregard or dismiss other theories but is an acknowledgment of the point made by Singer (1968) that it is going to take more than one kind of theoretical model to do justice to the variety, complexity and richness of human culture. However, I am pleased to have had the opportunity of criticising some of the populist theories that are, in my mind, misleading and damaging to the theoretical debate.

One of the issues that I should like to spend a short while reflecting on is the methodology that I have used. As Bhaskar (1975) pointed out, the social scientist can only say as much as the tools at his disposal, or those which he chooses to use, enable him to say. The tools used here to provide the sought-after explanation of organisational culture have been concepts from psycho-analysis. In the event it is felt that this has permitted a consistent and compatible investigation of a wide range of concepts that are associated with organisational culture. In more specific terms, by building on these concepts it has been possible to arrive at a theory which begins to answer a crucial question: how culture develops.

However, it may be appropriate at this point to adopt a cautionary note as it will be appreciated that working in the manner described is not a perfect art. But then, as we have seen, neither would it be if we were working with the other methodologies that are influenced by the old empirical-analytical approach; especially when they are applied to the study of human behaviour. Working in an interpretive manner will not provide certainty. However, as Sutherland has stated, 'The precise interpretation is not as important as long as enough of the underlying dynamics of the total situation are articulated' (1985, p. 81). We cannot possibly hope to know everything that is going through the mind of every member of a group or organisation. We cannot possibly know what is in their individual and collective perception. However, by the way that we are used by the members of an organisation we can discover enough 'of the underlying dynamics of the total situation'. That is, how the members of the organisation perceive their organisational holding environment.

This leads me to a further consideration of the notion of an 'organisation held in the mind'. We have seen that we will categorise data perceived by our sensory processes according to our previous knowledge and experience. As stated in Chapter 1, by the process of perception we impose some structure on new input, compare it with a pool of old information, and then either add to it or eliminate it. The basis for our perceptive process is the pool of internalised information which in turn provides the basis for our self-concepts which are the individual's views of himself. They begin in childhood with the bodily self-concept and expand rapidly through object relations; first with the mother, and then with other significant family members. The object relations with the parents provide a continual psycho-social basis for learning what is pleasurable and what is distressing. The memory bank grows throughout life to produce that rich mosaic which is the individual personality.

Although no longer conscious in adult life, the imaginings and memories of infantile experience, particularly when associated with anxiety, have a profound influence on subsequent mental development, and help to determine the character of personal and social relationships, cultural interests, and the way of living. The growth of an infant in a human environment creates a transactional field in which most affect becomes oriented to human objects, so that, even if the object is not human, it is associated with human activity.

The concept of an organisational holding environment provides the opportunity to add further clarification to the notion of an 'organisation held in the mind'. In much the same way that the infant creates 'the mother held in the mind' through the filters of the perceptive process which then becomes the object that the infant identifies with, so also do the members of an organisation create 'an organisation held in the mind' from the filtered experience of the organisation holding environment. Not all of the information about the holding environment could be held in the mind so we use our perceptual filters to create an image or construct. This will be influenced by major factors in the organisational holding environment which will differ from organisation to organisation.

Because of our ability to form concepts we can construct an object in the mind that is a non-human object. Having created the concept of an organisation the members of the organisation act 'as if' it exists and, because of our previous experience, even if the object is not human, it is associated with human activity. The result is that we therefore attach to this object the same attributes as other influential objects, especially the mother. We attach to the organisation (held in the mind) the same emotions so that, to a lesser or greater degree, the members of an organisation will experience the same feelings as a result of their inter-relatedness with the holding environment.

Affect, which exists at both the conscious and unconscious levels, is the subjective state which accompanies the expression or inhibition of behaviour. The social meaning of affect is obvious when it is viewed as communication: if language is the melody, then affect is the harmony and rhythm which transforms a bare tune into music. The representation of culture is chiefly through the use of language and words used as symbols, and each culture is represented by its own unique private language or idiom. The communication of affect supplies intonations and patterns to speech which may communicate more than the cognitive meaning of the language itself. Another sense of communicating affect is through posture and gesture which differ in meaning in different cultural groups: some gestures are nearly universal, while others are variable.

Since most human needs are supplied by other persons, adaptation to the world is with the world of other men and not with the world of nature. The members of an organisation test reality by comparing their own perceptions and evaluations with those of other persons who experience the same or similar events. All being subject to the same organisational holding environment, to a greater or lesser degree the members of the organisation share the same feelings about the organisation held in the mind. The 'truth' of reality concepts is finally tested in the bubbling cauldron of consensus, not in the isolation of lonely contemplation. Man is a social animal who knows that his existence is absolutely tied to the group. Thus reality testing – the need for continuity, consistency and confirmation – leads to consensual validation.

At a conscious level I can be aware of the affect being communicated to me through intonations and content of speech. I can also be aware of the level of anxiety by observing the respiration rates and rhythms of the members of the organisation, by studying their facial colouring, their posture and their gestures. However, it is by deliberate intervention and the deciphering of the responses – that is, the way that the consultant is used and experienced and the feelings evoked in him – that makes it possible to develop hypotheses about the unconscious processes of the members of the organisation. As consultants, we work with our feelings to identify what is happening in the group, to provide information about the commonality of the group, and about what is not being said by the group. It is in this context that Sutherland's (1985) remarks about 'articulating enough of the underlying dynamic' should be seen.

Let me now turn to some reflections about organisation holding environments. In providing data about the way the actors interpret their holding environment the theoretical framework is helpful in diagnosing the cause of an organisational problem. Without such an understanding we would address our attention to the symptoms, which would not provide a lasting solution to the problem. However, the framework also provides data at a deeper level of understanding. Too much anxiety will prevent progression and will result in a regression to paranoid-schizoid behaviour. A working hypothesis is that the consultant who is able to acquire such knowledge of culture will be able to reduce the anxiety by providing the members of the organisation with a temporary holding environment while they adjust to new behaviour and a new meaning system.

It is also important to bear in mind that all organisations are unique. Consequently, there can be no settled categorisation of what a holding environment is or is not. The question of what the holding environment includes and what it does not include can only be organisation specific. The significance of various aspects of the organisation holding environment will also be organisation specific. In addition, we need to assess how open the organisation system is and what the significant aspects are. For example, looked at from this theoretical basis, a significant aspect of the holding environment for Kets De Vries and Miller (1987) in their 'neurotic organisations' was the leader. For Jaques (1955) and Menzies Lyth (1988) in their 'social systems as a defence against anxiety', the significant aspect was the inappropriateness of the formal structures and strategies.

All cultures are unique but it seems that by using the concept of an organisation holding environment, we can influence culture indirectly. We cannot influence culture per se but we can influence the holding environment and through this the organisational culture, if the organisational holding environment is such that the members of an organisation have a basic trust in their organisation (held in the mind). If their concept of the organisation (the 'organisation held in the mind') is seen as a good object the culture is likely to be task related. However, should the organisation be experienced by its members as a bad object the culture is likely to be non-task related or even anti-task. For all of us as managers, leaders and consultants the aim then is to try to ensure that the holding environment is perceived by its members as good enough.

Knowing how culture develops and what is involved in its development raises the exciting prospect that we may have a genuine chance of shaping our organisations so that they are task related and not anti-task. Posing the question about what is required is rather the same as that which was posed by Winnicott when he asked: 'What is good enough mothering?' It is suggested that it cannot be defined with any certainty but what Winnicott (1965b) refers to as 'A Facilitating Environment' one which encouraged (or facilitates) the development of the child – seems to be the sort of organisation holding environment that is required in today's organisation.

BIBLIOGRAPHY

ABRAHAM, K. (1979) *Selected Papers on Psychoanalysis*. London: Hogarth Press.

ALLAIRE, Y. and FIRSIROTU, M. E. (1984) 'Theories of organisational culture', *Organisational Studies* 5(3): 193–226.

ALLPORT, G. W. (1955) *Becoming: Basic Considerations for a Psychology of Personality*. London: Yale University Press.

ANZIEU, D. (1984) *The Group and the Unconscious*. London: Routledge & Kegan Paul.

—— (1989) *The Skin Ego*. London: Yale University Press.

—— (1990) *A Skin for Thought*. London: Karnac Books.

ARGYRIS, C. and SCHON, D. A. (1978) *Organisational Learning: A Theory of Action Perspective*. Reading, MA: Addison-Wesley.

ARMELIUS, K. and ARMELIUS, B. A. (1985) 'Group personality, task and group culture', in M. Pines (ed.), *Bion and Group Psychotherapy*. London: Routledge & Kegan Paul, pp. 255–73.

ASTRACHAN, B. M. and FLYNN, H. R. (1976) 'The intergroup exercise: a paradigm for learning about the development of organisational structure', in E. J. Miller (ed.), *Task and Organisation*. London: John Wiley, pp. 47–68.

BAIN, A. (1982), *The Baric Experiment: The Design of Jobs and Organisation for the Expression of Growth of Human Capacity*. London: Tavistock Institute of Human Relations, Occasional Paper no. 4.

BATESON, G. (1973) *Steps to an Ecology of the Mind*. St Albans, Herts: Paladin.

—— (1979) *Mind and Nature*. New York: Dutton.

BENEDICT, R. (1935) *Patterns of Culture*. London: Routledge & Kegan Paul.

BERGER, P. L. and KELLNER, H. (1981) *Sociology Reinterpreted*. Harmondsworth: Penguin.

BERGER, P. L. and LUCKMANN, T. (1966) *The Social Construction of Reality*. Harmondsworth: Penguin.

BETTELHEIM, B. (1960) *The Informed Heart*. Harmondsworth: Penguin.

—— (1967) *The Empty Fortress*. Harmondsworth: Penguin.

—— (1969) *The Children of the Dream*. London: Thames & Hudson.

BHASKAR, R. (1975) *A Realist Theory of Science*. Brighton: Harvester.

BION, W. R. (1955) 'Group dynamics: a review', in M. Klein, P. Heimann and R. E. Money-Kyrle (eds), *New Directions in Psycho-analysis*. London: Tavistock, pp. 440–76.

—— (1961) *Experiences in Groups and Other Papers*. London: Tavistock.

—— (1962) *Learning from Experience*. London: Heinemann.

—— (1963) *Elements of Psycho-analysis*. London: Heinemann.

—— (1967) *Second Thoughts*. London: Heinemann.

—— (1970) *Attention and Interpretation*. London: Tavistock.

BLAY-NETO, B. (1985) 'The influence of Bion's ideas on my work', in M. Pines (ed.), *Bion and Group Psychotherapy*. London: Routledge & Kegan Paul, pp. 247–54.

BLEICHER, J. (1980) *Contemporary Hermeneutics*. London: Routledge & Kegan Paul.

BLIGHT, J. G. (1981) 'Must psycho-analysis retreat to hermeneutics?', *Psycho-analysis and Contemporary Thought* 4: 147–205.

BOHANNAN, P. (1962) *Social Anthropology*. London: Holt, Rinehart & Winston.

BOHM, D. and PEAT, F. D. (1991) 'Science, order and creativity', in J. Henry (ed.), *Creative Management*. London: Sage, pp. 24–33.

BOWLBY, J. (1969) *Attachment and Loss*: vol. 1, *Attachment*. Harmondsworth: Penguin.

BRITTON, J. (1970) *Language and Learning*. Harmondsworth: Penguin.

BUCHANAN, D. A. and HUCZYNSKI, A. A. (1985) *Organisational Behaviour: An Introductory Text*. London: Prentice-Hall.

BURRELL, G. and MORGAN, G. (1979) *Sociological Paradigms and Organisational Analysis*. London: Gower.

CARTWRIGHT, D. and ZANDER, A. (1953) *Group Dynamics*. London: Tavistock.

CAUDWELL, C. (1937) *Illusion and Reality*. London: Lawrence & Wishart.

CHILD, J. (1984) Organisation: *A Guide to Problems and Practice*. London: Harper & Row.

CSIKSZENTMIHALYI, M. (1975) *Beyond Boredom and Anxiety*. London: Jossey-Bass.

CUPITT, D. (1990) *Creation Out of Nothing*. London: SCM Press.

CYERT, R. M. and MARCH, J. G. (1963), *A Behavioral Theory of the Firm*. Englewood Cliffs, NJ: Prentice-Hall.

DAVIS, M. and WALLBRIDGE, D. (1987) *Boundary and Space: An Introduction to the Work of D. W. Winnicott*. London: Karnac Books.

DAVIS, S. M. (1984) *Managing Corporate Culture*. Cambridge, MA: Ballinger.

DEAL, T. (1985) 'Cultural change: opportunity, silent killer, or metamorphosis', in R. H. Kilmann, M. J. Saxton, R. Serpa, and Associates (eds), *Gaining Control of the Corporate Culture*. London: Jossey-Bass, pp. 292–331.

DEAL, T. E. and KENNEDY, A. A. (1982) *Corporate Cultures: The Rites and Rituals of Corporate Life*. Reading, MA: Addison-Wesley.

DOISE, W. (1978) *Groups and Individuals: Explanations in Social Psychology*. Cambridge: Cambridge University Press.

DOUGLAS, J. D. (1976) *Investigative Social Research: Individual and Team Field Research*. London: Sage.

ELIAS, N. (1991) *The Symbol Theory*. London: Sage.

ERIKSON, E. H. (1950) *Childhood and Society*. New York: Norton.

—— (1959) *Identity and the Life Cycle*. London: Norton.

—— (1968) *Identity, Youth and Crisis*. New York: Norton.

—— (1977) *Toys and Reasons*. New York: Norton.

EVANS, P. and DEEHAN, G. (1988) *The Keys to Creativity*. London: Grafton Books.

EYSENCK, H. J. and WILSON, G. D. (1973) *The Experimental Study of Freudian Theories*. London: Routledge & Kegan Paul.

FAIRBAIRN, W. R. D. (1952) *Psycho-analytic Studies of the Personality*. London: Routledge & Kegan Paul.

FENICHEL, O. (1946) *The Psycho-analytic Theory of Neurosis*. London: Routledge & Kegan Paul.

FERENCI, S. (1952) *First Contributions to Psycho-analysis*. London: Hogarth Press.

FREUD, A. (1966) *The Ego and the Mechanisms of Defence*. London: Hogarth Press.

FREUD, S. (1895) 'Project for a Scientific Psychology', in James Strachey (ed.), *The Standard Edition of the Complete Psychological Works of Sigmund Freud*, 24 vols. London: Hogarth Press, 1953–73, vol.1, pp. 295–387.

—— (1908) 'Creative Writers and Day Dreaming'. *S.E.* 14, pp. 129–42.

—— (1910) 'Five lectures on psycho-analysis', in *Two Short Accounts of Psycho-analysis*. Harmondsworth: Penguin.

—— (1911) 'Formulations on the Two Principles of Mental Functioning'. *S.E.* 11, pp. 29–43.

—— (1915) 'Instincts and Their Vicissitudes'. *S.E.* 11, pp. 113–38.

—— (1917) 'Mourning and Melancholia'. *S.E.* 11, pp. 245–68.

—— (1920) 'Beyond the Pleasure Principle'. *S.E.* 11, pp. 269–338.

—— (1921) 'Group Psychology and the Analysis of the Ego'. *S.E.* 12, pp. 95–178.

—— (1923) 'The Ego and the Id'. S.E. 11, pp. 339–404.

—— (1926) *'Inhibitions, Symptoms and Anxiety'*. *S.E.* 10, pp. 237–315.

—— (1940a) 'Some Elementary Lessons in Psycho-analysis'. *S.E.* 23, pp. 281–86.

—— (1940b) 'An Outline of Psycho-analysis'. *S.E.* 15, pp. 375–444.

FLUGEL, J. C. (1921) *The Psycho-analytic Study of the Family.* London: Hogarth Press.

FROMM, E. (1955) *The Sane Society.* New York: Holt, Rinehart & Winston.

—— (1962) *Beyond the Chains of Illusion.* London: Sphere Books.

FROST, P. J., MOORE, L. F., LOUIS, L. F., LUNDBERG, C. C., and MARTIN, J. (1985) *Organisational Culture.* London: Sage.

FURTH, H. G. (1981) *Piaget and Knowledge: Theoretical Foundations.* Second Edition. Chicago, IL: University of Chicago Press.

GADAMER, H-G. (1962) *Truth and Method.* New York: Seabury Press (1979).

GARZA-GUERRERO, A. C. (1974) 'Culture shock: its mourning and the vicissitudes of identity', *Journal of the American Psychoanalytic Association* 22: 408–29.

GEERTZ, C. (1973) *The Interpretation of Culture.* London: Hutchinson.

GELNER, E. (1985) *The Psycho-analytic Movement.* London: Paladin.

GIDDENS, A. (1976) *New Rules of Sociological Method.* London: Hutchinson.

GOODENOUGH, W. H. (1964), 'Rethinking "Status" and "Role": Toward a general model of the cultural organisation of social relationships', in S. A. Tyler (ed.), *Cognitive Anthropology.* New York: Holt, Rinehart & Winston.

—— (1971) *Culture, Language and Society: McCaleb Module in Anthropology.* Reading: MA: Addison-Wesley.

GREENSON, R. (1965) 'The working alliance and the transference neurosis', *Psychoanalytic Quarterly* 34: 155–81.

GUMMESSON, E. (1991) *Qualitative Methods in Management Research.* London: Sage.

GUMPERZ, J. J. (1969) 'Communication in multi-lingual societies', in S. A. Tyler (ed.), *Cognitive Anthropology*. New York: Holt, Rinehart & Winston.

GUNTRIP, H. (1971) *Psycho-analytic Theory, Therapy and the Self.* New York: Basic.

HABERMAS, J. (1968) *Knowledge and Human Interests.* Cambridge: Polity Press.

HABERMAS, J. (1976) *Communication and the Evolution of Society.* Boston, MA: Beacon Press.

HANDY, B. C. (1976) *Understanding Organisations.* Harmondsworth: Penguin.

HEALY, D. (1990) *The Suspended Revolution.* London: Faber.

HENRY, J. (1991) *Creative Management.* London: Sage.

HORWITZ, L. (1985) 'Projective identification in dyads and groups', in A. D. Colman and W. H. Bexton (eds), *Group Relations Reader 2.* Washington, DC: A. K. Rice Institute, pp. 21–36.

HUNT, J. C. (1989) *Psycho-analytic Aspects of Fieldwork.* London: Sage.

ISAACS, S. (1952) 'The Nature and Function of Phantasy', in M. Klein, P. Heinemann, S. Isaacs, and J. Riviere (eds), *Developments in Psycho-analysis* London: Hogarth.

JACOBSON, E. (1964) *The Self and the Object World.* Connecticut: International Universities Press.

JAQUES, E. (1953) 'On the dynamics of social structure', *Human Relations* 6: 3–24.

—— (1955) 'Social systems as a defence against persecutory and depressive anxiety', in M. Klein, P. Heimann and P.E. Money-Kyrle (eds), *New Directions in Psycho-analysis.* London: Tavistock, pp. 478–98.

—— (1970) *Work, Creativity and Social Justice.* London: Heinemann.

JUNG, C.G. (1956) *Symbols of Transformation.* London: Routledge & Kegan Paul.

—— (1961) *Modern Man in Search of a Soul.* London: Routledge & Kegan Paul.

JURAN, J. M. (1989) *Juran on Leadership for Quality.* New York: Free Press.

KAES, R. (1971) 'Travail et Illusion dans la Formation', *Mouvement Psychiatrique* 2: 34–36.

KATZ, D. (1969) *Gestalt Psychology.* New York: Ronald Press.

KEGAN, R. (1982) *The Evolving Self.* London: Harvard University Press.

KERNBERG, O. (1966) 'Structural derivatives of object relationships', *International Journal of Psycho-analysis* 47: 236–53.

KETS DE VRIES, M. and MILLER, D. (1987) *The Neurotic Organisation*. London: Jossey-Bass.

KHAN, R. L. (1976) 'Individual and corporation: the problem of responsibility', in E. J. Miller (ed.), *Task and Organisation*. London: John Wiley, pp. 69–83.

KILMANN, R. H. (1989) *Managing Beyond the Quick Fix*. London: Jossey-Bass.

KLEIN, M. (1923) 'Early analysis', in M. Klein, *Love, Guilt and Reparation and Other Works 1921–1945*, London: Virago, 1975, pp. 77–105.

—— (1930) 'The importance of symbol-formation in the development of the ego', in M. Klein, *Love, Guilt and Reparation and Other Works 1921–1945*. London: Virago, 1975, pp. 219–32.

—— (1940) 'Mourning and its relation to manic-depressive states', in M. Klein, *Love, Guilt and Reparation and Other Works 1921–1945*. London: Virago, 1975, pp. 344–69.

—— (1948) 'On the theory of anxiety and guilt', in M. Klein, *Envy and Gratitude and Other Works 1946–1963*. London: Virago, 1975, pp. 25–42.

—— (1952) 'Some theoretical conclusions regarding the emotional life of the infant', in M. Klein, *Envy and Gratitude and Other Works 1946–1963*. London: Virago, 1975, pp. 61–93.

—— (1955) 'On identification', in M. Klein, *Envy and Gratitude and Other Works 1946–1963*. London: Virago, 1975, pp. 141–175.

—— (1959) 'Our adult world and its roots in infancy', in M. Klein, *Envy and Gratitude and Other Works 1946–1963*. London: Virago, 1975, pp. 247–263.

—— (1960) 'On mental health', in M. Klein, *Envy and Gratitude and Other Works 1946–1963*. London: Virago, 1975, pp. 268–274.

KOESTLER, A. (1964) *The Act of Creation*. Harmondsworth: Penguin.

KONIG, K. (1985) 'Basic assumption groups and working groups revisited', in M. Pines (ed.), *Bion and Group Psychotherapy*. London: Routledge & Kegan Paul, pp 151–6.

KROEBER, A. L. and KLUCKHOLM, C. (1952) *Culture: A Critical Review of Concepts and Definitions*. Cambridge, MA: Harvard University Press.

KUHN, T. S. (1962) *The Structure of Scientific Revolutions*. Second edition enlarged with a Postscript. Chicago, IL: University of Chicago Press, 1970.

LACAN, J. (1977) *Ecrits: A Selection*. London: Tavistock/Routledge.

LAING, R. D. (1967) *The Politics of Experience and the Bird of Paradise*. Harmondsworth: Penguin.

LANGER, S. (1951) *Philosophy in a New Key*. New York: New American Library.

LAWRENCE, W. G. and MILLER, E. J. (1976) 'Epilogue', in E. J. Miller (ed.), *Task and Organisation*. London: John Wiley.

LEACH, E. (1976) *Culture and Communication*. Cambridge: Cambridge University Press.

LEVI-STRAUSS, C. (1958) *Anthropologie Structurale*. Paris: Librairie Plon.

—— (1973) *Anthropologie Structurale Deux*. Paris: Librairie Plon.

LEWIN, K. (1951) *Field Theory in Social Science*. New York: Harper.

LIDDELL, H. S. (1956) 'Emotional hazards in animal and man', in C. Rycroft, *Anxiety and Neurosis*. Harmondsworth: Penguin.

LOFGREN, L. B. (1975) 'Organisational design and therapeutic effect', in A. D. Colman and W. H. Bexton (eds), *Group Relations Reader 1*. Washington, DC: A. K. Rice Institute, pp. 185–192.

LOUIS, M. (1980) 'Surprise and sense making: what newcomers experience in entering unfamiliar organisational settings', *Administrative Science Quarterly*, June, vol. 25: 226–51.

LYNN MEEK, V. (1988) 'Organisational culture: origins and weaknesses', *Organisation Studies* 9(4): 453–73.

MARRIS, P. (1974) *Loss and Change*. London: Routledge & Kegan Paul.

MASLOW, A. H. (1943) 'A theory of human motivation', in H. J. Leavitt, L. R. Pondy and D. M. Boje (eds), *Readings in Managerial Psychology*. Third edition, 1980. Chicago, IL: University of Chicago Press, pp. 5–22.

—— (1969) *The Psychology of Science*. New York: Gateway.

—— (1970) *Motivation and Personality*. Third edition. New York: Harper & Row.

—— (1971) *The Farther Reaches of Human Nature*. Harmondsworth: Penguin.

MAY, R. (1975) *The Courage To Create*. New York: Norton.

—— (1977) 'Gregory Bateson and humanistic psychology', in J. Brockman (ed.), *About Bateson*. London: Wildwood House, pp. 77–102.

MENZIES LYTH, I. (1988) *Containing Anxiety in Institutions: Selected Essays vol. I*. London: Free Association Books, pp. 43–88.

MENZIES LYTH, I. (1989) *The Dynamics of the Social: Selected Essays vol. II*. London: Free Association Books, pp. 26–44.

MERRY, U. and BROWN, G. I. (1987) *The Neurotic Behaviour of Organisations*. New York: Gestalt Institute of Cleveland Press.

MERTON, R. (1957) *Social Theory and Social Structure*. Glencoe, IL: Free Press.

MESSER, S. B., SASS, L. A. and WOOLFOLK, R. L. (1988) *Hermeneutics and Psychological Theory*. London: Rutgers University Press.

MILLER, E. J. (1976) 'Introductory essay: role perspective and the understanding of organisational behaviour', in E. J. Miller (ed.), *Task and Organisation*. London: John Wiley, pp. 1–16.

—— (1983) *Work and Creativity*. London: Tavistock Institute of Human Relations, Occasional Paper no. 6.

—— (1985) 'Organisational development and industrial democracy: a current case study', in E. J. Miller (ed.), *Task and Organisation*. London: John Wiley, pp. 243–72.

—— (1990) 'Experimental learning in groups 1: the development of the Leicester model', in E. Trist and H. Murray (eds), *The Social Engagement of Social Science*. London, Free Association Books: 165–87.

—— and RICE, A. K. (1967) *Systems of Organisation: Task and Sentient Systems and their Boundary Control*. London: Tavistock.

MINTZBERG, H. (1988) 'The machine bureaucracy', in J. B. Quinn, H. Mintzberg and R. M. James (eds), *The Strategy Process*. London: Prentice-Hall.

MITROFF, I. I. (1989) *Stakeholders of the Organisational Mind*. London: Jossey-Bass.

MONEY-KYRLE, R. (1950) 'Varieties of group formation', *Psychoanalysis and the Social Sciences* 4: 7–25.

MORGAN, G. (1983) *Beyond Method*. London: Sage.

MUELLER-VOLLER, K. (1986) *The Hermeneutics Reader*. Oxford: Blackwell.

NEVIS, E. C. (1987) *Organisational Consulting*. New York: Gestalt Institute of Cleveland Press.

ORNSTEIN, R. E. (1977), 'Two sides of the brain', in H. J. Leavitt, L. R. Pondy and D. M. Boje (eds), *Readings in Managerial Psychology*. Third edition, 1980. Chicago, IL: University of Chicago Press, pp. 106–25.

PALMER, B. (1972) 'Thinking about thought', *Human Relations* 26 (1): 127–41.

—— (1979) 'Learning and the group experience', in W. G. Lawrence (ed.), *Exploring Individual and Organisational Boundaries*. London: John Wiley, pp. 169–92.

PALMER, R. E. (1969) *Hermeneutics*. Evanston, IL: Northwestern University Press.

PARKES, C. M. (1972) *Bereavement*. Harmondsworth: Penguin.

PETERS, T. J. and WATERMAN, R. H. (1982) *In Search of Excellence*. London: Harper & Row.

PETTIGREW, A. M. (1979) 'On studying organisational cultures', *Administrative Science Quarterly* 24: 570–81.

—— (1985) *The Awakening Giant: Continuity and Change in ICI.* Oxford: Blackwell.

PIAGET, J. (1951) *Play, Dreams and Imitation in Childhood.* London: Routledge & Kegan Paul.

PONDY, L. R., FROST, P. J., MORGAN, G. and DANDRIDGE, T. (1983) *Organisational Symbolism.* London: JAI Press.

POPPER, K. R. (1934) *The Logic of Scientific Discovery.* London: Hutchinson, 1959.

POZZI, L. (1990) 'Creative shadows', in K. Barnaby and P. D'Acierno (ed.), *C. G. Jung and the Humanities: Towards a Hermeneutics of Culture.* Princeton, NJ: Princeton University Press, pp. 150–2.

PRUYSER, P. W. (1979) 'An essay on creativity', *Bulletin of the Menninger Clinic*, July, 43(4): 294–352.

RACKER, H. (1968) *Transference and Countertransference.* London: Hogarth Press.

RANK, O. (1945) *Will Therapy and Truth and Reality.* New York: Alfred A. Knopf.

REASON, P. (1988) *Human Inquiry in Action.* London: Sage.

REDLICH, F. C. and ASTRACHAN, B. (1975) 'Group dynamics training', in A. D. Colman and W. H. Bexton (eds), *Group Relations Reader 1.* Washington DC: A. K. Rice Institute, pp. 225–34.

REED, B. and PALMER, B. (1976) 'The local church and its environment', in E. J. Miller (ed.), *Task and Organisation.* London: John Wiley, pp. 261–82.

RICE, A. K. (1963) *The Enterprise and its Environment.* London: Tavistock.

—— (1976) 'Individual, group and intergroup processes', in E. J. Miller (ed.), *Task and Organisation.* London: John Wiley, pp. 25–46.

RICOEUR, P. (1970) *Freud and Philosophy: An Essay on Interpretation.* New Haven, CT: Yale University Press.

—— (1974) *The Conflict of Interpretations.* Evanston, IL: Northwestern University Press.

RIOCH, M. (1985) 'Why I work as a consultant in the conferences of the A. K. Rice Institute', in A. D. Colman and M. H. Geller (eds), *Group Relations Reader 2.* Washington, DC: A. K. Rice Institute, pp. 365–82.

ROGERS, C. R. (1954) 'Towards a theory of creativity', in P. E. Vernon (ed.), *Creativity.* Harmondsworth: Penguin, pp. 137–52.

RYCROFT, C. (1968a) *Anxiety and Neurosis*. Harmondsworth: Penguin.
—— (1968b) *Imagination and Reality*. London: Hogarth Press.
—— (1981) *The Innocence of Dreams*. Oxford: University Press.
SACKMANN, S. A. (1992) 'Culture and subcultures: An analysis of organisational knowledge', *Administrative Science Quarterly* 37: 140–61.
SADLER, P. (1976) 'Task and organising structure in marketing', in E. J. Miller (ed.), *Task and Organisation*. London: John Wiley, pp. 173–92.
SANDLER, J. (1987) *Projection, Identification, Projective Identification*. London: Karnac Books.
SAPIR, E. (1961) *Culture Language and Personality*. Berkeley, CA: University of California Press.
SCHEIDLINGER, P. (1980) *Psycho-analytic Group Dynamics*. New York: International Universities Press.
SCHEIN, E. H. (1987a) *The Clinical Perspective in Fieldwork*. London: Sage.
—— (1987b) *Organisational Culture and Leadership*. London: Jossey-Bass.
—— (1988) 'Organisational socialisation and the profession of management', *Sloan Management Review*, Fall, pp. 52–65.
SCHNEIDER, B. (1979) 'Organisational climates: an essay', *Personnel Psychology* 28: 447–79.
SCHINDLER, W. (1952) 'The "group personality" concept in group psychotherapy', *International Journal of Group Psychotherapy* 2: 311–15.
SEGAL, H. (1981) *The Work of Hanna Segal: A Kleinian Approach to Clinical Practice*. London: Free Association Books.
SHERIF, M. (1936) *The Psychology of Social Norms*. New York: Harper.
SINGER, M. (1968) 'Culture: the concept of culture', *International Encyclopedia of the Social Sciences* 3: 527–41
SINNOTT, E. W. (1959) 'The creativeness of life', in P. E. Vernon (ed.), *Creativity*. Harmondsworth: Penguin, pp. 107–115.
SKYNNER, R. (1989) *Institutes and How To Survive Them*, J. R. Schlapobersky (ed.), London: Tavistock/Routledge.
SMIRCICH, L. (1983) 'Concepts of culture and organisational analysis', *Administrative Science Quarterly* 28: 339–58.
STEELE, R. S. (1979) 'Psycho-analysis and hermeneutics', *International Review of Psycho-Analysis* 6: 389–411.
STERN, D. N. (1985) *The Interpersonal World of the Infant: A View from Psycho-analysis and Developmental Psychology*. New York: Basic.

STORR, A. (1963) *The Integrity of the Personality*. Harmondsworth: Penguin.

—— (1972) *The Dynamics of Creation*. Harmondsworth: Penguin.

—— (1988) *The School of Genius*. London: Andre Deutsch.

SUTHERLAND, J. D. (1985) 'Bion revisited: group dynamics and group psychotherapy', in M. Pines (ed.), *Bion and Group Psychotherapy*. London: Routledge & Kegan Paul, pp. 47–86.

SYMINGTON, N. (1986) *The Analytic Experience*. London: Free Association Books.

SZMIDLA, A. and KHALEELEE, O. (1975) 'Unpublished memorandum', in A. D. Colman and M. H. Geller (eds), *Group Relations Reader 2*. Washington, DC: A. K. Rice Institute, 1985.

TAJFEL, H. and FRASER, C. (1978) *Introducing Social Psychology*. Harmondsworth: Penguin.

TERWEE, S. J. S. (1990) *Hermeneutics in Psychology and Psychoanalysis*. Berlin: Springer-Verlag.

THOULESS, R. H. (1958) *General and Social Psychology*. Fourth edition, London: University Tutorial Press.

TRIST, E. (1985) 'Working with Bion in the 1940s: the group decade', in M. Pines (ed.), *Bion and Group Psychotherapy*. London: Routledge & Kegan Paul, pp. 1–46.

—— (1990) 'Culture as a psycho-social process', in E. Trist and H. Murray (eds), *The Social Engagement of Social Science*. London: Free Association Books, pp. 539–45.

—— and MURRAY, H. (1990) *The Social Engagement of Social Science: A Tavistock Anthology*. London: Free Association Books.

TUNSTALL, W. (1985) 'Cultural transition at AT&T', *Sloan Management Review* 25(1): 1–12.

TURNER, B. A. (1971) *Exploring the Industrial Sub-culture*. London: Macmillan.

—— (1986) 'Sociological aspects of organisational symbolism', *Organisation Studies* 7(2): 101–15.

TURQUET, P. M. (1974) 'Leadership: the individual and the group', in G. S. Gibbard, J. J. Hartmann and R. D. Mann (eds), *Analysis of Groups*. San Francisco, CA: Jossey-Bass, pp. 337–71.

TYLER, S. A. (1969) *Cognitive Anthropology*. New York: Holt, Rinehart & Winston.

VROOM, V. H. (1964) *Work and Motivation*. New York: John Wiley.

WALLACE, A. F. C. (1970) *Culture and Personality*. New York: Random House.

WEISBERG, R. W. (1986) *Creativity*. London: W. H. Freeman.

WHITE, L. A. (1949) *The Science of Culture*. New York: Grove Press.

WHYTE, W. F. and BRAUN, R. R. (1968) 'On language and culture', in E. C. Hughes (ed.), *Institutions and the Person.* Chicago, IL: Aldine Publishing.

WINNICOTT, D. W. (1957) *The Child and the Outside World.* London: Tavistock.

—— (1965a) *The Family and Individual Development.* London: Tavistock.

—— (1965b) *The Maturational Processes and the Facilitating Environment.* New York: International Universities Press.

—— (1971) *Playing and Reality.* Harmondsworth: Penguin.

—— (1988) *Human Nature.* London: Free Association Books.

WITTGENSTEIN, L. (1953) *Philosophical Investigations.* Oxford: Blackwell.

—— (1969) *On Certainty.* Oxford: Blackwell.

VAN MAANEN, J. (1979) *Qualitative Methodology.* London: Sage.

YOUNG, E. (1989) 'On the naming of the rose: interests and multiple meanings as elements of organisational culture', *Organisation Studies* 10(2): 187–206.

ZIMAN, J. (1978) *Reliable Knowledge.* Cambridge: Cambridge University Press.

Index

Index by Linda English